Ethics of

"In *Ethics of Hope*, Jürgen Moltmann makes a significant contribution to Christian ethics that will be of interest not only to scholars but to students, pastors, and lay people as well. Addressing the central ethical issues facing our time, Moltmann's distinctively Christian way of doing ethics—from the standpoint of a 'transformative eschatology'—presents a highly refreshing alternative to existing approaches to Christian ethics."

Lois Malcolm
Luther Seminary

Ethics of Hope

Jürgen Moltmann

Translated by Margaret Kohl

Fortress Press
Minneapolis

ETHICS OF HOPE
First Fortress Press edition, 2012

Cover design: Ivy Palmer Skrade
Book design and typesetting: Josh Messner

Library of Congress Cataloging-in-Publication Data

Moltmann, Jürgen.
[Ethik der Hoffnung. English]
Ethics of hope / Jürgen Moltmann ; translated by Margaret Kohl.—1st Fortress Press ed.
    p. cm.
Includes bibliographical references (p.   ) and index.
ISBN 978-0-8006-9858-4 (alk. paper)
1. Christian ethics. 2. Hope. I. Title.
BJ1253.M6513 2012
241—dc23   2011047080

The paper used in this publication meets the minimum requirements of American National Standard for Information Sciences—Permanence of Paper for Printed Library Materials, ANSI Z329.48-1984.
Manufactured in the U.S.A.

16 15 14 13   2 3 4 5 6 7 8 9 10

Contents

Part 2. An Ethics of Life

Part 3. Earth Ethics

Part 4. Ethics of Just Peace

Part 5. Joy in God: Aesthetic Counterpoints

To Johannes Rau

Preface

Ever since the publication of the *Theology of Hope* in 1964, an ethics of hope has been on my agenda. I had familiarized myself with bioethical questions at congresses with doctors and pharmaceutical concerns. The political and 'alternative' movements of the post-1968 years had provoked me to take up positions for which political and liberation theology provided the theological frameworks. In the ecumenical movement I came to know the north-south conflict and the theological struggles which went along with the antiracist programme. At the University of Tübingen, I regularly gave lectures on Christian ethics. So at the end of the 1970s, I wanted to write an *Ethics of Hope*. But instead, to the disappointment of my friends and colleagues, in 1980, with *The Trinity and the Kingdom of God*, I published a social doctrine of the Trinity instead. Why?

In discussions about questions of medical ethics, I became painfully aware of the limits of my knowledge. The need for an ecological ethics only grew from a perception of the limits of growth, which the Club of Rome made plain to us in 1973. But as yet I did not have an ecological doctrine of creation and could not make the individual specific decisions I had arrived at plausible in wider contexts. After 1968 the political circumstances of the time were so contradictory, and not just in West Germany, that decisions made one day were already obsolete by the next. In short, at the end of the 1970s, I was not yet ready. But the desire and the obligation have weighed on my theological conscience to the present day. So at the close of my contributions to theological discussions, I shall try to say what I mean by an ethics of hope, and how I have ethically perceived, judged and acted in line with that ethics. In what I have to say, I am also picking up ideas from the dissertations, essays and books which have come to the fore in this direction since the *Theology of Hope*, and as representative of many, should like to mention Timothy Harvie, *Jürgen Moltmann's Ethics of Hope: Eschatological Possibilities for Moral Action* (London, 2009).

This *Ethics of Hope* is not a textbook offering surveys and an introduction to ethical methods. Nor does it offer political advice such as is supplied in the memoranda of the German Protestant church, the EKD. I am turning to

Christians in order to make suggestions for action with hope as its horizon. This ethics is related to the ethos which has to do with endangered life, the threatened earth and the lack of justice and righteousness. It is not a discussion of timeless general principles; but in the face of these dangers, it focuses on what has to be done today and tomorrow with the courage of hope. I have therefore picked up specific statements of my own made about ecological and political ethics during the last forty years and have set these in a wider context. For me, this meant a critical revision of my ethical standpoints.

Ever since I became a member of the ecumenical Faith and Order Commission, I have taken my bearings from the ecumenical ethic which ever since the Fourth General Assembly of the World Council of Churches in Uppsala in 1968 has stood under the banner of transforming hope. That assembly's message ran: 'Trusting in God's renewing power, we call upon you to participate in the anticipation of God's kingdom and to allow now something of the new creation to become already visible which Christ will complete on his day.'

At that time ecumenical ethics served the renewal of the churches, not just—as today—their fellowship in 'reconciled difference'. I am therefore seeing the ecumenical dimension of this ethics of hope not as a collection and comparison of the ethical perspectives and positions of the different churches (although that would undoubtedly be desirable) but as an outline for a common answer by worldwide Christianity to the global dangers which threaten us all.

This ethics of hope is intended to be a *deliberately Christian ethics*. So at decisive points I have taken my bearings from the promises and the gospel of the Bible. Christians have no better answers to the questions about life, the earth and justice than secular people or people belonging to different religions; but Christians have to live in accordance with the divine hope and the claim of Christ. I have consequently described the great alternatives offered by the Anabaptists in the Reformation era to the *corpus Christianum*—Constantinian state Christianity—and have introduced these critically into the discussion about the Christian character of Christian ethics. In Europe and America, in the old countries of the *corpus Christianum*, we have entered into a post-Christian era, and for that era the ethical alternatives of the Anabaptists in their service for peace, in their experience of community and in the conduct of life are as important as is the ethos of the monastic orders for the ethics of the Catholic Church and as are the countercultural movements for the dominant culture of the Western world.

The principle behind this ethics of hope is:

—not to turn swords into Christian swords

—not to retreat from the swords to the ploughshares

—but to make ploughshares out of swords.

The hope for God's eschatological transformation of the world leads to a transformative ethics which tries to accord with this future in the inadequate material and with the feeble powers of the present and thus anticipates it.

As regards method, I have always started from theology in order to conceive and put forward an ethics of hope. That does not mean 'first the theory, then the practice', or that 'Christian ethics is part of the church's dogmatics', but it does mean that everything done and suffered must conform to what is believed, loved and hoped for. The relation between theory and practice is not a one-way affair. Theory is not in the vanguard, nor is practice. In the hope to which both are related, they share a dialectical relationship of reciprocal influence and correction.

I have preceded the ethics of life with a theological description of what 'life' is in the sense of the gospel. I have begun the ethics of the earth with the question of what the earth is according to the biblical message. I begin the political ethics with a discussion of concepts of justice. There is an ethics of ideas and definitions too. That immediately becomes obvious in bioethical questions, in the discussion about whether the embryo is assigned human status so that it shares the rights which life entails, or whether it is merely a preliminary stage to human life, or is simply human material. In ecological ethics too we don't know whether we ought to talk about the environment, the world we share, or nature. If an ethics allows its concepts to be predetermined by the dominant worldview, it cannot be innovative.

The ethics of terminological definitions of course raises the question about the right to interpretation. Who decides on the political correctness of the terms? Who lays down the rules for the way we speak? I reject authorities in thinking and speaking, and I claim the right to a democratization of terminological definitions. Communication can of course be nonviolent, but it cannot be free of interests and concerns. That means that the formation of theories is a field for ethics just as are directions for practice in conflicts of interest.

In introducing this outline of an ethics of hope, and in order to prevent disappointment, I must mention two deficits.

First, I have not included the development of Catholic social doctrine. My lectures on ethics at the University of Tübingen always went into the doctrine of natural law and the formative social encyclicals of the Catholic church, with their principles of solidarity and subsidiarity. I entered in detail into the encyclicals *Gaudium et Spes* and *Populorum Progressio*, which resulted from the changes brought about by the Second Vatican Council. But what prevented me from going into Catholic social doctrine in detail were two things. Ever since the middle ages, traditional Catholic theology has thought in a pattern of 'nature and grace' and has seen hope together with faith and love as a 'supernatural virtue'. In this way of thinking, it is hardly possible to discern the birth of the Christian hope out of God's future. Catholic liberation theology has, on the other hand, taken as its point of orientation the eschatological opening-up of the history of liberation. But up to now no convincing fusion between Catholic social doctrine and liberation theology has come into my hands. And since in this book I have not aimed to provide surveys of the various ethical concepts held in the ecumenical community of the Christian churches, I have not included in detail the broad field of Catholic social doctrine. For this I would ask the indulgence of my Catholic colleagues and readers.

Second, in the present book I have not yet ventured to add a chapter on economic ethics. In my lectures I always discussed the ethics of work, property, the systems of democratic liberty and social justice. I hope too that the chapters in this book about the ethics of life, the earth and justice draw upon so many fundamentals of an economic ethics that they will be able to make my ideas about a democratization of the global economy plain. But in light of the present chaotic globalization, which is destabilizing all conditions, and because of the breakdown of the capitalist financial systems since 2008, I know what I hope for but not what must specifically be done in order to transform the present economic conditions of our lives, which seem to be leading to the global bankruptcy of humanity. The alternatives required if life is to be preserved and if God's expectations are to be fulfilled are probably much more radical, and for the present time more urgent, than we dare to think. A valuable prophetic word is the statement on the global financial and economic crisis issued in June 2009 by the Council of the Protestant Church in Germany (EKD) entitled *Wie ein Riss in einer hohen Mauer* ('Like a Crack in a High Wall'). I may perhaps publish a comment on the matter at a later point.

With regard to the ecumenical discussions, I draw attention to Konrad Raiser's comprehensive and informative report 'Globalisierung in der ökumenisch-ethischen Diskussion',[1] as well as to Michael Haspel's excellent article in the same issue, 'Globalisierung—Theologisch-ethisch'.[2] On the international level there are enough talented moral philosophers in the younger generation who are able to turn economics, that 'science of dismay', into a science of hope, provided that they do not remain caught up for too long in the fundamental problems of a formal ethics but go on to the practical freedoms and necessities of material ethics.

Finally, I should like to thank my former assistant Dr Claudia Rehberger, who read the chapter on the ethics of life and provided criticism and suggestions, and Dr Geiko Müller-Fahrenholz, who read the whole manuscript and offered constructive questions and advice. In this book I have experienced particularly strongly the help of faithful companions and know how to value it. Nevertheless, I alone am responsible for all the judgments.

Anyone not interested in the specifically theological discussion about the correlation between eschatology and ethics can begin with the section on 'transformative eschatology', which is fundamental for these ethics, and can come back later to the alternatives I have put forward in chapter 1.

In this ethics I am turning to a wide public, and I have therefore dispensed as far as possible with technical terms in the interests of general comprehensibility. But because this is a consciously Christian ethics, I have been compelled to present the heart of Christian hope and of the Christian faith in as much detail as I have here.

I am dedicating this book to my old friend Johannes Rau, whose political development I accompanied as attentively and sympathetically as Rau accompanied my theological journeyings. As former president of the German Federal Republic, he unfortunately died early on 27 October 2006, but the warmth of his humanity and his natural confidence can still be felt and are unforgotten as a shining model of convincing Christian life in politics. His sermons and addresses at the church's lay assemblies (*Kirchentage*) were published in 2006 under the fine title *Wer hofft, kann handeln* —'the one who hopes can act'.[3]

Part 1
Eschatology and Ethics

Introduction

What Can I Hope For? What Can I Do? Free Action

In this first chapter we will look at the theological connection between hope and action. The different answers to Immanuel Kant's question, 'What can I hope for?' always affect the various choices of action open to us in response to the question, 'What should I do?' We become active in so far as we hope. We hope in so far as we can see into the sphere of future possibilities. We undertake what we think is possible. If, for example, we hope that the world will continue to be as it is now, we shall keep things as they are. If we hope for an alternative future, we shall already change things now as far as possible in accord with that. If the future is closed, then nothing more is possible; we cannot do anything more. Unlike Kant, I am talking about an acting impelled by hope, one not in the mode of 'ought' but in the mode of 'can'. An action sustained by hope is a free action, not one under compulsion.

Hope is always a tense expectation and rouses the attentiveness of all our senses, so that we can grasp the chances for the things we hope for, wherever and whenever they present themselves. That distinguishes hope from mere expectation or a patient waiting. When all the senses are attentive, reason is the vehicle which conveys the knowledge of change. We then perceive things not just as they have become and now exist but also in the different ways they could be. We perceive things not only *sic stantibus* but also *sic fluentibus*, as fluid not static, and try to realize their potentialities for change in a positive direction.

Realism teaches us a sense for reality—for what is. Hope awakens our sense for potentiality—for what could be. In concrete action we always relate the potentiality to what exists, the present to the future. If our actions were directed only to the future, we should fall victim to utopias; if they were related only to the present, we should miss our chances.[1]

In hope we link far-off goals with goals within reach. What is last of all gives meaning to the next-to-last. So in the imaginations of hope there is always a superabundance of what is hoped for. It is only when we want what is now impossible that we arrive at the limits of our possibilities. It is good to stress this added value of hope, for we generally fall short of our possibilities. Lethargy is the real enemy of every hope.

What Must I Fear? What Should I Do? Necessary Action

We become aware of the future not only in our hopes for better times in the future but also, if not even for the most part, in our fears and anxieties. We are worried by the possibility of all the things that can happen. Fear and anxiety are early warning systems of possible dangers and are necessary for living. As long as potential dangers can be discerned and named, they give rise to fears which impel us to do what is necessary in good time, and so to avert the dangers. But if discernible threats swell into insubstantial dangers, they result in diffuse anxieties in the face of nothingness or the total write-off of the world and one's own existence. These anxieties generally lead to despairing resignation and paralysed inactivity or to overreactions which only intensify the dangers.

As well as the fundamental question, 'What can I hope for?' Immanuel Kant should have asked the reverse of this question, 'What must I fear?' But Kant was an 'Enlightened' optimist—theologically, as he himself said, a millennialist. Every answer to the question about our fear affects what we do. Our sense for the possible is roused at least as much by the fear as by the hope.[2] Anxiety is concerned for our lives—hope, for our fulfilled lives. Anxiety awakens all our senses, making them alive to imminent threats, and prepares our reason to recognize in the facts of the present 'the signs of the end'. Without these abilities we would be like the people in Pompeii who didn't notice the eruption of Vesuvius or couldn't accept that it was happening. We would feel as safe as the people before the Flood, who in spite of a biblical warning did not see anything coming (Matt. 24.38-39). Humanity would long since have become extinct. An ethics of fear sees the crises; an ethics of hope perceives the chances in the crises. In the exuberance of hope, the temptation is utopianism; in fear, the temptation is alarmism.

In Ernst Bloch's *Principle of Hope*, we find the foundation for an ethics of change; in *The Imperative of Responsibility*, Hans Jonas gives us an ethics of fear.[3] The hope for what can come is replaced by the fear for what perhaps will no longer be. So it becomes more important to retain what is old than to attain the new. Hans Jonas therefore maintained that the prediction of the bad takes precedence over the prediction of the good: 'It is the rule, to put it in primitive terms, that the prophecy of disaster has to be listened to more attentively than the prophecy of salvation.' For him, general anxiety about the continued existence of humanity is the foundation for the fear of the unforeseeable consequences of human technology. He uses the alarm over humanity's threat to its own existence in order to ensure authentic human being in the present. The 'heuristic of fear' awakens responsibility in the present. That is not pessimism any more than what Bloch disseminated was optimism. It is the reverse side of hope, although the two sides are not equal, since hope precedes fear: without hope there would be no fear, and without 'the prophecy of salvation' there would be no 'prophecy of disaster'.

In Jewish and Christian apocalyptic, the endtime is announced with every conceivable catastrophe scenario, but at the same time deliverance in the new divine beginning is proclaimed all the more intensively. In the catastrophes of the endtime, nothing less than God's Spirit itself will be poured out, so that everything mortal may live (Joel 2.28-32; Acts 2.16-21). With the outpouring of the divine Spirit of life, the new creation of all things begins in the downfall of the world. After 'the heavens pass away' and 'the earth is burnt up', on the Day of the Lord there will be 'a new earth on which righteousness dwells' (2 Peter 3.13).

> Near and hard to grasp the God,
> But where there is danger deliverance also grows.

So wrote Friedrich Hölderlin in his Patmos Hymn.[4] The Christian ethics of hope is called to life through the recollection of the raising of the crucified Christ and therefore expects the dawn of God's new world in the passing away of the old one (Rev. 21.1). The endtime is simultaneously the new-time. In the perils of time it lives from hope for the coming of God. It mobilizes energies out of surmounted fears. It holds instructions for resistance against the old world in anticipation of the new one. It presupposes a transformative eschatology and, correspondingly, is itself transforming action. It is this unity of messianic awareness of the time and transformative action that is meant in Romans 13.12:

> The night is far gone,
> the day is at hand.
> Let us then cast off the works of darkness
> and put on the armour of light.

Christian hope is founded on Christ's resurrection and opens up a life in the light of God's new world. Christian ethics anticipates the universal coming of God in the potentialities of history.

Praying and Watching

All Christian action is embedded in a particular spirituality. In the Benedictine tradition, this spirituality is *ora et labora*, pray and work. Prayer is directed towards God, work towards the world. But through prayer work in the world is seen *sub specie aeternitatis*, in the light of eternity, and is brought before the face of God. In other words, it is answerable to God. Consequently, it is not a pious irrelevance if we begin our daily work, or any special project, with a prayer.

What does hope add to prayer? I think what it adds is 'watching'.[5] In Christian life according to the New Testament, the call to prayer is always linked with the messianic wake-up call to watch. In the night of God in the Garden of Gethsemane, when the disciples are sunk into the deep sleep of hopelessness, Jesus does not ask them, 'Could you not pray with me' but 'Could you not watch with me one hour?' (Mark 14.37), and he warns them: 'Watch and pray that you may not enter into temptation.' Specifically, Christian prayer is always linked with expectation for what is to come, whether it be out of fear of evil and catastrophes or out of hope for the kingdom of God. Watching awakens all our senses for what is to come. Watching and being sober, watching and expecting, watching and being open-eyed, go together in the messianic hope.[6]

In watching we open our eyes and 'recognize' the hidden Christ who waits for us in the poor, the sick, the weary and heavy-laden (Matt. 25.37). In the faces of the poor, we 'see' the face of the crucified God. Today the messianic awakening for God's future is often translated into sensibility for the little things in everyday life. That makes it more realistic but also weaker. Attentiveness in the messianic awakening surely lies in attentiveness for the signs of the times, in which God's future is heralded, so that Christian action, inspired by hope, becomes the anticipation of the coming kingdom in which righteousness and peace kiss each other. So Christian action is accompanied by prayer and watching, by the trust of the heart, by wide open eyes, and by attentive senses.

Waiting and Hastening

Out of hope for God's future, all theologians of hope from Comenius to Blumhardt have praised these two attitudes towards life: Christoph Blumhardt called them *warten und pressieren* 'waiting and being in a hurry'. It is the Second Letter of Peter (3.12) which tells Christians they should be 'waiting for and hastening the coming of the Lord's future'. By this he means the new earth 'on which righteousness dwells'.

Waiting and hastening: that sounds like a contradiction. If we are waiting, then what we are waiting for is not yet there. If we are hastening, then what we have waited for is already in sight. These are the two extremes between which attitudes towards the future are played out. As boundary marks they do not have to be mutually contradictory. Let us translate 'waiting and hastening' into our own language and experience:

Waiting: that doesn't mean a passive waiting-it-out; it means an active expectation. A passage in the prophet Isaiah offers an apt example of the difference. When they are in exile and far from home, the prisoners come to the prophet and ask, 'Watchman, what of the night?'—and he replies: 'Morning is coming, but it is still night. If you will enquire, come back again' (21.11-12). The apostle Paul picks up this image about the night and proclaims the dawn of God's day in the light of Christ's resurrection: 'The night is far gone, the day is at hand' (Rom. 13.12). So waiting turns into expectation, and the dreams of the night become an awakening in the daybreak colours of the new day. The eclipse of God becomes the sunrise of God. As Paul, in his ethic of hope, calls for the 'weapons of light', so the awakening of hope carries the promised future of righteousness into one's own life. God's coming unfolds a transforming power in the present. In our tense expectation we are prepared for God's future, and that future acquires power in our present.

The ability to wait also means not conforming to the conditions of this world of injustice and violence. People who expect God's justice and righteousness no longer accept the so-called normative force of what is fact, because they know that a better world is possible and that changes in the present are necessary. Being able to wait means resisting the threats and seductions of the present, not letting oneself be brought into line, and not conforming.

The ability to wait means not giving oneself up, not capitulating, either before the supremacy of the powers of this world or before one's own helplessness, but living with head held high. The 'upright walk' Kant commends is deserving of every respect. It is the heroic stance of the unbowed back of the free. But 'the head held high' is a result of the approaching redemption (Luke 21.28).

The ability to wait is faithfulness in faith. Hope does not give faith only wings, as we say; it gives faith also the power to stand firm and to endure to the end. That is the famed 'perseverance of the saints' (*perservantia sanctorum*) to which Calvin and the Huguenots held fast. 'O Lord our God, other lords besides thee have ruled over us, but thy name alone we acknowledge'

(Isa. 26.13). For the resistance of the Confessing Church in Nazi Germany after 1933, these words were of vital importance.[7] The Huguenot Christian Marie Durand endured thirty-six years of captivity in the Tour de la constance in Aigues-Mortes and scratched her famous *resistez* on the door instead of denying her faith and so regaining her freedom.

Hastening: To hasten is really to go swiftly in space from one place to another. To hasten 'towards the future' transfers this movement from space into the time of history. The present becomes the transition from what has been to what will be, to the future. To 'hasten' in time means crossing the frontiers of present reality into the spheres of what is possible in the future. In crossing these frontiers we anticipate the future for which we hope. With every doing of the right, we prepare the way for the 'new earth' on which righteousness will 'dwell'. If we achieve some justice for those who are suffering violence, then God's future shines into their world. If we take up the cause of 'widows and orphans', a fragment of life comes into our own life. The earth is groaning under the unjust violence with which we are exploiting its resources and energies. We are 'hastening' towards the Lord's future when we anticipate the righteousness and justice out of which, on the Day of the Lord, a new and enduring earth is to come into being. Not to take things as they are but to see them as they can be in that future, and to bring about this 'can be' in the present, means living up to the future. So looking forward, perceiving possibilities and anticipating what will be tomorrow are fundamental concepts of an ethics of hope. Today 'waiting and hastening towards the Lord's future' means *resisting and anticipating*.

1

Apocalyptic Eschatology

Every Christian ethics is determined by a presupposed eschatology. In differing ethical decisions we must always deal not only with differing ethical conceptions but also with fundamental theological decisions in eschatology, and then in Christology. In this chapter we will make this clear from an apocalyptic eschatology, a christological eschatology, a separistic eschatology and a transformative eschatology.

The Lutheran Doctrine of the Two Kingdoms

Martin Luther was an Augustinian monk. In his early academic life he talks like Augustine about the struggle of the *civitas Dei* against the *civitas diaboli*, the city (or state) of God against the city (or state) of the devil, a struggle which will dominate world history apocalyptically until the end. Cain and Abel, Jerusalem and Babylon, the good and the evil forces, God and the devil are always engaged in the struggle for human beings and creation. Just as this conflict dominates world history, it also determines the personal life of Christians in the form of a struggle between spirit and flesh, a struggle of righteousness against sin, life against death, faith against unbelief.[1] This struggle finds an end only in the resurrection of the dead and eternal life. It is eschatologically interpreted in conformity with an apocalyptic eschatology, which talks about a future not yet decided and hence a final struggle still to be expected. Inasmuch as this doctrine of the two kingdoms means the struggle between God and the devil for rule over the world, it is not a dualism; it is a doctrine of conflict, and its distinctions are polemical in kind.

Understood in Christian terms, the reason for this endtime conflict of history is found in the coming of Christ, in the proclamation of the gospel, and the awakening of faith. In the light of Christ, the Antichrist too will be manifested; the proclamation of the gospel awakens unbelief as well. Faith's decision for God goes with a decision against the devil. The separation between believers and unbelievers anticipates the endtime judgment. In his accord with God, the believer is in opposition to the godless world, and the world opposes him and leads him into temptations, persecutions and suffering. For Luther, the human being stands between God and the devil to the very end. He has to 'renounce' the Devil in baptism and must daily fight against the 'age-old wicked enemy'. Since he is at once 'righteous and a sinner', he is involved in continual conflict between his correspondence and his opposition to God, between faith and unbelief: 'Lord, I believe, help thou mine unbelief'. This apocalyptic doctrine of the two kingdoms does not make a distinction between two different spheres, divided from each other. It perceives two complete aspects of the human being in miniature and of the world as a whole.

Because the *civitas Dei* means the lordship of the creator of the world and of human beings, the church does not stand alone in the struggle against the realm of the devil. There are created orders in this world of evil which are nonetheless in conformity with the kingdom of Christ in the church. Within the great distinction between the kingdom of God and the kingdom of the devil—a distinction which dominates world history as a whole—Luther makes a second one between the saving kingdom of Christ and the life-sustaining kingdom of the world.[2] In order to restrict and disperse the power of the devil, God has established two different rules or governments: the worldly one and the spiritual one. Within the great distinction, these two kingdoms or rules are directed in God's name against the power of the devil but in different ways, and these must therefore be distinguished from one another. The one is *justitia civilis*, civil justice, the other *justitia Dei*, divine justice. In the worldly realm, rule is by law, reason and the sword—in the spiritual kingdom, it is only by God's Word and Spirit, grace and faith. In the spiritual realm God provides for eternal salvation; in the worldly realm human beings provide for the wellbeing of life.

The two rules limit and complement each other mutually. In the worldly rule, law and force contribute to external order and earthly peace. In the spiritual rule the word of God contributes to faith and salvation. In our confused world this distinction between the two rules is also very much a polemical one: it is directed against every kind of religious politics and every political religion. The worldly realm must not intervene in the spiritual one, for no one can be forced to believe. The spiritual rule must not interfere in the worldly one, for no state can be ruled by means of the gospel. This division of functions would certainly seem to be an ideal state of things, but it always needed to be critically related to the religious and political situation of the time, as it must still. Religion is continually being 'made' using politics, and that leads souls astray. Politics are continually being 'made' using religion, and that is the ruin of the worldly order. The spiritual rule acts indirectly on the worldly one inasmuch as it de-divinizes and de-demonizes political power. We should deal with the world, with law and force, objectively and rationally. This world is not going to become the kingdom of God on earth, but it is a good earthly order which counters the chaos disseminated by the devil. We should act towards God and the gospel in a spiritual way. The gospel does not create any better orders in the world, but it does save human beings through faith and requires that in the orders that exist we should practise love.

Although the apocalyptic doctrine about the struggle of the two kingdoms and the practical doctrine about the two earthly rules seem convincing in their limited sense, they become difficult where the political life of Christians is concerned. Does the Christian serve two masters? Is he simultaneously a citizen of two different kingdoms? Should he follow the Sermon on the Mount or the law and force? Luther made a corresponding distinction in the personal life of Christians between the faith which justifies before God without works and the works which ought to be performed simply for the sake of one's neighbour: in relation to God, faith alone; in relation to one's neighbour, love alone. In faith someone is a 'Christian person', in works 'a worldly person'. Anyone who mixes the two will act appropriately towards neither God nor his neighbour.

But what criterion determines good works for one's neighbour? Article XVI of the Augsburg Confession says: 'The Gospel does not destroy the state or the family. On the contrary, it especially requires their preservation as ordinances of God and the exercise of love in these ordinances'.[3] The state, economic life and the family are named as 'divine ordinances'. Are these mentioned only as the fields for love's activity, or are there also authorities and laws to determine our conduct politically, economically and in the family? We should obey 'the powers that be' and keep their laws 'in so far as that may be done without sin'. Resistance is required only if authority and the law want to compel us to sin. But normally speaking harmony reigns, for God rules through both forms of government, and Christ manifests his kingdom against the power of the devil through faith and good works. The more that God's two rules are seen in their common struggle against the realm of the devil, the more they move into proximity to each other. In politics, economic life and in the family, Christians will then become coworkers with God and witnesses to Christ against the kingdom of the devil. Christian love follows Christ's guidelines in life's diverse sectors. In these different sectors Christians act appropriately and rationally but not under their constraints. In the struggle against the power of the devil, the church and the worldly orders come close to each other. The orders are then viewed as spheres of God's good creation 'which should all include Christ'.[4] In dictatorships, the Christian churches did in fact often become the refuge of humanity and freedom and the place of truth.

There are two fundamental questions:

1. The doctrine of the two kingdoms sets the gospel of Christ and the worldly orders within an apocalyptic eschatology about the struggle between the lordship of Christ and the power of the devil. Is this right? Shouldn't the gospel of Christ announce the victory of God over sin, death and devil? 'Hell, where is thy victory!' (1 Cor. 15.55)? Apocalyptic eschatology sees Christ in the light of God's struggle against the devil at the end of history, but it does not see history and the end of history in the light of Christ. It fits Christ into an apocalyptic picture of history and does not let him be the lord of history and its end. For the doctrine of the two kingdoms, the victory of God Paul saw in the resurrection of Christ stands in the apocalyptic future tense, not in the prophetic and apostolic present.

It follows from this that the worldly orders, and preeminently the state, are regarded as God's repressive powers against the evil and chaos of the devil. They are not seen as processes open to the future in which the justice, righteousness and peace of God's kingdom are anticipated. In God's struggle against the machinations of the devil, what counts is the politics of friend or enemy relations and the permanent struggle against evil.

2. The doctrine of the two kingdoms puts worldly government under the law, as distinct from the gospel. But what is the law? The law of Israel's covenant? The natural law of ancient times? The law which is in force in each individual state? If the 'orders' are accepted as they are, what is meant has to be the law in force in any given state. There are no criteria here bearing on 'justice and righteousness'—criteria, that is to say, whereby the justice or injustice of the laws in force are to be judged. If Christianity is supposed to practise love only in the existing structures, this leaves out the creative power of this love in its bearing on law and its power to change structures.

According to the doctrine of the two kingdoms, in worldly structures the Christian acts no differently from other people, appropriately and rationally. But that makes him invisible. So in worldly life Christians become anonymous. There is no plan for a specifically and distinguishable *Christian* ethics.

This doctrine brings into Christian life the realism which takes account of the facts and grasps the normative power of the factual. But it provides no motivation for the world-changing hope which gives effect to what is possible. It is in the best sense conservative, but it is in no way innovative.

The Apocalyptic Catechon

In apocalyptic eschatology there is a mysterious biblical passage which has led to ever-new speculations down to the present day: 'For the mystery of lawlessness is already at work, but only until the one who now restrains it is removed. And then the lawless one will be revealed, whom the Lord Jesus will destroy with the breath of his mouth, annihilating him by the manifestation of his coming' (2 Thess. 2.7-8, NRSV).

Who is this 'restrainer', in Greek the κατέχον, the 'catechon'? In whose name does he hold back the complete revelation of the evil and therefore delay the victory of 'the Lord Jesus' over the evil one?

It is impossible to discover exegetically whom Paul means in the Second Epistle to the Thessalonians. After the Constantinian turn of events, Christian tradition saw the catechon as being the Roman state. It was that which restrained the power of endtime evil, thus winning time for the church to spread. Whereas persecuted early Christendom tried to hurry on the end, praying 'Amen, come Lord Jesus, come soon' (see Rev. 22.20), the imperial Constantinian church prayed *pro mora finis*—that the end might be delayed. Whereas the early Christians suffered from the delay of the parousia (2 Pet. 3.4), the imperial church deliberately went along with this delay of the parousia and fortified 'the restrainer' by legitimating it theologically.

Dietrich Bonhoeffer praised the 'restrainer' as being the ordering power of the state,[5] which with immense physical power stood successfully in the way of what would have led to disaster. 'The restraining power...is the force that is made effective within history by God's rule in the world which sets limits to evil. The 'restrainer' itself is not itself God, and is not without guilt, but God uses it to protect the world from disintegration....The 'restraining force' is the ordering power of the state.[6] According to Bonhoeffer, this ordering power sees its ally in the church, and such elements of order as still exist seek the proximity of the church. Bonhoeffer wrote this during the Second World War, after he had already joined the resistance. At that time the mystery of wickedness was by no means restrained by the state. On the contrary, the German state served the cause of wickedness. It was empowered by the evil which through the agency of the German state spread death and destruction. The Nazi dictatorship was organized 'wickedness'. In the resistance Bonhoeffer evidently looked for the true power of the state, which can 'restrain' this destructive power. And what gathered around the Confessing Church was in fact the political and cultural resistance against the Nazi barbarity.

In its power against evil, the catechon does not merely hold back the complete development of evil, but in doing so it also corresponds in time to the final annihilation of evil which will come about through Christ's appearance. In so far, it is at the service of God and ministers to the lordship of Christ. Unless it could be understood in this sense, the 'restrainer' would hinder not only the culmination of evil but the coming of Christ too. But then it would be impermissible for Christians to support the ordering power of the state. They would have to be anarchists, so as to hasten Christ's coming; for after all they expect with Paul that at the end Christ will 'destroy every rule and every authority and power…that God may be all in all' (1 Cor. 1.24, 28).

The political theology of the conservative constitutional theorist Carl Schmitt was rooted in his apocalyptic eschatology and was intended to serve solely its expectation of the final struggle.[7] Consequently in his speculations about the theology of history, he again and again came to speak about the mysterious catechon which the Second Epistle to the Thessalonians talks about. His political theology begins with the revelation of God, the truth of which is accepted only in faith. Unbelief is therefore not only an enemy of faith; it is an enemy of God as well. The divine revelation divides friend from enemy. It is the revelation itself which brings about this separation. 'It is only because of God's revelation that there is enmity against God.' So unbelief is not an inability to believe; it is rebellion against God. What Carl Schmitt calls in his politics the fundamental 'friend-enemy' relationship originates in the division between belief and unbelief. The primal metaphysical image of the political friend-enemy relationship is the relationship between God and Satan in the conflict of world history. The eschatological orientation in history is given by the relation between Christ and Antichrist in the decisive battle of the endtime.[8]

'I believe in the catechon; for me as a Christian it is the only way in which to understand history and to find meaning in it.'[9] There are three reasons impelling Schmitt to this belief. 1. The idea of the catechon explains the delay of the parousia without surrendering the expectation. 2. It explains why there is still history at all after the coming of Christ. 3. It gives the state a meaning in the context of salvation history. Since Christ's coming, there must have been a catechon in every era. 'Its place was never unoccupied; if it had been we should no longer exist', said Schmitt, and yet he was unable to give the catechon a name. If it is meant to be the state, which state? Every state or only legitimate states? Up to now there has been no universal state which could have held back the end of world history. Are there as many catechons as there are national states? Or is it individual persons important in world history who are meant? Or is it an angel? After all, Paul talks about the catechon in the singular. So the catechon must be universal. Not without a certain ironic recollection of Carl Schmitt's anti-Semitism, one is reminded of the story about the 'ten righteous men' for whose sake God was to spare Sodom, as Abraham prays (Gen. 18.22-33). That has found its place in the Jewish legend about the few righteous in every generation for whose sake the world still exists and because of whom the Last Judgment is still deferred.

However it may be with the deferring of the final struggle, the catechon doctrine lends state power a sacred status in salvation history, and for Carl Schmitt that was the point. From an eschatological viewpoint it preserves human beings, but only in an extreme state of alert, as German Lutheran theologian Wilhelm Stählin thought;[10] or to put it more precisely: it awakens an apocalyptic alarmism which is hardly conducive to the surmounting of historical crises, because it paralyses the power to act. It defines the task of the state one-sidedly as being the repression of evil, chaos and anarchy. It confers apocalyptic legitimation on this repression. This of course is no protection against the hostile takeover of state power by evil itself. But state terrorism and anti-Christian politics have put their stamp on twentieth-century experience.

In the twenty-first century, we are facing another threat to the state: international terrorism, particularly of an Islamic kind. Suicide activists cannot be punished by death. They have departed from the foundation of all international agreements, which is the will to survive. Their desire is annihilation, the annihilation of others, of themselves and often of this whole wicked world. Terrorist groups are recruited from states in which the state's monopoly of power cannot be sustained.[11] These are disintegrating states, such as Somalia and Pakistan. But even in the wealthy countries of the West, the state's power monopoly is surrendered once security is privatized and made a commodity only the rich can still afford. These people then live in gated communities and pay private security personnel. On the other hand, in these same countries there are slums in which the police are powerless. In this briefly outlined situation, to which we shall return, the catechon must first enforce its constitutionally legitimated monopoly of power, and out of many catechons a worldwide catechon must emerge to organize humanity's will to survive, suppress apocalyptically aligned terrorism and hold back the manmade destructions of the world.

Armageddon

This prophecy can be found in the book of Revelation in the chapter about the outpouring of God's wrath through seven angels.

> For they are demonic spirits, performing signs, who go abroad to the kings of the whole world, to assemble them for battle on the great day of God the Almighty…and they assembled them at the place which is called in Hebrew Armageddon. (Rev. 16.14, 16)

The prophecy has no connection with the victory of Christ and the downfall of Babylon. Since the name 'Armageddon' is not explained any further, it is probably meant to remain a mystery. Historically, there may be an echo here of an old myth about the onslaught of the demonic army against the mountain of the gods, the demons then being annihilated by light-emanating divine beings.[12] The struggle between the Almighty God and the demons talked about here does not play a central role in the Apocalypse of John because it does not talk about 'the victory of the Lamb'.[13]

In the apocalyptic tradition of the English Reformation, the central point from the beginning was the struggle between Christ and the Antichrist, God and the devil, believers and unbelievers.[14] Nowhere else in Europe were so many commentaries on the book of Revelation written as in England. Among them we may especially mention one written by King James I and another by Sir Isaac Newton. In the political mythology of the Pilgrim Fathers in the American colonies, the Exodus from Egypt (Europe) and the arrival in the promised land (America) always played a legitimizing role for the occupation of the lands belonging to America's original inhabitants. So the apocalyptic dualism of the English Reformation itself was adopted too, brought over and became deeply anchored in the American soul. American expectations of the end of the world were always concentrated on the final struggle between God and the devil, the good and the wicked. Nowhere else in worldwide Christianity did this mysterious name 'Armageddon' play such a key role for churches, politics, world history and 'the rest of the world'.[15]

In the middle of the seventeenth century, a Christian Zionism emerged in England.[16] The Jews no longer counted as agents of the Antichrist, as they had in the Reformation period. They were now seen as agents of the apocalyptic redemption of the world.[17] The scenario has remained the same down to the present day. Act I: The Jews return home from the Dispersion and build the state of Israel. Act II: The demonically ruled Gentile nations make an assault on Israel. Act III: These nations will be annihilated by God in the battle of battles at Armageddon. Act IV: Then Christ will come with his own, who have been 'caught up' or 'raptured' before the great tribulation; he will appear on Zion and set up his thousand years' kingdom. So all the Jews must first be compelled to return to Israel. Christian Zionists such as the television preacher Pat Robertson have collected millions of dollars in order to finance the return of Russian Jews to Israel. In Jerusalem, the 'Christian Embassy' sees to the distribution of the money. Then the true believers must be prepared for the final struggle in Armageddon by being made certain that they will be snatched away and by cutting themselves off from all those who remain behind. In the scenario Hal Lindsay developed in *The Late Great Planet Earth*,[18] in the first wave Soviet Russia's 'Red Army' will move against Jerusalem and will be annihilated in Armageddon by US atomic bombs; then the People's Army from China will move up; it will be annihilated in the same place by US hydrogen bombs. And then Christ, 'the Lion of Judah', will appear with those who are his and will bring about the millennium.

One can brush all this aside as apocalyptic nonsense, but unfortunately that kind of thinking influences American politicians too. In October 1983, United States President Ronald Reagan told a journalist from the *Jerusalem Post*: 'I turn back to the Old Testament prophets and to the signs which announce the Armageddon, and I ask myself whether we are not the generation that will experience it. I don't know if you have recently come across any of these prophecies, but believe me, they certainly describe the time we are living in.' Asked later by *Time Magazine* whether he meant a 'nuclear Armageddon', Reagan said 'yes';[19] but then said no more; for in order to bring about a nuclear Armageddon it was he himself, not God Almighty, who would have had to press the button.

However it may be with the apocalyptic Armageddon, this expectation of the endtime struggle puts the present, both religiously and politically, into a permanent state of war: religiously by separating believers from unbelievers, politically by continually fanning anew the flames of 'friend-enemy' thinking. Enemies—in the Cold War it was the Red East, the Soviet Union and China; after that came the 'rogue states': Iraq, Iran and North Korea. Without an enemy there can be no struggle, and without a struggle there is no expectation of the final battle and the victory of the good and its God over the wicked.[20]

2

Christological Eschatology[1]

Calvinist Kingdom-of-God Theology

The Lutheran Reformation came into being in the German princely states and the Reformed churches in the city-states of Zurich, Geneva and Strasbourg. These cities had already developed what were to some extent democratic forms of government in the magistrate constitutions. There, every Christian was also a responsible citizen of his city. Reformed faith and political responsibility were more closely interwoven among the ordinary people than they were in the Lutheran principalities. The fundamental idea of a *civitas Christiana*, a Christian city or state, linked faith and politics in the Christian and the civil communities. In political negotiations, the citizens' representatives sought to discern the will of God; and Zwingli in Zurich, Calvin in Geneva, and Bucer in Strasbourg came to the town hall armed with the Bible. In the Zurich Disputation of 1523, Zwingli subjected the city's politics to 'the guideline of Christ'. It was from the teaching and acts of Christ that the authorities took their power and consolidation. If they proceeded without the guideline of Christ, they were to be deposed in the name of God.[2] The theocracy was manifested in the law of Moses and in Christ's interpretation of that law: *Politia Moisi* and *Politia Christi*. These Reformers saw no antithesis to the gospel in the biblically attested divine law but viewed it as a 'form of the gospel' (Karl Barth) and understood the gospel as being the law of Christ. They certainly distinguished between the spiritual and the worldly rule, as Luther did too, but according to their interpretation Christians do not live simultaneously in two different worlds but in the one, inclusive rule of Christ in life's different sectors. They did not view the state as merely an earthly order but always formulated its significance and its functions in the context of the kingdom of God. We might call this a theocratic interpretation of the state. In the Swiss city-states, this theological perspective on politics led to a theocratic interpretation of democracy. Luther had stressed 'the general priesthood of all believers' over against the clerical tyranny in Rome, and with that he discovered the rights of the congregation. Against the onset of political absolutism in France and England, the Calvinist theologians stressed 'the general kingship of all believers' and discovered the political significance of the covenant as the foundation of constitutional democracy. 'The crown sitteth not on the head of any man, but on the constitution of free citizens', said John Milton.[3]

Karl Barth's Christological Eschatology

The most convincing contemporary form of Reformed kingdom-of-God theology in our time was formulated by Karl Barth in the era of the Confessing Church's struggle against the total claim of the Nazi dictatorship in Germany.[4] The Barmen Theological Declaration of 1934, written by Barth, proceeds in Thesis 1 from the assertion that God has revealed himself completely and finally in Jesus Christ and that for the church of Christ there is therefore no other source of revelation. God reveals himself in his Word Jesus Christ. He does not reveal himself additionally in history or nature, in political events or through political leaders. Thesis 2 concludes from this that Jesus Christ is already Lord over the cosmos, the principalities and powers, and hence over all sectors of human life. So there are no sectors in which Christians should listen to any voices other than the voice of Christ. 'We reject the false doctrine that there could be areas of life in which we would not belong to Jesus Christ but to other lords.' 'All things and conditions are subject to the liberating and demanding lordship of Christ. In all areas we are in need of justification and sanctification.'[5]

The fundamental theological decision in support of this doctrine about the sole and all-comprehensive lordship of Christ derives from Karl Barth's *Church Dogmatics*.[6] We may sum it up in three points, without claiming completeness for the summary.

First, objectively speaking, the whole world is already in Christ and subject to his rule, for God has raised him, exalted him and given him all power in heaven and on earth. Death has already been swallowed up in the victory of the living God. So the struggle in world history between the *regnum Dei* and the *regnum diaboli* is already decided. In Christian faith we see the world in the light of the resurrection and live in the certainty of Christ's victory. Objectively, seen from God's standpoint, all human beings are already reconciled in Christ, even if subjectively there are still those who already believe and those who do not yet believe. Here Augustinian-Lutheran apocalyptic Christology is replaced by a christological eschatology. God's struggle against Satan, which continues to the end, now becomes the victory God has attained once and for all in Christ over sin, death and the devil. The eschatological future can only be the universal and manifested epiphany of that which in Christ is already 'finished'.

Second, in those years, in three topical writings, Barth tried to present the relationship between church and world along the lines of this christological eschatology: in *Evangelium und Gesetz* ('Gospel and Law', 1935)[7]; in *Recht-fertigung und Recht* ('Justification and Law', 1938),[8] and in *Christengemeinde und Bürgergemeinde* ('The Christian Community and the Civil Community', 1946).[9] If Christ is Lord, then all power in heaven and on earth has already been given to him. It follows that 'that power, the State as such, belongs originally and ultimately to Jesus Christ; that in its comparatively independent substance, in its dignity, its function and its purpose, it should serve the Person and the Work of Jesus Christ and therefore the justification of the sinner'.[10] Is the consequence of this a christological metaphysics of the state, or is this meant as theological justification for the political activity of Christians?

Finally, Barth points out above all, however, that the order of the kingdom of God and the new creation of all things in the New Testament is described not with religious concepts but with political ones: the kingdom, the heavenly *polis* Jerusalem, the heavenly citizenship. 'The Church sees its future and its hope, not in any heavenly image of its own existence, but in the real heavenly State.'[11] The future of the church is more than church, it is the universal kingdom of God, 'on earth as it is in heaven'. Through politically relevant preaching and action, the Christian community manifests this political eschatology to the civil community in which it lives. Because the whole world is the space of the liberating rule of Christ, Christianity assumes its responsibility in all sectors of life.

The perception of the sovereign rule of Christ which surmounts all frontiers leads to a christocratic ethic. But what will the criteria and perspectives for this political discipleship of Christ be?

Political Parables of the Kingdom of God

Barth does not distinguish between church and state from the top down, according to their ways of ruling, but from below, according to their types of community: the Christian community and the civil community. The state is the legally constituted community of citizens and their unified social community. It is not characterized as 'the powers that be' in the first place because of its monopoly of power. The foundation of the political community is law, not power, and its monopoly of power must be bound to the law. The Christian community certainly sees the state order of the civil community as an

order of divine grace but mainly as an exponent of the kingdom of God—
outside the Christian community but not outside the lordship of Christ.

Barth conceives the relationship between Christian community and civil
community in the image of two concentric circles: the central point is Christ
the Lord; the inner circle of the lordship of Christ is the believing Christian community, which proclaims Christ's liberating lordship and the hope
for God's coming kingdom. The outer circle is the civil community, which
orders social and political life in accordance with justice. It is not meant to
become the Christian community but should be independently responsible for its own tasks. The state is not the kingdom of God, but it belongs
within the promise of the coming universal peace and righteousness and
justice. In describing this relationship between the state and the kingdom
of God, Barth uses the concept and language of parable. The parable—the
correspondence—the resonance—bridge the gap between similarity and
dissimilarity. Just as in 1928 Barth already considered culture to be in need
of parable and open to parable,[12] this is also true of the political community
and the politics of the state. The Christian community will press towards
correspondences with the lordship of Christ and towards parables of the
hoped-for kingdom of God in the civil community. It wants human law
to correspond to the divine righteousness and not to contradict it. It wants
human beings and civil laws to correspond to the freedom of God's children.
It wants politics to be pursued with honesty, because it itself lives in the
light of God's truth. It will resist both a deification of political power and
a demonization of the state. It will support moderation in human affairs. It
will resist the Moloch of 'nationalism' and try to tame predatory capitalism.

However questionable the examples are that Barth puts forward, his fundamental idea is clear: politics is capable of acting as a parable for the lordship of Christ, which the church believes in, and for the hoped-for kingdom
of God, in which the whole creation will become new. This means that 'the
true state must have its prototype and model in the true church'.[13]

We have to ask some critical questions.

Where can we find 'the true church' which could be a 'prototype and model'
for the civil community and the state? Of course, historically speaking, such
instances can be shown, but they are moments of chance, 'providential', as we
say. And a few fortunate moments give the church no claim to the allegiance
of political life. Where there has been any such allegiance in modern times,
the church has been conservative in a traditional sense and has supported
authoritarian, undemocratic forms of government, for example, in Spain

and Portugal. Ever since the French Revolution, the Christian churches in Europe have been laggards in cultural development rather than pioneers. This does not refute the view that politics in the form of social and peace policies are capable of being parables of the kingdom of God for which Christians hope and that politics should be such parables more than is the case. The state is a form of the kingdom of God parallel to the church and should be respected by the church and influenced by it.

Karl Barth's christological eschatology is a realized, or presentative, eschatology in which hardly anything is left for futurist eschatology except the universal unveiling of what God has already brought in Christ. This means that the Old Testament's surplus of promise beyond the coming of Christ to which the New Testament testifies is annulled. It means that Israel too has no future other than conversion to the Christ who has come. But still ahead is the resurrection of the dead and the new creation of all things, the future of Israel and the establishment of the kingdom of God on a new earth where righteousness dwells. Christian life is certainly discipleship of Christ, but in that discipleship it is also an anticipation of the coming kingdom and the new creation of all things. Consequently, for an ethics of hope, a futurist eschatology is indispensible.

Theocratic Democracy

I am going beyond Barth but, I hope, along the same lines when I point out that democracy proceeded from belief in the sovereignty of God and the limitation which imposes on all human powers.[14] Today the word 'theocracy' is used for religious dictatorships which want to dominate everything in the name of God. That is wrong. Literally speaking, 'theocracy' says that all power and force belongs to God alone and that it is therefore in principle withdrawn from human scope. No one has the right to rule over other human beings, for God alone is the Lord. If human beings are to rule over the earth, they have to be given the charge by God (Gen. 1.26), since 'the earth is the LORD's, and the fullness thereof, the world and those who dwell therein' (Ps. 24.1). Understood in this way, in a theocracy the fear of God permits no one to rule by the grace of God. If human beings act as representatives of other human beings, and thus exercise rule, that rule must be humanely based and is answerable to God, to whom all power belongs.

Through the influence of Christianity, the cult of the God-emperor came to an end in Europe and was replaced by intercession for the ruler, for whom power was a danger and a temptation. Under the absolutism of Louis XIV, the sovereign was not answerable to the people. In the Nazi dictatorship, the Führer's will counted as law. In the Communist totalitarian state, the party 'was always right'. Calvinist theocracy taught absolute and total resistance to these absolute and total deifications of the state, providing the justification for the alternative of modern times: constitutional democracy. The prohibition of images and the fight against idolatry had lasting political consequences. In America, democracy is always viewed as the Christian form of the state and is put in relation to the kingdom of God.[15] It was only in the old countries of Europe that democracy counted as atheistic or relativistic, because in France it had to prevail not only against political absolutism but also against the clericalism and papism of the Roman Catholic Church. True tolerance, springing from concern for other people, is rooted in the theocracy which withdraws human beings from the absolutist claim of others or of a state. Since modern democracy was founded on the basis of universal human rights, it has a charge for humanity and a missionary character of its own: 'To save the world for democracy.' In this slogan parables of God's universal kingdom of peace and his righteousness are evident.

3

Separatist Eschatology

An Interim Reflection: Did Jesus Teach a Special Ethics? Is There Such a Thing as a Christian Ethics?

Christian moral philosophers in Germany think that a special Christian ethics is not possible:

1. Christians have no better ideas about the solution of ethical problems in today's society than other people. There is only one natural or general human ethics which Christians observe, like other people. There are no specifically Christian solutions to questions about nuclear energy or genetic engineering.

2. Christians have to act as pragmatically and responsibly in society as other people.

3. In disputed ethical questions there is no common answer to which all Christians assent. The differences in public opinion run right through Christianity as well. When the Roman Catholic Church sets up ethical norms, these are based not on Jesus' teaching but on natural law, because that makes them reasonable and generally acceptable.

The upshot of these arguments is that, as far as public ethical action is concerned, Christians are indistinguishable. According to the Lutheran doctrine of the two kingdoms as we have described it, Christians act in worldly matters according to law and reason, even if also in love. According to the Reformed doctrine about the royal rule of Christ, they make special identifiable characteristics of the Christian community relevant in a general human sense in civil society. But the Christian origin of their good orientations and decisions are no longer seen.

Underlying the unidentifiable quality of a specifically Christian ethos explained in this way is not just a fundamental problem of Christian ethics; there is also the fundamental theological problem of Christology itself. If Jesus is the Christ who has come into the world, as the confession of Peter and Martha affirms (Matt. 16.16; John 11.27), then he is the Messiah promised by the prophets. But indispensable to the Messiah is the messianic era and the changes the Messiah brings to his people and the world of the nations: indispensable to the Messiah is divine justice for the wretched and the peace of the nations. So the discussion about the Christian character of an ethics has to do with nothing less than the acknowledgment of Christ itself. The question asked of Christian ethics is not whether it has good or better solutions for general social or political problems. The question is preeminently whether the way and teaching of Jesus has to be taken seriously. Christian ethics should first and foremost put its stamp on a form of living which accords with Jesus' way of life and his teaching. That is where its identity lies. The question about general relevance then follows, but it cannot take first place.

Ever since the era of the Reformation, this has been precisely the question posed by the Anabaptists, the Mennonites and the Gemeinschaft der Brüder to the Lutheran state churches and to the Reformed congregational churches.[1] The knowledge that Christ alone is Lord cannot be confined to faith. It must encompass the whole of life. Why is the saving significance of the cross of Christ at the centre of Lutheran belief, and the resurrection of Christ at the centre of Reformed belief, and in neither of them is the way of life and the teaching for which Christ was crucified by the Romans and which as the Gospels show were endorsed by God when he raised him from the dead? Jesus' self-surrender to death on the cross and his raising and exaltation to be Lord are events in the vertical dimension—the dimension of eternity—but his way of life and his teachings are horizontal recollections in time and hopes for the future of his kingdom. Faith is related to Jesus' giving of himself for many; hope is related to his raising and exaltation to be Lord; but the discipleship of Jesus corresponds to his way of life and his teaching. The ethical idea of discipleship was 'a stepchild of the Reformation'.[2] But for the Anabaptists, the idea of discipleship was fundamental.

Christo-logic and Christo-praxis form a unity. It is not only with our reason that we know Christ, and it is not only with the faith of the heart that we trust him; we also confess him through the way we live. That was the fundamental perception of the Anabaptists in the years of Luther, Zwingli and Calvin. As Hans Denk put it: 'No one is able verily to know Christ unless he follows him with his life.'[3]

The praxis of the discipleship of Jesus becomes intellectually relevant when it contributes to the assurance of faith as well as in witness to other people. The slogan of the Reformers was *solus Christus*. The slogan of the Anabaptists was *totus Christus*. The only place I have found a 'Chapel of the Sermon on the Mount' was in the Mennonite seminary in Elkhart, Indiana.

Who Were the Anabaptists?

The third force in the Reformation of the sixteenth century were the so-called Anabaptists, or 're-baptizers'. Although they were condemned, persecuted and put to death in great numbers by Catholic, Lutheran and Reformed Christians, the Anabaptist movement sprang up among the people and was a Christian reformation of a special kind. One root of this movement reaches back to the beginnings of the Reformation in Zurich. In 1525 a group of people around Felix Mantz, Jörg Blaurock and Konrad Grebel met together in the fishing village of Zollikon and baptized each other afresh, in order to surrender their lives entirely to Christ. They had been moved by Zwingli's sermons and had learned from Erasmus of Rotterdam. They were educated people. With their believers' baptism they called into question obligatory infant baptism, which was the very foundation of the state church in the *Corpus Christianum*. By doing so they called into question the *Corpus Christianum* itself. The movement spread rapidly in southern Germany and Bohemia. Michael Sattler, formerly prior in the monastery of St Peter in the Black Forest, gathered Anabaptist congregations in Swabia and in 1527 drew up the Schleitheim Confession,[4] the first confession of the Anabaptists. A few months later Sattler was taken prisoner in Rottenburg together with his adherents, was interrogated, tortured and executed. His wife was drowned in the River Neckar. Other regions where the Anabaptists spread were the Netherlands and Friesland. Whereas when the princes and the free imperial cities adopted the Reformation they were always simultaneously pursuing political interests, the Anabaptist movement was a reformation for Christ's sake. It was often monks who carried into worldly life the monastic way of consistent discipleship of Jesus and founded Christian communes. Many priests were converted; Balthasar Hubmaier was rector of the university in Ingolstadt and cathedral preacher in Regensburg; Hans Denk was a humanist; Pilgram Marbeck was an honourable citizen of Augsburg; there were also many theologians among the ranks of the Anabaptists.

What is generally known is only the attempt by the Anabaptists to establish 'the New Jerusalem' in Münster by force and the catastrophe of 1534. Because of the violent persecutions, one section of the Anabaptists, the 'Gladiari', took to the sword, while another group, the 'Stabulari', refused to do so. Both groups were punished as heretics 'by fire, sword and the like, as the occasion demanded'. Between 1529 and 1555 at least fifty thousand Anabaptists were put to death in the Netherlands alone. Not a few of them shared the protest of the peasant farmers against their oppression and exploitation and together with Thomas Müntzer participated in the peasant revolts. The well-known Anabaptist missionary Hans Hut was one of them. Even after their catastrophic defeat in the battle of Frankenhausen in 1525, they held on to the economic and social demands of the peasant rebels and tried to realize them through the ideal of the community of property. Anabaptists founded the communities of the Hutterite brethren in Moravia and organized social networks for mutual help.

According to Article 6 of the Schleitheim Confession and the influential teachings of Menno Simons (1496–1561), the Anabaptist movement in the broad sense was committed to a violence-free life of nonresistance, following 'the way of the cross'. For the Anabaptists, the kingdom of God on earth was not to be established in Münster but was to be found in the heavenly Christ. For them, Jesus' way of life and teachings were the presence of the kingdom of God in person. The Anabaptists of the Reformation period lived out the great refusal and suffered and died for it. They refused infant baptism. They refused service with the sword, because 'the sword is an ordinance of God outside the perfection of Christ', as Article 6 of the Schleitheim Confession says. They refused to participate in tasks imposed by the authorities because 'the rule of the powers that be' was 'according to the flesh, but that of Christians is according to the Spirit'. They refused to swear the oath of allegiance, following Jesus' command, rejecting for themselves this foundation of the *Corpus Christianum* although accepting it for others. The sword is a 'divine ordinance' but not for Christians. They wanted to live only in the voluntary community of Christ. The 'powers that be', both Catholic and Protestant, saw the Anabaptist refusal as an attack on the *Corpus Christianum* which imperilled its life. In 1528 the emperor issued a mandate against them which in 1529 was raised to an imperial law. This reactivated against 'Anabaptists' a thousand-year-old law promulgated by the Emperor Justinian which imposed on them the sentence of death. Catholic and Protestant authorities alike persecuted the Anabaptists with the sanction of the imperial law, because the 'Holy Empire' was under attack.

What Did the Anabaptists Believe?

The theological thinking of the Anabaptists was as varied as their dissemination, but about one thing they were united: this old, corrupt world is going to be replaced by a completely new creation.[5] With Christ, the new Adam, the heavenly human being, has appeared, one who has nothing more to do with the old Adam, the earthly human being. They replaced the apocalyptic dualism of the two eras of the transitory and the coming world by the ontological dualism of heaven and earth. As the bride of Christ, the heavenly man, the church is itself heavenly in nature and can have nothing more to do with the earthly, fleshly institutions of the 'world'. Responsibility for the world gives way to denial of the world and detachment from worldly affairs.

For this viewpoint, the sixteenth-century reformer Melchior Hofmann developed a specifically Anabaptist Christology which was in fact Gnostic: at his incarnation, the heavenly Christ did not take upon himself flesh from Mary but brought his heavenly humanity with him. In this way he became the new Adam, who had nothing more in common with the old one. According to Roman Catholic teaching, Christ's humanity was supposed to be of a sinless nature; consequently, Mary had to be excepted from original sin by way of her own immaculate conception. The Anabaptists were only going a step further along the same docetic path when they identified sin with the flesh of earthly human beings and replaced it with the new heavenly humanity.

Anthropologically, what follows from this is a doctrine not of rebirth but of new birth. Melchior Hofmann's theology (also followed by Menno Simons, who gave his name to the Mennonites) was marked by the absolute antithesis between the heavenly and the earthly in Christology, soteriology and ecclesiology. 'His theme was not the reconciliation of the human being with God but the deification of the human being—not the justification of the godless but the sanctification of the redeemed—not the sanctification of believers through their incorporation in the body of Christ but the presentation of the church as Christ's holy bride through the gathering of the saints.'[6] In this way the mission of the community of Christians following the sending of Christ into the world was replaced by the gathering of the heavenly community and the zeal for their purity.

How Did the Anabaptists Live?

'No one is able verily to know Christ unless he follows him with his life', declared the Anabaptist leader Hans Denk (1500–1527). This discipleship though the believer's life takes its impress from the path and teaching of Jesus, above all from the Sermon on the Mount, and is accentuated through its antithesis to 'the world'. 'It shall not be so among you' (Matt. 20.26).[7] Christ became human 'just like us, yet without sin'. Jesus was the one who was sinless and pure. To follow him 'with one's life' makes believers sinless and pure in a new human existence. In the heavenly fellowship of believers there is only admonition, no coercion; forgiveness, no judgment; love, no retaliation.

This voluntary community is the counter-picture to the violent society of laws and constraints. 'The perfection of Christ' is manifested through the refusal to participate in state violence. The Anabaptists did not believe, like Luther, that hangmen and soldiers 'could belong to a blessed estate'. The discipleship of Jesus demands a life lived for peace, with defencelessness and vulnerability for oneself and hence with preparedness for suffering and martyrdom. A moving Anabaptist hymn of 1527 begins 'Wie köstlich ist der Heilgen Tod ('How precious is the death of the saints'). Michael Sattler was an Anabaptist leader martyred in 1527. When during his interrogation in Rottenburg he was asked about resistance against the Turks, with their threat to the Christian empire, his answer was 'Live defencelessly'.[8] The sole concern of the Anabaptists was to come to resemble Christ through discipleship but not to regulate the powers of this earth justly and peacefully. They confronted the world with a great rejection, but they did not want to transform it. They were not revolutionaries, although through their rejection they shook the foundations of the *Corpus Christianum* and through the voluntary principle they maintained they anticipated the coming age of subjectivity and the autonomous individual.

As history went on, the Mennonites, and even more the Baptists, became increasingly tame and were less and less persecuted. 'The quiet in the land' were peaceful and were left in peace. Their forms of life developed best in agricultural settings and in rural communes. The Hutterites in the United States and Canada are a good example. In communities of the brethren, they can arrange their affairs for themselves and can preserve a pure communal life.[9] It was the Baptist Martin Luther King who was required 'to show the Mennonites that Jesus' teaching about non-resistance in fact possesses a power to change society and that the love of enemies proves itself in the streets.'[10]

In the sixteenth century, Catholics, Lutherans and Reformed defended the Holy Empire Constantine had once established. They were prepared to transform 'swords' into Christian swords. The Anabaptists wanted to live in accordance with the standards of the early and pre-Constantinian church. They let swords be swords, withdrawing to the ploughshares. But the essential thing is to reforge the swords into ploughshares.

The Post-Liberal Separation between "Church" and "World": Stanley Hauerwas

In the twenty-first century, Stanley Hauerwas took up a position similar to that of the Anabaptists in the sixteenth century.[11] But he did so not in the context of the old *Corpus Christianum* but in the liberal democracy of the United States. If the context changes so much, the results of a similar position can be very different. In the sixteenth century the Anabaptists were persecuted under imperial law. Modern liberal democracy does not persecute any religious communities but makes them ineffective through relativist tolerance.

What is 'post-liberal' in the United States today? In the nineteenth century, liberal Christianity extolled its era as 'the Christian century'. Church and culture, faith and morality, Christianity and democracy merged to the point of unrecognizability. This civil religion became the soul of the American empire. Modern post-liberal theologians in the United States link on to the new era of dialectical theology which emerged from German culture-Christianity after the First World War. Karl Barth and Dietrich Bonhoeffer are the sources and authorities for the new retreat from compromised Christianity to the church of Christ: it is only in the church that Christian identity in faith and life is to be found. Worldly disengagement and political disentanglement are required so that the church can come to itself and therefore to Christ. 'The Christian must be uninvolved in the politics of our society and involved in the policy that is the church.'[12] Theology becomes church dogmatics in the sense that it can be understood only in church circles. According to George Lindbeck's cultural-linguistic theory, religion, like a language, can be understood only in the light of its own presuppositions; it cannot be translated into other discourses.[13] In this way theology becomes the witness of its own concern but not a partner in the public discourse. The 'Yale school' maintains this position in American theology and calls it 'post-liberal'. But one asks what then really happened at Pentecost?

Hauerwas is a moral philosopher and transfers into life this retreat by theology into the church. The result is a radical antagonism between what 'church' is supposed to be and what 'world' is. In the church there are 'forgiven sinners', in the world unforgiven sins; the church is obedient to God, the world is disobedient; the church is holy, the world is full of lies and violence; the church is *the peaceable kingdom*, the sinful world is marked by violence; the church shows the unity of human beings, the world is engaged in permanent conflict and disunity. The church's prime task is to follow Jesus' way of life and teaching, in this way showing the world that it is 'world'. The church does not proclaim any social ethic but is itself an alternative social reality of truth and peace in a world of violence. Nonviolence and a rejection of every war through a refusal to perform military service is a fundamental obligation of the church of Christ.[14] Like the Mennonite theologian John Howard

Yoder, Hauerwas too condemns the 'Constantinianism' in which the Christian witness is superfluous and Christians have become unrecognizable. God
becomes visible through the holiness of the church; the church must leave it
to God to change the world. The heart of the church is worship. Christian
ethics takes its bearings from the essential parts of the liturgy, especially the
Eucharist, and describes life in Christ. Christian ethics is ethics for Christians, no more than that. Hauerwas rightly traces Christian ethics back to
Christian identity and its resources, but he wrongly surrenders the public
relevance of God, or of liberal democracy in its postmodern do-as-you-like
form.[15] He has therefore been reproached with sectarianism. But my own
impression is that with the crass antagonism he postulates between church
and world, he fails to confront the world with the gospel at all and does not
disturb the world either, let alone call it into question. Why does he follow
the Mennonite Yoder and not the Baptist Martin Luther King? Why does
the pure but innocuous little flock seem to him holier than the march on
Washington of the blacks, the poor and the opponents of the Vietnam War?[16]

Here I would like to add a few critical comments:

1. The righteousness and justice of God in the world does not begin with
the justification of the perpetrators of sin; it begins with the justification of
the victims of sin, injustice and violence. The justification of sinners comes
into effect by way of the justified victims. That is why justification cannot
be reduced to the forgiveness of sins. The forgiveness of sins is only half the
truth, for Christ has been raised for our justification (Rom. 4.25). It is only
through that that the conversion will be complete.[17]

2. Do the 'forgiven sinners' acknowledge only their own sins or the sins of
their people too? In 1945, in the Stuttgart Confession of Guilt, the Protestant churches acknowledged not only their own failures but also the wrongs
done to other countries by Nazi Germany. But if the forgiven sinners confess
the sins of their nation too, then the confession must be public, must be an
impeachment of public lies, and must be a call to public conversion. Here
again Martin Luther King is the best example.

3. Nonviolence is good, but it is merely the presupposition for the creation of peace through justice. The nonviolent creation of peace is not a powerless creation of peace. It will be brought about by intelligence and the force
of conviction. Nonviolence, like the forgiveness of sins, is only a negation of
the negative, out of which nothing positive as yet proceeds. Positive conclu-
sions can never be drawn from negative premises.

4. We are not told: 'Blessed are the peaceful' but 'blessed are the peace-makers.' *Eirenopoesis* is what the Preacher on the Mount calls blessed. So the church of Christ is not a 'peaceable kingdom', as Hauerwas calls it; it is the *peacemaking kingdom*.

5. Finally, 'church' as a nonviolent community of forgiven sinners is an ideal construction. In the church as it really exists there are violent people too. And 'world', again, is the description of an 'ideal' type of non-churchly reality. In the world as it exists there are many nonviolent people who do what is good and right simply in order to preserve the life of this world in spite of its corruption. Consequently, the confrontation between these constructs of ideal types is abstract and impracticable.

6. In the United States, the Hutterites were always peaceable and did not protest against any war; nor did they protest against racism, poverty and homelessness. Apparently, the general rejection of war hinders practical involvement in the protest against particular wars. Apparently, the protest against particular wars also requires the principles of 'the just war' in order to declare as lawless and unjust the undeclared war in Vietnam and the unjustified war against Iraq.

4
Transformative Eschatology

First Orientations

My early ideas about an ethics of hope were stimulated by the civil rights movement in the United States and by Martin Luther King's proclamation of his 'dream' in Washington on August 28, 1963. These ideas took on more concrete form in the message of the Fourth General Assembly of the WCC in Uppsala, which met under the motto: 'Behold, I make all things new.' I took up this message in 1973 at the World Missionary Conference in Bangkok in the report from Section II, and in lectures in Tübingen on Christian ethics, which I wanted to see interpreted as messianic ethics. Since 1978 I have tried to expand this message and to deepen it.

In 1963 Martin Luther King composed his vision of the liberation of the suppressed black people from white racism in this way:

> I have a dream that one day this nation will rise up and live out the true meaning of its creed: 'We hold these truths to be self-evident: that all men are created equal.'
> I have a dream that one day on the red hills of Georgia the sons of former slaves and the sons of former slaveholders will be able to sit together at the table of brotherhood . . .
> I have a dream that one day every valley shall be exalted, every hill and mountain shall be made low . . . and the glory of the Lord shall be revealed, and all flesh shall see it together.
> This is our hope.'[1]

King set the liberation of Afro-Americans from white racism within the framework of the American Declaration of Independence and the United States Constitution, where it is stated that all human beings, white and black, men and women, poor and rich 'are created equal'. The democratic principle of equality makes the liberation of the oppressed the public duty of society. Going beyond that, Martin Luther King set democracy and liberation against the horizon of the messianic hope for the coming kingdom of God

on earth. In order that 'all flesh'—that is all the living—may see the glory
of God 'together', the mountains must be made low and the valleys must be
raised up, so that in human history equal living conditions for everyone are
created, together with a life-furthering community of human beings with all
living things on earth. This messianic hope of the prophets gives a thrust to
the forward hope. It calls people out of their apathy and pessimism to active
participation in the movements for liberation. Martin Luther King was not
just concerned to overcome racism. After the march of African Americans
on Washington, he wanted to organize a march to Washington by the poor.
He was also a strict opponent of the Vietnam War and a supporter of nonviolent political actions. For these reasons he was murdered on April 4, 1968.

In 1968 I was roused to enthusiasm by the message issued by the Assembly of the World Council of Churches in Uppsala, because it captured exactly
what I wanted to arrive at in 1964 with the *Theology of Hope*: the category
of the new in the biblical history of promise and the glance into the future
of the world in that light of Christ's resurrection. In the experience of faith
God's promise 'Behold, I make all things new' (Rev. 21.5) already becomes
reality: 'If anyone is in Christ, he is a new creature. Behold, everything has
become new (2 Cor. 5.17). It is with this assurance that Christianity goes
to meet God's great future for the world. The active connection between
the promised future and the experienced coming of the new creation of all
things was described in Uppsala through the term 'anticipation'. [2] And this
anticipation also means preparing the way:

> We hear the cry of those who long for peace. The hungry and the exploited
> cry out for justice. The despised and the disadvantaged demand their
> human dignity. Millions are seeking a meaning in their lives....Trusting
> in God's renewing power, we call upon you to participate in the anticipa-
> tion of God's kingdom and to allow now something of the new creation
> to become already visible which Christ will complete on his day.'[3]

Practical suggestions for these 'anticipations of the kingdom of God'
included: (1) efforts for peace and cooperation at the time of the Vietnam War,
(2) efforts for social justice in the gulf between rich and poor in our societies
and between the nations, and (3) efforts for an orientation toward the shared
life of human beings and all living things in the living space of the earth.

Because the kingdom of God is the future of all history, it transcends the
historical future and all anticipations within history. But in this very way, the

kingdom will become the power of hope in history and the source of these anticipations with which we prepare the way for the coming of God.

At the World Missionary Conference in Bangkok in 1972–1973, I worked on the draft report of 'Section II: Salvation and Social Justice'. This was headed 'Salvation Is Hope in Action'.[4] At that time I wrote, 'The salvation which Christ brings and in which we share offers us total life in this divided world: we understand salvation to be a renewal of life—as the development of true humanity in the fullness of the Godhead. It is the salvation of the soul and the body, of the individual and the community of humanity and 'the sighing and groaning creation'.' Understood in its totality, the salvation of the world finds its testimony through a mission of Christianity which encompasses the whole of life. I saw four social dimensions of salvation:

1. Salvation takes effect in the struggle for economic justice and against the exploitation of human beings by human beings;

2. Salvation takes effect in the struggle for human dignity against political oppression by other human beings;

3. Salvation takes effect in the struggle for solidarity against the alienation of human beings;

4. Salvation takes effect in the struggle for hope against despair in individual life. Without social justice there is no political liberty; without political liberty cultural alienations cannot be overcome; without cultural identity there is no personal hope—and vice versa.

These four dimensions are interconnected, but different situations call for different priorities. There are varying gifts and tasks, but there is one Spirit and one salvation. 'Salvation is all-embracing, if we embrace the world with the heart of Christ.'[5]

Eschatological Christology

As has been shown, Christian ethics is always stamped by the Christology it premises. I developed my own Christology in dispute with the Christology of Karl Barth, which had convinced me earlier. I have called Barth's position a *christological eschatology* because he carried eschatology into Christology: In Christ's death and resurrection salvation has already been 'finished' (John 19.30). So the future of Christ will bring only the universal unveiling of the salvation of the world which has already been 'finished' or completed in Christ.

I have presented my own Christology 'in messianic dimensions'[6] and over against Barth have maintained an *eschatological Christology,* according to which the beginning of the coming consummation of salvation has

already taken place in the coming of Christ, and with Christ the eschatological future has already begun. That is to say, Christology is the beginning
of eschatology: for in Christ 'all the promises of God are Yes and Amen' (2
Cor. 1.20). In contrast to Barth's time-eternity eschatology, I took up his
initial 'forward eschatology', which he pursued in the spirit of Christoph
Blumhardt and took it further. A Christology in 'messianic dimensions' must
be followed by a messianic ethics. By 'messianic' I mean in this connection a
present already gripped and determined by the eschatological future. Eschatological future becomes present without ceasing to be future. In this way it
makes of the present a present future.

If in the coming of Christ all God's promises are endorsed, then in Christ
the prophetic promises of Isaiah are put into universal force. These promises
point beyond the coming of Christ into the kingdom of glory, for the sake of
which Christ was sent into the world. This does not put the church of Christ
above Israel but beside it. A single hope links the two communities. So Israel's
Torah also includes practical directions for a Christian messianic ethics.

If we understand eschatologically the life and teaching of Jesus, his self-
surrender to death on the cross and his raising from the dead, we discover in
his Sermon on the Mount a messianic interpretation of the Torah, and in the
death and resurrection of Jesus we see the kingdom of God taking form in
the world. In Christ's baptism, God the Father made the Son the Lord and
revealer of the kingdom; in his resurrection from the dead and the annihilation of death the handing over of the completed kingdom by the Son to the
Father begins (1 Cor. 1.28).

Kingdom of God ethics is discipleship-ethics, and the ethics of the discipleship of Jesus is the anticipation-ethics of his future.

Not least, an eschatologically open Christology opens our eyes to perceive the subsequent outpouring of the Spirit, and the experiences of the
vital powers of the divine Spirit, as being 'powers of the world to come' (Heb.
6.5). The coming of the Holy Spirit is nothing other than the beginning of
Christ's parousia. That is why the Spirit is called 'the pledge (or guarantee)
of glory' (2 Cor. 1.22; Eph. 1.14). What begins here in the Spirit will be
completed there in the kingdom of glory. The kingdom of God's glory, which
is the consummation of all human history and the whole open creation, does
not come without preparation. It has its beginning in the coming of Christ,
is already heralded in the kingdom of the Spirit and in the Spirit lays hold
of the present.

The grounding of the experience of the Spirit is also eschatological. That is why the prophet Joel looks ahead, seeing it together with the coming of the great and terrible Day of the Lord (Joel 2.31) and in conjunction with the corresponding apocalyptic signs. But what does this kingdom of the Spirit reveal? According to Joel 2 and Acts 2.17ff, it will be poured out 'on all flesh', that is, on all the living inasmuch as they are 'flesh'—weak, helpless and hopeless—in order to make them living for eternal life.[7] 'Your sons and your daughters will prophesy.' Men and women will receive these gifts of the Spirit equally. There are no male privileges. A charismatic community comes into being where men and women have the same dignity and the same rights. 'The old shall dream dreams and the young shall see visions', so no one is too old and no one is too young. The generations are equal in their reception of the Spirit. The Spirit 'will be poured out on menservants and maidservants', so the divine Spirit takes no account of slavery and social subjugations; it does away with them. All the Spirit-filled revival movements in Christianity have these socially revolutionary aspects, as we can see from the Anabaptists in the Reformation period. Through its forward-pointing existence, the new Spirit-possessed community of men and women, old and young, former slaves and slave-owners, testifies to the world that there is salvation even in danger, testifies to what is permanent in a world passing away and to an eternal future in transitory time.

Transformative Ethics

Walter Rauschenbusch, the pioneer of the Social Gospel movement in the United States, declared: 'Ascetic Christianity called the world evil and left it. Humanity is waiting for a revolutionary Christianity which will call the world evil and change it.'[8] Are there theological reasons why Christians should change the world for the better? The world is certainly in a poor way, but it doesn't have to remain so, said Johannes Rau!

In the raising of the crucified Christ, Christians have behind them the great turning point of all things, and they therefore hope for the eschatological turning point for the world. They work for a corresponding reevaluation of this world's values, so that they may be in conformity with the coming world of God. In the raising and exaltation of Christ, God has chosen the one whom the moral and political powers of this world rejected—the poor, humiliated, suffering and forsaken Christ. God identified himself with him and made him Lord of the new world. That corresponds to Israel's experience of God according to the Old Testament:

He has shown strength with his arm,
He has scattered the proud in the imagination of their hearts,
He has put down the mighty from their thrones,
    and exalted those of low degree.
He has filled the hungry with good things,
and the rich he has sent empty away (Luke 1.51–53, following 1 Sam. 2.1–10).

That is the experience of God in the Christian community:

Consider your call; not many of you were wise according to worldly standards, not many were powerful, not many were of noble birth; but God chose what is foolish in the world to shame the wise, God chose what is weak in the word to shame the strong, God chose what is low and despised in the world, even things that are not, to bring to nothing things that are, so that no human being might boast (1 Cor. 1.26-29a).

The God who creates justice for those who suffer violence, the God who exalts the humiliated and executed Christ—that is the God of hope for the new world of righteousness and justice and peace. In this world he comes to the poor, to the humiliated and to the sick so as to raise them up and heal them, and with them to begin his new world, as we can see from the life and teaching of Jesus.

In these dimensions Christian ethics is neither a conformist responsibility in the world nor a separatist flight from the world. It is guidance for changing the world. But those who want to change the conditions in which they suffer and are imprisoned must take three steps:[9]

First, they must free themselves from the world around them and resist its pressures: 'You know that those who are supposed to rule over the Gentiles lord it over them, and their great men exercise authority over them. But it shall not be so among you; but whoever would be great among you must be your servant' (Mark 10.42-45).

Next, they must find a new identity and fellowship: 'If anyone is in Christ he is a new creation' (2 Cor. 5.17). This new identity must be more important for them than the old one: we are Christians first of all, and only after that are we members of our own particular country. For us, Christian solidarity is more important than loyalty to our nation or culture.

Finally, it is only people changed in this way who are prepared to enter into an alternative change in their conditions and who can link with the ethos of change the solemnity of the new era: 'The night is far gone, the day is at hand. Let us then cast off the works of darkness and put on the armour of light' (Rom. 13.12). The darkness of this world's night means the God-forsakenness of this world of violence and deadly powers. The light of God's new day and the 'armour of light' means the passion and the striving for life, for fulfilled, for shared and for eternal life. It is out of this that the world-changing conflicts emerge—the conflict of life against death, of love against God-forsakenness, of righteousness and justice against violence—conflicts which will find an end only in the kingdom of God.

An ethics of hope sees the future in the light of Christ's resurrection. The reasonableness it presupposes and employs is the knowledge of change. This points the way to transforming action so as to anticipate as far as possible, and as far as strength goes, the new creation of all things, which God has promised and which Christ has put into force. The liberation of the oppressed, the raising up of the humiliated, the healing of the sick and justice for the poor are their familiar and practicable keywords.

This is distinguished from the Lutheran ethics under apocalyptic portents because it brings out the recognizability of Christian life and action; but it incorporates the principle of 'responsibility for the world'.

This is distinguished from the Reformed ethics under Christocratic portents because of its transforming anticipations in the process of Christ's coming; but it incorporates the principle of 'resistance'.

This is distinguished from the ethics of the Anabaptists and their quietism because of its active intervention in the social and public processes of public life; but it incorporates the principle of an 'alternative life'.

Part 2
An Ethics of Life

In this part, I want to develop an ethics of life which is based on a theology of life and which is a response to the manifold deadly dangers to life at the present time. At the beginning I will discuss some ideas about a culture of life which resists individual and collective desires for annihilation and therefore the terrorism of death.[1] Then, in a more limited framework, I will go into questions about the biomedical ethics of life and will try to answer questions about the beginning of life and its end, as well as questions about health and illness, in the framework of the previously discussed contexts.

5

A Culture of Life

Terror of Death

Today human life itself is in acute danger. It is not in danger because it is threatened with death—that was always so. It is in acute danger because it is no longer loved.

After World War II, Albert Camus wrote: "The secret of Europe is that it no longer loves life."[1] It was true that at that time my generation had become so used to the killing and the being killed, to the mass deaths and the cities destroyed in the fire-storm of nights of bombing, that we no longer got excited about death. Life was for us a matter of indifference, because it had been made meaningless. We had stopped loving life so as not to be so deeply touched by our own death and the death of people we loved. We wanted to make ourselves untouchable through an emotional armour of indifference. We fled into the death of the soul. It was only slowly, and years after the end of the war, that the survivors of my generation woke up out of this deadly paralysis of the soul and came back to life.

Terrorism

Today we are experiencing a new and frightening 'religion of death'. 'Your young people love life; our young people love death', the Taliban leader Mullah Omar once said to a Western journalist. After the bomb explosions in the commuter trains in Madrid on March 11, 2004, letters claiming responsibility were found with the same tenor: 'You love life, we love death.' This is the expression of an Islamic terror ideology against the Western world which is spreading but which is first of all costing the Islamic world itself unnumbered victims. Yet 'this love for death' could once be found in Europe too: '*Viva la muerte!*' cried an old Facist general in the Spanish civil war. 'Give death—accept death' was the slogan of the German SS, whose symbol was a skull and crossbones—the death's head.

45

Deterrence

Behind this terrorist surface lurks a greater danger still. All peace treaties, disarmament treaties and nuclear non-proliferation treaties have one self-evident premise: they presuppose the will of all the signatories to survive. But what if someone doesn't want to survive but wants to die? What if he can perhaps drag this whole depraved world into the abyss with him at the same time? What if in their attack terrorists use biochemical methods of mass destruction against which there is no defence? Up to now we have had to deal only with an international network of suicidal mass murderers. But what if a whole nation in possession of weapons of mass destruction wants not to live but to die if by so doing it can destroy a 'wicked' or 'unbelieving' world? A deterrent works only if the opponent wants to survive as well. The person whose own life has become a matter of indifference to him has left the terror of the deterrent behind him. He can no longer be threatened. We saw a terrible example of this in Nazi Germany, which began the Second World War in 1939. We see this attitude reflected in one of the SA's favourite songs, written by the Nazi songwriter Hans Baumann:

> The rotten bones of the world
> are trembling before the great war.
> But we have broken the terror,
> and victory beckons us on.
> So we will march onwards and forwards
> till nothing but potsherds are left.[2]

The attraction of annihilating a world viewed as 'rotten', corrupt or unbelieving can become a universal death wish for which one's own life is willingly sacrificed. 'Death' becomes a fascinating and a terrible deity. This 'religion of death' is the true enemy of the love for life. Necrophilia is the sombre attendant of every biophilia. Every affirmation of life also implies the possibility of its negation.

The Nuclear Suicide Program

Behind this real and deadly political danger to the shared life of the peoples of the earth is a greater danger still. When the atomic bomb was invented and dropped on Hiroshima and Nagasaki in August of 1945, it was not just the Second World War that was ended. The whole human race entered its endtime as well. That is meant in an entirely non-religious sense. The endtime is the age in which the end of humanity is possible at any time.[3] Through the potentialities for a global nuclear war, the human race as a whole became mortal. No human being could survive the nuclear winter that would follow a major nuclear war. It is true that, since the end of the Cold War in 1989, a major nuclear war is for the moment not very likely, but there are still giant arsenals of atomic and nitrogen bombs in the United States, Russia, China, England, France, India, Pakistan and Israel, ready for 'the final solution' of the question about humanity. 'The one who shoots first dies second.' That is humanity's latent but always-present suicide programme. Today it has been forgotten and suppressed, pushed out of public awareness. But it hangs over humanity as a sombre fate.

The Decline into Social Destitution

For more than forty years, we have been continually hearing on every side the lament that the gap between rich and poor is getting wider and wider. A small, wealthy upper class dominates the masses of impoverished people, and not just in the poor countries of the Third World (I am still deliberately using this term even today). In the democracies of the First World too the gap between the top executives with their millions and the people living on social security benefits is becoming grotesque. But democracy does not depend merely on liberty. It also rests on a balance felt to be equitable. Without social justice with regard to chances in life and living conditions, the common good dies—that is to say, the good of the whole community and with it the bonds that hold a society together. The liberty enjoyed by individuals and the wealthy classes becomes a public danger if 'privatize profits, socialize losses' becomes the ruling motto. Ever since the deregulation of the economy and the financial world in the great economic nations of the earth, the imbalance for many people between liberty and equality has become life-threatening, because the outcome is their impoverishment. A political capitalism—a capitalism no longer controlled by the common good—is the enemy of democracy, because it destroys a society's sense of community. We are on a downward path, socially speaking.

Where do we find the destructive drive behind this decline into poverty in modern societies? Let us pick out here only the social and psychological perspective. 'There is not enough for everyone': this impression, deliberately disseminated, postulates a general state of emergency which plunges many people into existential anxiety. The pointer to deficits in every sector of life justifies an ideology of growth as being the motor for the modern belief in progress. The general struggle for jobs, earnings and profits is supposed to mobilize the energies of the general public. 'Every man for himself' is the slogan, and solidarity gets left behind. In modern societies the community falls apart into winners and losers, 'the winner takes all' and the devil takes the losers. The existential fear of 'not making it' leads to a boundless greed for life and an insatiable hunger for power. 'It's cool'—'it's a must-have'—is already dinned into the ears of the young so as to make them buy designer clothes. Competition in modern societies has nothing to do with satisfying the basic needs of life. It has to do with social prestige, recognition in one's own social class. Modern existential anxiety tells people: 'You're nothing if you don't have anything—make something of yourself. If you don't you will be despised and looked down on'; and so the social struggles begin. Everyone competes against everyone else. It is a fight of each against all. This greed for life and this hunger for recognition are the reverse of the suppressed fears of dropping down the social ladder and of death. 'You only live once.' 'Look out for yourself.' 'You might miss out on something.' These deadly games with fear are really at the bottom of the modern competitive society. If solidarity gets left behind, if concern about the general good gets lost, if what belongs to everyone is viewed only as unclaimed property which can be grabbed without punishment—the result is a socially frigid world. In this dog-eats-dog society, everyone's neighbour is himself.

Once public spirit disappears from a society, trust disappears too. Conviction is no longer needed, only control. 'Trust is good, control is better', said Lenin, and most capitalists today still believe him. But 'who controls the controllers?' Even Karl Marx couldn't find an answer to this age-old question posed by the Roman poet Juvenal, for the answers to it reach, practically speaking, into infinity. So modern controlled economies and surveillance states come up against a dead end and spread mistrust.

It is the loss of solidarity and commitment to the common good, together with the loss of trust, which brings about society's divisions into poor and rich, the differences between the present and the future generation, the impoverishment of people in the countries of the Third World. These consequences are not a matter of fate, and are not inevitable; they are the sicknesses which the modern world has brought on itself. They can be healed. 'Another world is possible', as the international ATTAC[4] critically and rightly proclaims.

The Ecological Annihilation Trap

Unlike the nuclear catastrophe, the climate catastrophe—and together with it a general ecological catastrophe—is no longer merely latent, nor can it be pushed out of public awareness any longer. It has come about exactly as Donella Meadows and the Club of Rome's study *The Limits of Growth* already in 1972 said that it would.[5] Nevertheless, public awareness lags behind the true development. Some people don't know what they are doing and others are not doing what they know they should. Although we know better, little has been done up to now because—in spite of the limits that have been demonstrated—the ideology of quantitative 'growth' reigns unbroken, and to this ideology human beings, animals, plants and the earth are being sacrificed. Growth is a 'must'. If there is no growth, that is called 'zero growth', because growth is hope, and recession is depression. The greed for growth and enrichment cannot be halted. That is why today hardly anyone still talks publicly about the natural limits of growth. Yet the biosphere of the blue planet earth is *our limited space for living*. A human civilization that spans the world and is based on growth and consumption has long since arrived at these limits and is beginning permanently to destroy the living conditions of this living space in the earth's organism. Year after year, animal and plant species are becoming extinct; atmospheric pollution is destroying the ozone layer and raising the climatic temperature; the polar ice caps are melting; the water level of the oceans is rising; the deserts are spreading, and storms and hurricanes are on the increase. We know all this, or we can know it, but it is as if we were paralysed, changing neither our economic growth ideology nor our private and public way of life. *We are not acting on what we know.*

If we were to recognize the natural limits of growth, we would have to overthrow the idols of growth and learn to be moderate ourselves. We are like smokers—who know that smoking can damage your health and is deadly—but we still cannot stop believing that growth is a good thing. We are publicly showing ourselves to be suicide-prone, because ecologically we are living on the brink.

But there is another side to this growth crisis, although it is not much talked about. That is the *overpopulation* in countries in the Third World, which to an astonishing degree corresponds proportionately to the ageing of the population in the First World. This overpopulation destroys living spaces and triggers the migrations of millions of people. It is the poor, the neglected and the people who expect to die young who react to their situation with an immoderate population increase. Proportionately, the highest fertility rate is to be found in the poorest and most dangerous city on earth: Gaza City. A population bomb is developing in the Third World which threatens the wealth of the less-fertile populations of the West. In the long run, the fortresses of the more prosperous countries will not be able to barricade themselves against mass immigration.

But population growth can be encouraged and deliberately used to advance a particular aim or viewpoint. By rejecting birth control, popes want to increase the number of Catholics in the world and, with the same policy, the mullahs the number of Muslims. Ironically, this used to be called 'bedroom mission'. But to reject and resist responsible birth control is irresponsible. The resulting overpopulation has a catastrophic effect—and for many people even a deadly one. Whole regions become poverty-stricken, children die, and young people have to leave the region where they belong. 'Poverty is the worst pollution', said Indira Gandhi rightly. No animal species destroys its habitat through overpopulation; it is only the human being who possesses no ecological wisdom. Even the dinosaurs were wiser and will probably have lived longer on earth than the human species if human beings go on as they have up to now.

We don't know whether humanity will survive its self-made fate and whether it can free itself from this suicide trap. And that is just as well: for if we knew that we were not going to survive, we would not do anything more to ward off our annihilation—while if we knew that we were going to survive in any case, we would do nothing to practise new ways of dealing with our habitat, the earth. It is only when the future is open for both possibilities that we are compelled to do what is necessary, here and now, to avert the crash. Because we cannot know if humanity will survive, we have to act now as if its future depended on us today.

Humanity's Existential Question: Is There an 'Anthropic Principle'
in the Cosmos?

That brings us finally up against humanity's existential question in general. Today there are more than six billion human beings on this earth. But the earth could also be uninhabited by humans. It existed for millions of years without them and probably would go on for millions more if the human race disappeared from the earth. So if there were an 'anthropic principle' in nature—that is, if the development of intelligent life in nature had a certain inevitability—then humanity could feel 'at home in the universe', as the American biologist Stuart Kauffman suggests in the title of his book.[6]

However, the difference between a strong and a weak 'anthropic principle' diminishes this assurance.

As far as the development of intelligent human life is concerned, there are only three possible perspectives:

Human life is a fortuitous product of nature, perhaps even a malformation of life.

In human life the universe reveals the plan of its creator: in human knowledge nature comes to the awareness of itself. That would be the 'strong anthropic principle'.

Human life is the result of a self-organization on the part of life. That would be the 'weak anthropic principle'.[7]

I assume that the phenomenon of life in all the wealth of its forms and in the build-up of its complexities did not inevitably follow from the 'Big Bang', nor did it come about entirely fortuitously, but that it is an emergent phenomenon, that is to say, a wholly new thing in the history of the universe and of nature on the earth.[8] This phenomenon cannot be reduced to something different, nor can it be viewed in isolation; but it can be interpreted as an anticipation of a new future for the universe.

The universe provides no answer to whether there should be a human race or not, nor does it tell us whether the human race can survive or whether it is going to perish. In view of what human beings are doing today to the earth they live in, it is hard to give self-evident reasons for their survival. As the German philosopher Hans Jonas recognized, the survival of the human race is a matter of belief, the answer to which precedes all worldly reasoning.[9] He answers the question: 'Ought the human being to exist?' by saying that existence is an obligation.

If we search for an answer in the universe, we will arrive at the American physicist Steven Weinberg's sad assessment: 'The more the universe seems comprehensible, the more it also seems pointless.'[10] Even the Catholic philosopher Romano Guardini was reduced to 'the innermost core of melancholy' by the silence, the coldness, and the indifference of the universe to human beings.

The Terrorized Consciousness

Let us look finally at the mental and spiritual effects of the threatening scenarios of the present as we have described them. I am talking only about public awareness, not about the diversity of individual consciousness. Yet all individuals participate in the public awareness and relate to it either positively or critically.

Ie said that some people do not know what they are doing and are not concerned about its effect on others and the consequences for succeeding generations, while the others do not act on what they know; so they do not do the good they want, but the evil they do not want is what they do. If this analysis is correct, then public awareness is profoundly confused and the result is a general lack of orientation. People feel that they have no overview, and the result is stress. This stressful situation evokes contrary reactions. On the one hand there are *panic* attacks—on the other, people sink into apathy; on the one hand the public scene is stirred up by an alarmism which at every piece of bad news sees the end of the world on the way, and pop-apocalyptic books are in vogue—on the other hand fatalism spreads and people sink into social frigidity and a creeping lack of feeling called 'psychic numbing'.[11]

The threats of universal death exist and are felt, but the reactions to the threats are themselves life-threatening, because they do not ward off the threats but bring about the very thing that is threatened. It is like a kidnapping in which the victim does not defend himself but cooperates and gives himself up. A typical reaction of this kind is to enjoy life in the present at the cost of those who come later. 'Let us eat, drink and be merry, for tomorrow we die'—though then, of course, our children too! To run up unlimited debts means living at the cost of coming generations. Since they are unable to protest, it is easy to thrust the burden on them. So it is best to stay single, let alone to burden oneself with children. This hedonistic attitude is in actual fact the expression of an extremely nihilistic apocalypticism: we celebrate the end and bring it about—today! The banking crisis of 2008 was brought on by the greed for life in the here and now.

Another evasion tactic is *escapism*. If a threat emerges, one ducks down and plays dead, hoping that one won't be affected or at least won't feel the blow. One resigns oneself, becomes indifferent. Nothing much matters if one no longer loves life, and then death no longer touches one either. One becomes apathetic, anticipating death in mind and heart, and then one no longer feels it physically when it comes. With an attitude like this, we no longer withstand the threats either; we surrender ourselves to them and by doing so actually make what is threatened happen.

Here a *religious* escapism is coming to the fore especially in the present spread of a vague Gnostic religiosity of redemption. The person who surrenders himself to this religiosity feels at home in 'the world beyond' and on earth sees himself merely as a guest. So it is only by the way he is concerned about the fate of life on this earth. His soul is going to heaven, that is the main thing. In the body and on this earth, it was no more than a guest, so the fate of this hostelry really has nothing to do with him. Religious practices lauding an indifference to life are offered under many high-sounding names. A Western form of Buddhism has many adherents but has little to do with original Indian Buddhism. American pop-apocalyptic offers an especially dramatic escapism. Before the great afflictions at the end of the world, true believers will be 'raptured'—snatched away to heaven, so that they can then build the new world with Christ at his Second Coming. All unbelievers unfortunately belong to the 'Left Behind', the people who are not 'caught up' and who will perish in the downfall of the world ('Left Behind' is the title of an American book series read by millions).[12] Whether people throw themselves into the pleasures of the present or flee into the next world because they either cannot or will not withstand the threats, they destroy the love for life and put themselves at the service of terror and the annihilation of the world. Today life itself is in acute danger because in one way or the other it is no longer loved but is delivered over to the forces of destruction.

The Gospel of Life

According to the Synoptic Gospels, salvation is the kingdom of God which Jesus anticipated, proclaimed and practised. According to Paul, salvation is to be found in the conversion to righteousness which God brings about. In the Gospel of John and in the Johannine epistles, it is the fullness of life, which has appeared in Christ. In this sequence we can detect an intensification of salvation and a heightened perception of it.

The Synoptic Gospels

Everything Jesus proclaims according to the Synoptic Gospels derives from the conceptual material of the Judaism of the time. Nevertheless, while some people welcomed it, for others it was annoyingly new. Although what Jesus preaches and does is not new in detail, it is nonetheless new in the form of its totality, as one must put it in the terms of today's emergence theories. What is new in Jesus is identified by the name 'gospel'.

What kind of life is manifested through the earthly Jesus, the Son of God? Luke 4 sums up Jesus' divine mission in words taken from the prophet Isaiah:

> The Spirit of the Lord is upon me,
> because he has anointed me
> to preach good news to the poor.

He has sent me to proclaim release to the captives
 and recovery of sight to the blind,
to set at liberty those who are oppressed,
to proclaim the acceptable year of the Lord (Luke 4:18-19).

In Isaiah 61 this is followed by the words: 'and the day of vengeance of our God'. Luke leaves this out. The gospel to the poor says that it is to the poor that the kingdom of God belongs. 'The acceptable year of the Lord' is the messianic Sabbath, in which debts are forgiven and prisoners are set free. When the Messiah comes, the demons disappear from the earth and the sick are healed. When the blind see, the lame walk, lepers become clean and the poor hear their gospel about the kingdom—then the Messiah has come, and with his coming the messianic era dawns. The miracles of healing Jesus performs, or which take place in his proximity, are not intended to present him as a divine exceptional human being; they are miracles of the kingdom and signs of the messianic future which, with Jesus, breaks into the present in its sickness. They are 'miracles' only in an unchanged world. If the kingdom of God becomes powerful in the present, healings and liberations are not 'miracles' at all; they are a matter of course. The kingdom of the living God is health and life, and the fullness of life. The kingdom of God embraces the whole creation and is as protean and multicoloured as creation itself. This kingdom is not merely an ethical ideal of righteousness and justice and peace. It is that too, but in its fullness it is earthly and bodily and is experienced with the senses, just as the sick experience their healing and just as people who have been imprisoned outwardly and inwardly experience their liberty with all their senses. Everything that lives and has to die longs for the fullness of life of God's kingdom. That is why the kingdom of glory on earth will fulfil the longings of the whole earthly creation. For human beings, this bodily dimension of the kingdom is especially important, because men and women are inclined to flee from the mortality of the body into a dreamed-of immortality of the soul and to leave earthly life with its infirmities and frailties to itself. But the life Jesus brings and makes a truly living life is the harbinger and beginning of the bodily life of the new creation.

Mark sums up Jesus' message by saying: 'The time is fulfilled, and the kingdom of God is at hand; repent, and believe in the gospel' (1.15). At the centre of his message is the kingdom of God. The phrase 'at hand' does not mean that this is chronological information. What is meant is the presence of his future here and now. People who are reached by this message are freed from the existing world and the fabric of its life and are brought by it to the beginning of a life that is new. 'Repent and believe' is the call. Conversion means turning away from the old world and turning towards the new one; it is a turn to the future. This turn comprehends the entire life of the people addressed. What is talked about is not a freedom they already have. Conversion is the new birth of a freedom that overcomes the world, a freedom capable of future. The kingdom of God which is 'at hand' opens up for these people the liberty to begin a new life. Conversion is the anticipation of life in the kingdom of God in the conditions of the old world. It is the new way of living for people who do not 'conform' to this world and do not allow themselves be brought into line. They have this world's possessions 'as if they did not have them'.

Resistance against the forces of death and unconditional love for life are characteristics of this new, free way of living. Faith is the trusting self-surrender to the coming kingdom and an experience of freedom in its proximity. The apocalyptic aeon doctrine which lies behind Jesus' message about the kingdom of God makes it clear that this is not a matter of improvements to the old system; it has to do with a fundamental alternative. In Christian terms this is no longer meant apocalyptically: in Christ the kingdom has already come so close—it is actually 'at hand'—that people no longer have just to expect it, but in community with it can also already actively 'seek' it, and should and can make its righteousness and beauty the goal of the way they shape the world and life. That does not mean that the kingdom of God is in their hands, but their hands are supposed to prepare the way for God's coming, and should open closed doors and lethargic hearts in expectation of his coming.

Paul

For Paul, salvation is concentrated in the righteousness of God manifested in the self-giving and raising of Jesus, 'who was put to death for our trespasses and raised for our justification' (Rom 4.25). It is the *transition* from death on the cross to the raising from the dead which in the light of the resurrection reveals the death of Jesus to be a self-giving for godless and God-forsaken sinners, and which allows the Jesus who appears in the light of the resurrection to be recognized as the one crucified. It is this *turn* from self-giving to raising, from humiliation to exaltation, from death to life, which is decisive, because with this turn in Christ *the eschatological turn of the world* begins, from transience to non-transience, from the night of the world to the morning of God's new day and to the new creation of all things.[13]

It is therefore mistaken to reduce the justification of sinners to the for-giveness of their sins. We become just only in the power of the Spirit of Christ's resurrection. But it is of course also mistaken to celebrate the resur-rection only on Easter morning. Without liberation from the burden of the sins of the past, there is no future for a just life.

In his Christ mysticism, Paul perceives a mutual indwelling between Christ and believers: we in Christ—Christ in us.[14] Believers become 'like in form' to the crucified and risen Christ: 'always carrying in the body the death of Jesus, so that the life of Jesus may also be manifested in our bodies' (2 Cor. 4.10). The sufferings of Christ and the resurrection life of Christ mark the existence of believers simultaneously, and do so paradoxically 'as dying, and behold we live' (2 Cor. 6.9).

Because Paul starts from the raising of Christ *from the dead*, he reaches out beyond Israel's expectation of the messianic future to the promise of creation, and sees in Christ not only Israel's messiah but also the head of the new humanity. 'The first man Adam became a living being but the last (new) man became a life-giving spirit' (1 Cor. 15.45). 'For as in Adam *all* die, so in Christ shall *all* be made alive' (15.22). According to Jewish Wisdom teaching, God has created human beings for eternal life. So when mortality is overcome in the raising of Christ, that begins the fulfilment of the creation promise: eternal life in the new creation, which will be without the possibili-ties of sinning and of death, because the living God is present in all things.

John

In the Gospel of John, salvation is fully understood for the first time as life and is identified with Christ himself. The eternal God has the fullness of life in himself, and is therefore rightly called 'the living God'. In the same way, the Son of God also has life in himself and through his coming into this world becomes the source of the world's life, and life-giving life for others (John 5.26). 'In him was life, and the life was the light of all people', says the prologue to John's Gospel (1.4), and in the same Gospel Jesus says about himself 'I am the bread of life; I am the light of the world; I am the resur-rection and the life' (6.35, 8.12, 11.25). This make clear which life of Jesus is meant here; it is the eternal life in which the risen Christ appeared to the disciples and which they perceived with all their senses:

> That which was from the beginning,
> which we have heard,

which we have seen with our eyes,
which we have looked upon
and touched with our hands,
concerning the word of life—
the life was made manifest,
and we saw it, and testify to it, and
proclaim to you the life which is eternal (1 John 1.1-2).

That is the fullness of life, the life that is wholly and entirely filled with livingness. It is a life which by virtue of the risen Christ, the Christ who is present in the presence of God, is liberated from terror, from death, and from anxiety. It is an entirely and wholly human life participating wholly and entirely in the divine life. It is a human life which God indwells and which, for its part, dwells in God. Where do we find a life like this?

The answer given in John's Gospel is clear: it has appeared in Jesus Christ, is experienced in the life-giving Spirit, and will one day become the life of the whole future world.

This eternal life is synonymous with *the love of God* the Synoptic Gospels, Paul and the Gospel of John talk about. For the eternal life God has within himself presses in love beyond him to the creation of a beloved world, to the redemption of this world from terror and death and to the perfecting of this creation. Love is the self-communication of life. So in this way eternal life becomes loving and loved life. In the sending of the Son into this world, which is not merely threatened by powers hostile to life but is actually dominated by them, the love of God appears, and with that love true life (Rom. 8.38-39; 1 John 4.9). And in that way, this loved and loving life becomes a possibility for human beings:

God is *love*, and he who abides in love
abides *in God*
and God abides *in him* (1 John 4.16).

In the Synoptic Gospels the ethos of hope is conversion in faith to the gospel of the kingdom of God. In Paul it is the effect of the raising of the crucified Christ in the justification of the godless. In John it is eternal life in love. The turn to the future, resurrection into life, and the life lived in love: these things constitute the Christian ethos of hope.

What Follows from This for a Theology of Life?

What follows from this for a theology of life relevant for a culture of life today? We ask first of all: in what way is eternal life eternal? As the word 'eternal' is used in the Old and New Testament, it does not define the quantity of life but its quality. Eternal life is not an endless life; it is a life full-filled by God.[15] So eternal life has nothing to do with life-prolonging projects and tedious longevity. Nor is eternal life timeless life. According to Plato indeed (whose belief in immortality is followed by many Christians and theologians) we experience time as a sequence of fleeting moments in life which cannot be brought back. That is the time signified by the Greek word *chronos*. According to the Greek interpretation, *chronos* is the brother of death, *thanatos*. Time is transitory, and transience is the time of death. If time is the quintessence of the transitory, then eternity must, in contrast, be what abides, what is timeless and non-transient. It we apply this antithesis between time and eternity to life, we can conceive of timelessness, but not of a timeless life. Applied to God, the idea of a timeless eternity makes God a non-living being without relation. But the God of the biblical traditions is the 'living' God, who has a living relationship to his temporal creatures. His eternal life is the wellspring of the livingness of all temporal living things. So we have to measure eternity against the concept of life, not life against the concept of eternity. Over against Plato, Boethius proposed a different concept of eternity: *Aeternitas est interminabilis vitae tota simul et perfecta possessio*[16]—'Eternity is the unlimited, complete, simultaneous and perfect enjoyment of life.' Applied to God, God's eternity then means his unrestricted and perfect livingness in his inexhaustibly creative fullness of life. Applied to human beings, eternal life means the perfect fullness of life in unhindered participation in the life of God.

Eternal life is life filled by God's presence in the risen Christ and in the vital powers of his Spirit. That is the lived experience of God in the full-filled moment. Every moment of life full-filled in this way is 'an atom of eternity', as Kierkegaard said,[17] and a promise of the coming completion.

The corresponding experience of time is not transience; it is futurity. The essence of this is not the experience of time in the evening, but time as it is experienced at daybreak. What is important is not the time of death but the time of birth. *Chronos* disappears, its place being taken by *kairos*, for *kairos* is a brother of life, *zoe*. Empty, transitory time is transformed into fulfilled time, and every full-filled moment becomes the foretaste of the eternal and perfect enjoyment of life.

We go on to ask: In what way is eternal life living? What belongs to the livingness of life?

Human life lives from being *affirmed*, since it can also be denied. For human life to be destined for eternal life means its unequivocal and unconditional affirmation by the living God. If God himself becomes a human being, and if in Christ eternal life appears among mortal men and women on this earth, then the human race is wanted by God, and every individual person can have confidence in his own existence. Every woman, every man, and every child is desired and wanted and expected. The creation of human beings in the earth's community of creation, the taking flesh of the eternal Word among us, and the outpouring on 'all flesh' of the life-creating Spirit are an affirmation of humanity within the community of all the living in the living space of the earth. Humanity is affirmed by God in this way not just for itself, and not for heaven, but in the community of life and for this earth.

The only answer to the question 'why are you alive?' is, as Meister Eckhart said, 'I live because I live'. 'The rose blooms, it blooms without a why, it blooms because it blooms', says Angelus Silesius in a poem. Life is an end in itself—that it to say, it is beyond utility or uselessness. It has its meaning in itself. So it must be lived. It has no 'value', so it cannot be 'utilized'. There is no 'valueless life' which can be destroyed, neither the life of others nor one's own. Every life holds within itself the spark of eternal life. 'The right to life' is an uninfringeable human right, and its dignity must be protected against commercialization through patents and licences.

In spite of the evil people suffer and inflict on each other and on life itself, people become 'good, whole and beautiful'[18] through the righteousness of God which rectifies and justifies. God even affirms the human life which has destroyed itself and other life, in order to put it right and to heal it. That is the meaning of the Pauline doctrine of justification. Solely out of grace and solely through grace the victims and the perpetrators of sin are made just. Through the divine righteousness they are delivered from evil and liberated from 'the body of sin', as Paul describes in Romans 7. God's righteousness is not a righteousness that pins people down to what they have done, and retaliates; it is the healing 'sun of righteousness' which puts things to rights and awakens everything to life. Once the compulsion of evil is broken, death too will lose its power. Right through the night of terror, the terror of evil, God's affirmation of life becomes visible. There is no reason to deny life, to despair of this world, or to give up on oneself. Even the life burdened with sin and given over to death will be accepted by God and recognized and loved as the life he has created. So the most succinct definition of being human is that the human being is justi-fied by God.[19] It follows from this that human life is aligned towards *acceptance* as well as affirmation, for in this world it is often rejected and handicapped. The fear of guilt, on the other hand, condemns it to meaninglessness.

The gospel of life is God's yes to loved and loving life, to personal life and to a life of fellowship, to human and natural life on God's beloved earth. At the same time it is God's No to terror and death, to injustice and violence against life, to resignation, apathy and the death wish.

If we really want to live life, we must fight against the forces of death in the very midst of life. We must not surrender to lethargy of heart. We must not withdraw into private or churchly life. The resurrection hope of Christ encourages us to commit ourselves to a love for life everywhere and at all times, because it allows us to look for the universal victory of life beyond death. The love for life against death *here* is a wonderful resonance of the future of eternal life *there*. The resurrection hope reveals humanity's destiny to survive. It justifies life against the claims of death. But that already brings us to the heart of the question about a 'culture of life'.

Love for Life
But What Is Life? What Is Human Life? In What Does the Humanity of Life Consist?

The concept of life must include all the knowledge collected by biology.[20] But this is hardly possible, because there are transitional fields, and through a concept we would limit the creative future of life itself. It is easier to draw up some boundaries that mark the negation of life: life as a state of being is contrasted with death and with things that are dead; life as a process of activity and movement is contrasted with inactive and immobile life; life as being that is limited in time between beginning and end is contrasted with unlimited being; organic life is differentiated from inorganic matter. But here too there are so many transitional fields that a definition of life as distinct from its negation can only be provisional and heuristic. Nor must we forget that 'life' is not merely a biological concept; in general use it has so many connotations and evokes so many expectations that its reduction to biology would abbreviate and impoverish the understanding of what life is. For a full understanding of life, the biological concept of life has to be integrated into the social, political, philosophical and theological concepts of what life is. It is only the observation of its interacting relations that makes a life-furthering understanding of life possible.

Human life is life engendered and given birth to by human beings. It has a livingness specific to its own species, is bracketed by birth and death, and is closely connected with organic stages. It is numbered among the self-referential forms of life; it is lived socially in the spaces of human communities and in the times of human generations; it exists in an exchange of energy with the atmosphere and in exchange of the means of life with the biosphere, and in its body-soul totality it is part of the earth's organism; not least, it is aligned towards transcendence, and as long as it is alive it is involved in the process of transcending. It is being and ability-to-be, it is at once the reality and the potentiality of itself.

Modern anthropology has with particular interest stressed the special position of the human being in the cosmos of living things, and has judged that what is specifically human is what differentiates human beings from animals, the purpose here being to justify the human being's dominant role.[21] This is the origin of the view that human existence is hostile to nature, the view that characterizes modern human beings: the animal is tied to its environment, the human being is open to the world; the animal has no spirit, the human being is a spiritual being; the animal is soulless, the human being is ensouled. Behind this stand the great disjunctions which legitimate human domination in the bourgeois and industrial age: subject—object; history—nature; spirit—matter; necessity—freedom; civilization—nature. The new psychosomatic view of the human being, and the ecological viewpoint which stresses the community between nature and civilization, are steps with which to surmount these divisions, which are deadly for both sides.

We ask about a human life that corresponds to the life that has appeared in Christ.

According to the biblical interpretation, human life is experienced and lived only in a warp and weft with all the living, with animals and plants; for human beings are earthly beings (Genesis 2), and it was together with the animals that they were saved from the Flood. The covenant with Noah is a covenant of life made with human beings and 'every living creature' (Gen. 9.9-10). The biblical word 'flesh' (*kol' basar*) means 'all the living', and embraces human life together with all the living on earth. The 'becoming flesh of the Word' (John 1.14) and the outpouring of God's Spirit 'on all flesh' are not meant anthropocentrically.

The new psychosomatic, ecological and theological anthropologies are orientated towards a comprehensive concept of life, and are well suited to overcome Western anthropocentricism. It is not the human being that is at the centre of the earth; it is life. Human life is part of universal life, even if a special part. Human beings will only fulfil their special task as 'the image of God' if they recognize the community of creation in which and from which and with which they live.

Human life is not as yet identical with the true *humanity of life*, as a task for living. Every man or woman is a human being, but he or she has also *to be* a human being. Human beings are intended to live and act as such, for they can also live and act inhumanly. We may gather together some factors which are indispensible for the humanity of human life:

1. *The affirmation of life*: Human life must be affirmed, for it can also be denied. Even before it is born, a child must already be affirmed in its mother's womb, for it can only grow, develop and live healthily in an atmosphere of affirmation. If it lives in an atmosphere of rejection, as an 'unwanted child', it withers spiritually and deteriorates physically. It is only when a child feels that its life is affirmed that it can learn to affirm itself, and that is essential for living.

2. The same is true for the conscious *acceptance of life*. Human life must be affirmed and actively accepted. Only then will it become a life that is lived and experienced. It is only positive acceptance and esteem which activates the motivation system in body and soul.[22] If a child feels that its existence is rejected, it becomes ill, and withers away in its innermost being. If a grown-up feels rejected and despised, that person withdraws into himself, becomes defensive, or begins to despise himself and lose his vitality. Unless he experiences confidence, he never learns self-confidence. But if a life can no longer be experienced as a human life, it grows numb and turns to stone. This used to be called 'the death of the soul'.

3. Human life is *participation and sympathy*. Life comes alive when it finds that other people enter into it, and when it can enter into other life. Again we can easily make the cross-check: lack of sym-pathy leads to a-pathy, and that is a symptom of illness. Complete lack of sympathy is unlived life, 'death in life'. Human existence is social existence. To be humanly present means to be interested. As long as you are interested you are alive. Human life is alive as long as it exists in relationships. The loss of relationships which play an important part in a person's life leads to 'social death', which is generally a preliminary stage to the real death of the human being as a whole.

4. Human life is marked by a *striving for fulfilment*. It is this striving that lends it its dynamic. The striving for fulfilment is part of 'the struggle for existence'. It is what the American Constitution when it is talking

about human rights calls 'the pursuit of happiness'.[23] We also talk about the 'fulfilled life', the 'good life', the 'successful life,' or the 'meaningful life'. But what we mean is nearly always the same: the potential of human life is supposed to be fulfilled in such a way that life can be completely affirmed, and that the person can feel satisfied. Two ways of leading a meaningful life have developed—either through participation in human responsibility for the world, or through self-fulfilment. But at bottom the two belong together and cannot be separated, because the human self belongs within the world, and the world belongs to the human self.

To sum up: *Human life is affirmed, accepted, interested and fulfilled life.* It has to be lived and experienced, accepted and loved.

From this the second principle follows: *Consciously lived life is therefore a life which holds the contradictions within itself and find the strength to endure and surmount them.* 'The life of the Spirit is not the life that is afraid of death and keeps itself untouched by devastation but the life that endures death and maintains itself in it'.[24]

Can the *eternal* life we talked about in the previous section be experienced in this life and on earth? Or can we expect it only in the life beyond death? The answer is that in the loved and loving life, eternal life can be experienced in every moment with the senses, for love—Hegel calls it 'spirit'—is as strong as death and is the real beginning of a life which overcomes death.

Preliminary Orientations: Politics for the Whole of Life

1. When the atomic bomb was dropped on Hiroshima in 1945, the quality of human history was fundamentally changed: our time has become time with a time limit. The dream about 'a world without nuclear weapons' is certainly a beautiful dream, but it is only wishful thinking. Nobody seriously expects that one day people will again stop being able to do what they can do now. Anyone who has once learnt the formula can never again forget it. Ever since Hiroshima, humanity has lost its 'nuclear innocence' and will never get it back again.

If the nuclear age is humanity's final age, this means that today the fight for human survival is the fight for time. The fight for life is the fight against the nuclear end. If this is our endtime, we try to make it as endless as possible by continually giving threatened life on earth new time limits. This fight to postpone the end is a permanent fight for survival. It is a fight without victory, a fight without an end—and that at best. We can extend this nuclear endtime, but we and all the generations that follow us must eke out life in this endtime under the Damoclean sword of the bomb. The lifetime of the human race is no longer guaranteed by nature as it has been up to now; it must be ensured by human beings through deliberate policies of survival. Up to now nature has regenerated the human race after epidemics and world wars. Up to now nature has protected the human race from annihilation by individuals. From now on this will no longer be the case. Ever since Hiroshima life has irrefutably become the primary task for human culture, for political culture too. This means that all our decisions today must be considered in the light of the life of coming generations. That is the new, hitherto unknown responsibility of all human beings.

2. The nuclear age is the first age shared by all nations and all human beings. Ever since Hiroshima, the many different histories of the peoples on earth have become the shared world history of the one, single humanity—but initially only in a negative sense, in the mutual threat and the shared danger of annihilation.

Today the nations have entered the first common age of humanity, because they have all become the potential common object of nuclear annihilation. In this situation the survival of the human race is only conceivable if the peoples organize themselves into becoming the collective determining subject of action on behalf of survival. Ever since Hiroshima, the survival of humanity has become indissolubly linked with the uniting of the peoples for the purpose of together averting these deadly dangers. Only the unity of humanity will guarantee survival, and the premise for the survival of every individual is the unity of humanity. The life-saving unification of humanity in the age of nuclear threat demands the relativization of national interests, the democratization of the conflict-laden ideologies, the recognition and acceptance of different religions, and the general subordination of the peoples as a whole to their common concern for life.

Justice—Not Security—Creates Peace

Today deterrents no longer safeguard peace, because suicide assassins can no longer be deterred, and because there is hardly any protection against attacks with biological weapons. The biblical traditions and the Christian experience of faith tell us that it is only righteousness and justice which create lasting peace (*shalom*). So there is no road to peace other than just action and concern for worldwide righteousness and justice. All Christian memoranda have correctly maintained this thesis. But what is righteousness and justice?

If Jews and Christians want to bring righteousness into the world, they will start from their experience of God's righteousness. They experience his righteousness as a creative righteousness and justice that makes people just and creates justice. God is just and righteous because he creates justice for people who are without rights and puts to rights the unjust. His righteousness is a saving righteousness, through which he creates the peace which endures: *shalom*.

From this it follows that there is no peace where injustice and violence prevail, even if 'law and order' are enforced. It is not security and deterrents that bring peace; it is righteousness and justice. Injustice always creates inequalities and destroys just balances. Unjust systems can only be kept alive with the help of violence. There is no peace where violence prevails, for where violence prevails it is death, not life, that rules.

The biblical traditions and the Jewish and Christian experience of faith talk about an all-embracing peace because they talk about God's peace. Shalom means the sanctification of the whole of life God has created, in all its relationships. It is life blessed in fellowship with the life-giving God, with other people, and with all other created being: peace with God, peace among human beings, peace with nature. For God's sake, it is impossible to restrict shalom religiously or individually. Shalom is in tendency universal and enduring. What Jews and Christians experience of this peace in history is, as they see it, also the beginning and anticipation of the peace of God which will one day bring all created being to eternal life. Judaism and Christianity at their best are movements of practical hope for peace for all peoples and all creatures.

It follows from this that in history peace is a process not a state, a shared path not an individual possession. Peace is not the absence of violence; it is the presence of righteousness and justice.

In history, lasting peace is never there only for a particular generation alone, but also springs from responsibility for justice between the generations. Humanity has been created as a sequence of generations. Consequently, every generation is indebted to the generations that have gone before, and consequently, every generation bears responsibility for the life of the generations to come. Only justice in this unwritten human generation contract contributes to a lasting peace. Peace in history is not a condition in which one could sit back and rest on one's oars; it is always a way forward which has to be pursued, so as to create time for humanity, and so as to make life for coming generations possible.

From Powerlessness to Community

The qualitative alternative to poverty and wealth is *community*. In a community determined by solidarity, all its members become rich in relationships, in brothers and sisters, friends and neighbours, comrades and colleagues, rich in trust. In communities like this, in most cases we can help ourselves. Men and women are there for each other, so their ideas, their abilities, and the means at their disposal are available for all of them. In communities united in solidarity we take our lives into our own hands, and out of the hands of the people who dominate us and want to exploit us. Helpful initiatives are not ordered from above but come into being at the grass roots. Kindergartens, neighbourly help, co-operatives, trade unions, and many citizens' action groups originated when men and women combined spontaneously in manageable groups. It was only as they developed that these groups became professionalized and bureaucratically organized. In society's great bureaucratic institutions, there are always deficits to be administered. When people join forces for the purpose of mutual help, the richness of life emerges. When people find the courage to say 'we are the people', dictatorships collapse, as they did in 1989 in East Germany, in what was then the GDR. When Christian congregations say 'We are the church', they come of age.

The stress on individualization rather than community makes people in modern societies powerless and open to manipulation, in accordance with the old Roman motto *divide et impera,* divide and rule. On the other hand amalgamations at the grass roots for the purpose of a shared life call up the power of the people, and a community for the common good is created in which everyone can acquire a just share. This is also true on the level of the world market: if the nations take the liberty to provide for themselves first of all, before they produce for the world market, there will be enough for everyone. For this to be possible they must demand their right to their own land, which is taken from them by alien forces and global concerns.

It is quite possible to live in poverty if the poverty is borne by everyone together and is justly distributed. Only injustice makes poverty a torment. Only the dissolution of community kindles just anger. If everyone is in the same boat, people help one another. Once there ceases to be equality, the mutual help often stops too. We shall come back later to forms of the common life.

The Turn from Domination to Community

If in a biosystem where human society is linked with nature there is a crisis in which nature dies, this logically becomes a crisis in the system as a whole—

in the attitude to life, in the conduct of life, and not least in fundamental values and convictions. The dying of the forests finds its correspondence in the spread of mental and spiritual neuroses, the pollution of the seas and rivers is paralleled by the nihilist feeling about life which is prevalent among many people who live in the mega cities. The crisis we are experiencing is not just an ecological crisis, nor can it be solved merely technologically. A reversal in convictions and basic values is necessary as well as a reversal in the attitude to life and in the conduct of life. What are the interests and values governing our scientific and technological civilization? To put it simply: the main concern is the boundless will for domination which has driven men and women to seize power over nature, and continues to do so. It is modern Western civilizations which for the first time have been programmed with a bias towards growth, expansion and conquest. To gain power and to secure power are the fundamental values in force, regulating everything in our society. Why has this come about?

Its deepest reason is probably to be found in the religion of modern men and women. In Western Europe, ever since the Renaissance, God has always been interpreted in an increasingly one-sided way as 'the Almighty'. Omnipotence has counted as the preeminent attribute of his divinity. God is the Lord, the world is his property, and God can do with it what he likes. He is the absolute determining subject, and the world is the passive object of his rule. In Western tradition, God moved more and more into the sphere of transcendence, and the world came to be seen as purely immanent and earthly. God was thought of as world-less and so the world could be conceived of as god-less. It lost its divine creative mystery and through science could be stripped of its magic, as Max Weber aptly described this process. The strict monotheism of modern Western Christianity has become a decisive reason for the secularization of the world and nature.

As God's image on earth, the human being was obliged to see himself quite correspondingly as lord and master, as the determining subject of knowledge and will, and had to stand over against his world, which was his passive object, and to subjugate it. For it is only through his rule over the earth that he can correspond to God, the Lord of the world. God is the Lord and possessor of the whole creation so the human being must endeavour to become the lord and possessor of the earth, in order to prove that he is the image of his God. It is not through goodness and truth, not through patience and love, that the human being will come to resemble his God; it is through power and domination.

In order to experience that our place is within nature and that we belong to the same family as all other living things, we must undergo a reversal. This must begin with the picture of God from which we take our bearings. The consequence will be a turn away from one-sided domination, and a turn to mutual community.

The triune God—the very name makes this clear—is not a solitary, apathetic ruler in heaven who subjugates everything; he is a God rich in relationships and able to enter into relationships, a fellowship God: 'God is love.' The ancient doctrine of the Trinity was an interpretation of this experience. If this is true, then human beings can correspond to this triune God not through domination and subjugation but only through fellowship and life-furthering reciprocity. It is not the human being as a solitary determining subject who is God's image on earth; it is the true human community. It is not individual parts of creation which reflect his wisdom and his beauty; it is the community of creation as a whole.

The perception of the divine Spirit in all things engenders a new view of the world. If God's Spirit has been poured out on the whole creation, then the divine Spirit effects the unity and the community of all created beings with each other and with God. Life is communication. The life of creation is the communicating fellowship of creation. This warp and weft of mutual relationships in life is brought about by the divine Spirit, who in this respect can also be called the 'cosmic Spirit'.

The perception of the divine Spirit in the community of creation corresponds to the new ecological understanding of nature we are seeking. The era of the mechanistic world picture was also the era of subjectivity and of the sovereignty of human beings over against nature. The subjectivity of human existence and the reification of natural being conditioned each other mutually. If this bifurcation of the world we share is not to lead to the destruction both of nature and human beings, we must replace it by a new paradigm of a communicative community of culture and nature resting on reciprocity.

We Are Stardust

If the cosmos does not show any 'strong anthropic principle', why should this recognition cast us into melancholy? Does the silence of the universe offend us, as an insult to our narcissism? Are we then the 'crown' of the universe, or at least the summit in the development of matter and the organic stages? Or have we asked the wrong question? Even if there is no anthropic principle in the cosmos, is there not at least a *cosmic principle in anthropology*? The cosmos does not have to be aligned towards the appearance of the human race on the planet earth, but we human beings are aligned towards the cosmos and dependent on it. We are 'stardust'. The fundamental molecules making up human life derive from the explosions of supernovae and are distributed throughout the universe. The elements of the cosmos are present in our physical constitution. We are a part of the cosmos. The consequence of this fact is a *cosmic anthropology* in which the human microcosm corresponds to the universal macrocosm. It is an ancient and fascinating idea that the cosmos arrives at consciousness of itself in the human perception of it, and in the human consciousness in general. However fragmentary our cosmological knowledge may be, when we do not merely ask what something means for us, but also what it means for the cosmos, what emerges is an anthropological cosmology in correspondence to a cosmological anthropology. For it could well be that the future of human consciousness converges with the future of the cosmos. In a Christian eschatology of the cosmos, a cosmological Christology such as we find in the Epistles to the Ephesians and the Colossians will bind together the fate of humanity with the fate of the cosmos in the vision of the new creation. However speculations about the possible death of the universe through heat-death or the Big Freeze may frighten us with the senselessness of the universe, we believe for Christ's sake in the deification of the universe through the coming indwelling of the eternally living God in all things.

6
Medical Ethics

Some Benchmarks for a Judgment

Before we come to some problematic areas of modern bioethics, we have to clarify a few essential benchmarks if we are to form a judgment.

1. The greater the scientific and technological power over the vital processes becomes, the more far-reaching is the responsibility of everyone concerned.[1] Earlier, birth and death, health and sickness were largely regulated by nature and personal fate. People came to terms with the fact that here nothing much could be changed. They accepted the natural processes in their own bodies as being God's will, or surrendered themselves to their fate. The Hippocratic oath enjoined that life should be protected and furthered, but this meant life within the limits laid down by nature and personal destiny. The splendid advances in biogenetic research and reproductive medicine are continually pushing back human dependence on nature and progressively extending the area of what was humanly possible. Nothing is a matter of fate anymore—everything is possible: that seems to be the goal. The human being is to become the master of his own constitution and his own potentiality. But we do not have to do everything we can do. In order to handle the power that has been gained wisely and in a way that furthers life, society must set up ethical principles and rules, to which scientists and doctors have to conform. The Hippocratic oath applies not only to medical practice but already to the sciences themselves. It is foolish to develop more power than can be responsibly used ethically and controlled by law, the consequences of which cannot be foreseen. The natural regulating systems which have hitherto obtained are being replaced by imposed social systems. So we talk about health 'policies', population 'policies' and scientific 'policies'. We have to ask about ethical rules precisely at the points where nature and fate once reigned supreme. The powers of nature and fate were blind, as chance and fate are always portrayed as being. But the power of human beings must be clear-eyed if it is to protect and further human life, and the humane quality of that life. Today, instead of accepting nature and fate as 'God's will', we have to enquire about God's will in human ethics.

2. Human nature is a free nature. Of course every person's particular freedom is conditioned by his physical and mental constitution. Nor has he
any control over the place and time of his birth, and hence initially his life.
Yet his nature and his fate provide no directions for the way he should act.
I am unable to understand why the demand to be 'true to nature' has to be
an uninfringeable doctrine of the Catholic church, since the human being
has an 'ex-centric' position to his own nature. He *is* bodily and *has* a body,
so at the same time he is nature and has nature.[2] The freedom of his nature
is shown in the ambivalence of being and having. An ethics of life will try
to find tenable balances between being and having. Human beings must
take responsibility for what they do and leave undone. They cannot push off
that responsibility on to 'nature'. Birth control, with all the methods which
do not endanger life, is part of responsible parenthood. The ethical question is not whether the pill or condoms are used but *how* they are used. The
Knaus-Ogino method of abstinence during periods of ovulation leaves more
to nature but it is no better ethically. The biological concept of nature alone
(for nature is more than biology) does not tally with the responsibility of
human beings for the birth of human life. It seems to me more important to
stress the fact that every fusion between sperm and ovum brings about not
just a new human life but also a mother and a father who must stand up to
their responsibility. Discussions about birth control cannot be silenced when
it is a matter of the control over dying. Here too a purely biological concept
of nature fails to take account of the dignity of dying, and its human quality.

3. According to the Christian view, every human life is created to be
the image of God on earth and must be respected as such. This fact has
two dimensions: It means first of all God's relation to the human being,
and secondly the human being's relation to God.[3] God puts himself into
a relationship to human life which reflects his divinity in the way a mirror
does. God's relationship to the human being is universal, indestructible and
inalienable. The human being's relationship to God, on the other hand, is
potential: it can be realized through a life which corresponds to God and is
responsible, or—running counter to this—it can fail to be so realized. The
human being's relationship to God is visibly portrayed and given concrete
form in God's incarnation. This incarnation, or becoming human, in Jesus
Christ is also the incarnation or becoming human of God's eternal Word. 'All
the works of God end in bodiliness', the German theologian and theosophist
Friedrich Otinger said in the eighteenth century, in opposition to LaMettrie's
book *Man a Machine*. Today, to see divinity in human bodiliness is a necessary

contrast programme to the modern computerization of human bodiliness. That is 'the profound this-worldliness of Christianity' which Dietrich Bonhoeffer talked about, which 'includes the ever-present knowledge of death and resurrection'.[4] Love for life ensouls life's bodiliness and its sensory nature, and the resurrection hope gives the readiness to accept its mortality.

4. In order to arrive at exact scientific findings, we have to objectify the object to be investigated. It must be isolated from other contexts and reduced to one moment in its development so that it can be subjected to the interests of research. 'Reason has insight only into that which it produces after a plan of its own,' said Kant. 'It must not allow itself to be kept, as it were, in nature's leading-strings, but must itself show the way with principles of judgment based upon fixed laws, constraining nature to give answer to questions of reason's own determining'.[5]

The 'plan' establishes the question nature is constrained to answer and eliminates other questions as being irrelevant. It establishes the dimensions of meaning within which nature so questioned has to be understood. Perception and judgment are dependent on the perspective from which nature is seen. In the experiment, only the aspect is put forward in any given case in which nature is constrained to answer the question put to it. These are artificial situations made abstract through exclusion. The criterion for the correctness of the results is their repeatability.

Objectifications, isolations and reductions of this kind are methodologically necessary if scientific verifiable results are to be arrived at. But if we wish not merely to establish them but to understand them as well, we must integrate them once more into the wider contexts out of which they have been extracted. The investigation of the parts does not as yet lead to an understanding of the whole. The scientific methods must not lead to an ideological reductionism. If we want to avoid this reductionism, we shall gather specialist sciences together and build up integrative sciences, as in the geo-sciences, for example, and in researches into the brain. To put it rather more generally, we shall integrate anthropologically the parts of the body analysed in the specialist sciences into the total organism of the human body, and integrate the total organism of the body into the life history of the persons concerned, the persons into their societies, these societies into the community of humanity, and ecologically into the community of life on earth; and shall integrate all together into the systems of values and certainties in which we live and judge. We can make this clear to ourselves from our own experience of illness. Illnesses are objectified by the sick person. In severe cases he will be taken out of the world he lives in and put into hospital, possibly in an isolation ward. Once he is healed, the reverse process takes place: he is moved to the normal ward, is discharged, and returns to his own world. The reintegration process corresponds to the isolation process and is just as necessary—and occasionally even more difficult. What does this mean for ethics? We must not view the individual parts each for itself, but must comprehend their significance for their own relative totalities.

5. *Ultra posse nemo tenetur:* 'No one is obliged to do more than he can'. A Christian ethics must be neither abstract nor rigorous, but must take into consideration what the person can do 'as far as he can', and what is objectively possible for him. Immanuel Kant's motto, 'You ought, therefore you can', is an illusion, for the obligation does not provide the energies for an enabling. It is law without gospel. Anyone who sets up demands in God's name which people cannot fulfil is blaspheming God. Anyone who sets up demands which cannot be fulfilled does not want what he demands to be done; he is generally only ministering to his own self-righteousness and to the humiliation of other people. Excessive and impracticable demands are just as irresponsible as moral indifference. The mediaeval principle we quoted at the beginning of this section describes very well the limits of ethical demands and of human self-reproaches. We should do what we can and what it is possible for us to do, but should also recognize our limitations. No one is obliged to abrogate himself completely, because by doing so he would destroy himself as the determining ethical subject. What is impossible cannot be demanded or expected. An ethics of life is intended to serve life, the life of the acting person too. One should love one's neighbour as oneself, and that presupposes a healthy self-love. The person who despises himself will not be able to love his neighbour either. Someone who is uncertain in himself will make his neighbour uncertain too. The self-love which is presupposed has nothing to do with the egoism which seeks itself because it has lost itself or wants to fulfil itself but does not know itself. To accept oneself because one has been accepted by God purely out of love liberates us from the condition Kierkegaard described as despairing at being oneself or despairing at not being oneself.[6]

6. The more perfect therapeutic methods become, the more doctors find themselves in borderline situations in which they have to decide over life and death and are faced with an ethical dilemma: should they determine the 'value' of a patient according to external criteria? In that case the person must survive who clinically speaking has the greatest chances to live. Or should it

be the person who has the greater social 'value'? Does a positive judgment about the survivor imply a negative judgment about the one who cannot be helped? Can one weigh up people against one another in the way one weighs up commodities? Is one not destroying one's own integrity by making judgments of this kind? In borderline cases like this there are no simple solutions. Every decision in favour of one life at the expense of another leaves behind a feeling which I should like to describe as metaphysical sadness. It is not a feeling of moral guilt, for there are no alternatives, but it is certainly a feeling for the tragedy of history. It is good to be aware of this tragedy, for the awareness makes us immune against the tempting notion that the life that has been saved was after all of more value than the life that could not be saved. It is only if we remain aware that unavoidable decisions of this kind are not good decisions that we cease to be content with them. The medical decisions in borderline cases of life and death resemble political decisions in critical situations. One has to do the better under poor conditions and yet be aware that it is not good. In history, tragic action of this kind is aligned in a trans-moral sense towards reconciliation. This awareness keeps the ethos healthy, because it is a preservation against the temptation of rigorous ethics which lead to inactivity, and permits no one to play God over the life or death of other people.

Is there an ethical rule of thumb for a decision at the border between life and death? In a seminar meeting about medical ethics, an experienced doctor said to me *in dubio pro vita*—in case of doubt, decide for life. If there is still the faintest hope of saving life, try your utmost; if there is no longer any hope, accept the unavoidable.

The Birth of Life

It is really a matter of course that we should pass on the life we have ourselves received and should take our place in the sequence of generations. This sequence is the presupposition of the unwritten contract between generations, so often invoked today, which talks about equal chances in life for the generations of the future and the present. To pass life on is an expression of gratitude for one's own life and an expression of hope for the life of the future. No one should avoid the obligation to pass on life without good reasons.

Does that mean children are the purpose of marriage or life partnership?

No, in the Christian sector we start from the assumption that with the birth of Jesus, Israel's messiah and the saviour of the nations has been born, and that with him the 'child of the promise' has already come into the world.

So we are no longer waiting for the messiah in our male children. This makes the religious and legal privileges of fathers and sons null and void. Women and daughters are equally endowed with the Spirit, and receive the same baptism (Gal. 3.28). The right to inherit the kingdom of God is shared equally by daughters and sons. So children of both sexes are the bearers of hope for humanity. If through Jesus the kingdom of peace is already present in this world, there is no longer any religious duty to beget and bear children. Marriage is not a partnership for a particular purpose; it is a partnership lived in love, friendship, and mutual respect. Sexuality is a sphere of shared joy in one another.

Children are rightly said to be a gift of God's and they should be respected by their parents or the person to whom they relate most closely as 'God's children', to whom 'the kingdom of heaven belongs' (Mark 10.14 par.). A particular ray of hope therefore falls on every newborn child. Every child brings the beginning of a new life into the world, and grows into the dawn of God's new day. Children must be accepted and respected in the transcendent dimension where they can develop independently. A society which forces its children into traditional patterns of adult life is cheating itself of its own future. Every child brings something new into the world. We recognize the magic of this new beginning of life when a child is born, and so we must keep its own future open for every child. The message children have for adults is: 'Unless you turn and become like children, you will never enter the kingdom of heaven ' (Matt. 18.3). Because every human being is 'an *initium* and a newcomer and beginner by virtue of birth', people can 'take the initiative', become beginners and 'are prompted to action',[7] said Hannah Arendt, distinguishing freedom as an ability to begin from freedom as autonomy.

Birth Control by Means of Sterilization and Artificial Insemination[8]

By birth control we mean the deliberate restriction of the procreation and conception of life through sexual abstinence or the restriction of intercourse to the 'safe period', as well as through physical and biochemical methods and through sterilization. By birth control we also mean the deliberate surmounting of infertility by way of artificial insemination, in-vitro fertilization, surrogate mothers and genetic manipulation.

We shall first look at these two interventions in the nature of human beings, and ask whether they are responsible ones. We are starting from the assumption that people are by nature free in the sense defined above and so have the right to correct defects in their own physical constitution.

The ethical discussion about sterilization has always had to do with both a general problem and a specific one. Human beings have the right to engender and to give birth to life. They also have the right to protect life from illnesses. Do they also have the right to prevent life? Is sterilization, as the ultimate act of preventing life, contrary to nature, and therefore contrary to God's will? For a long time this was a problem in Catholic moral teaching. Today the right to birth control is generally accepted in Christianity, but this right has to be exercised only in the framework of responsible parenthood. Parents do not have to produce as many children as they can, although that would be logical if natural human fertility were a manifestation of God's creative will.

Sterilization raises the same problem as contraception but what in contraception is temporary, is here irreparable. It is an intervention in the bodily integrity of human beings which irreparably puts an end to the ability to engender and conceive. Here we are not thinking of the Nazi crime of the enforced sterilization of people with hereditary diseases or of the disabled; nor are we considering the sterilization of sex offenders. We mean voluntary sterilization at the wish of husband and wife or the two partners, perhaps after the fourth child, or because they have passed the age of forty. A case of this kind went through the German press fifty years ago. A Dr Dohrn had at a woman's wish undertaken a tubal legation. The discussion turned on whether a person has at all times a right of disposition over his or her body, whether a 'social duty' is involved, and whether this intervention is an offence against what was called 'the moral code'.

Article 2.2 of the Basic Law (the German Constitution) states that 'bodily integrity is uninfringeable'; but this is said in the social context, and this social aspect of bodily life cannot simply be determined in isolation, for in the case of physical deterioration society is supposed to intervene in helpful ways. No one is permitted to mutilate himself in order that other people may look after him. This certainly happens involuntarily when people make themselves the recipients of social benefits through drug addiction, but it is nevertheless irresponsible. So does voluntary sterilization infringe social obligations? Does it affect a bodily organ which has a social duty? No: voluntary sterilization is neither immoral nor does it make the person concerned antisocial. The preservation and exercise of fertility cannot be made a social or political duty.

To limit the number of children in a marriage is a responsible decision which does not infringe the dignity either of the woman or of the man. *Ultra posse nemo tenetur.* In spite of continual admonitions and considerable attempts, modern societies cannot be called exactly child-friendly. To have a large family of children still means in many cases a drop in the social scale. Voluntary sterilization does not lead to sexual excess and hedonism in the marriage, as often used to be said, and to limit the number of children in families is not the beginning of the country's ruin, as nationalists complain. Dr Dohrn defended himself at that earlier time by saying that through the voluntary sterilization of women he wanted to avert the horror of abortion. This is also true, but it points to the shameful fact that it is only with difficulty that men can be persuaded to such an intervention, although for them it is much more harmless than it is for women. Interventions of this kind are facilitated if the indications are made clear: the social indication, if families already have three or four children and are not in a position to bring up more, and the eugenic indication, if the couple has to fear for good reason that they will bring into the world severely handicapped children or children who cannot survive. Since the intervention must be undertaken by a doctor, it is important for all concerned to be clear about the adequacy of the reasons.

Artificial insemination is increasingly in demand today, because in modern industrial societies male fertility is rapidly declining. Here too the question was whether parents should accept their natural misfortune as 'God's will' or whether they could claim the right to correct their natural disability in God's name. When artificial insemination became possible, it brought about a new situation legally and ethically. Artificial insemination with the sperm of a man who is not the woman's husband or partner—that is to say heterological insemination—was legally excluded; homological insemination on the other hand was considered unobjectionable. In Western civilizations, heterological insemination has meanwhile also come to be widespread. Married couples or single women can order sperm from sperm banks. In the United States, I read in a university newspaper that sperm was on offer for payment. Where is the ethical problem and where are the legal ones?

The 'eugenic project': In 1962 the famous Ciba conference on 'The Eugenic Future of Humanity' took place in London. I participated in the subsequent Hoffmann-LaRoche Conference in Basel in 1972, giving a lecture and meeting the most important proponents of this project.[9] The fundamental ideas behind it were these:

Natural selection endangers the future of the human race because the number of untalented people increases and the highly talented hold back. As a result, in the advanced nations the genetic makeup of the human race in the civilized nations deteriorates. Consequently, we need to 'enhance' the genetic equipment of human beings. It is not enough to offer tax incentives as a way of encouraging the talented and educated to have more children; we must go over to artificial selection through AID (artificial insemination from a donor) in order on the one hand to exclude hereditary illnesses, and on the other to promote health, intelligence and competence.

For this purpose sperm banks should be set up with valuable genetic material such as 'excellent quality of heart, mind and body'. Correspondingly, genetically selected egg cells should be stored. Nanotechnology and genetic engineering make improvements in genetic material possible. In 1962 the American geneticist Herman Muller lauded the 'eugenic project', saying 'The idealist vanguard of humanity will introduce healthy genetic progress', and: 'which woman would not be proud to receive one of Darwin's sperm?' Joshua Lederberg, Nobel prize-winner from Stanford University, wanted to enlarge human brains through pre-natal genetic interventions: if the IQ of the population could be raised by 1.5 percent, 50 percent more geniuses would be born, and that is necessary because humanity is not yet intelligent enough to stop the whole world from being annihilated. Most people at the conference were agreed in believing that eugenics is merely the biological equivalent of the general moral education of the human race, and must be used to promote its further evolution.

Some critical points:

It remains unclear what we are supposed to understand by the enhancement of the human genetic make-up, because it is impossible to judge good and bad with the concepts of genetics.

The influence of genes on, for example, the intelligence of human beings was greatly overestimated, and is still overestimated today. As prominent intelligence researchers have shown, the social environment plays a more important part for the IQ than the genetic equipment. Neurobiologists have proved that the motivation system is decisive for the development of talents, not the genes as such, and the motivation system is stimulated or depressed through social communication.

Legally, artificial insemination raises the question: Who undertakes the responsibility? Who makes himself responsible for damage caused by a sperm from a sperm bank, or by an ovum from an ovum store? Can parents give back a 'designer baby' if they don't like it? Can children bring a case against their parents, or those responsible, or the society which allows or promotes it, on the grounds of neglected genetic optimization or wrong genetic regulation? The bio-scientific description of the human being as being the product of his genes cannot displace recognition of the person as a fully responsible and accountable determining subject; on the contrary, it promotes this recognition.

That brings us finally to the ethical question as to whether it can be considered responsible to fuse fatherless sperm with motherless egg cells. With the insemination of a female egg cell the result is not only a new human life; it is also a fatherhood and motherhood, and these conditions must be accepted and answered for by human persons. A surrogate motherhood changes nothing in this respect; a surrogate motherhood is merely lent, not accepted. Surrogate motherhood is incidentally an inhumane and unreasonable demand made on a woman unrelated to the child.

The 'eugenic project' presented here cannot serve the 'improvement' of the human race, for biological, legal and ethical reasons. It is not so much the genetic situation of human beings that has to be improved as their social situation.

Acceptance and Abortion

This brings us finally to the most difficult problem human beings have with their fertility, because here it is no longer a question of rights and obligations with regard to one's own body but of rights and obligations with regard to the body and life of unborn children.[10] In German law, for example, criminal acts committed 'against developing life' are distinguished from acts 'against life' itself, but the categories are nevertheless put together.

First of all we must ask: Who is speaking here, a pregnant woman or a man, a father or a celibate bishop? For in this question the existential conditions of the people who judge are highly influential. For a pregnant woman it is a matter of what used to be called 'the fruit of her womb'; for the father, it is a life he has engendered; for the bishop without children of his own, it is a moral problem.

We then have to ask what is the real point in question? For the definition of the case already predetermines the concern behind its solution. If it is a question of 'a terminated pregnancy', attention is concentrated only on the body of the pregnant woman; if it is a matter of what the German criminal law calls an *Abtötung*—a destruction or, more brutally, a 'killing off'—then the growing life is a life of inferior quality; if it is a homicidal offence, the developing life is stressed; if it is 'murder', the developing life is equated with a life after birth. We have the same problem with the bio-scientific and medical definitions of the developing human life. Is this at the beginning a fertilized ovum, then a cell cluster, then an embryo and finally a foetus—or is it a child from the very beginning? Of course these objective definitions imply evaluations of the human quality of developing life. If embryos are not yet human life, they can be produced for the purposes of research, or for the extraction of stem cells; if they are already human life, this is inadmissible.

Together with Karl Barth, I am starting from the assumption that 'every deliberate interruption of pregnancy…is a taking of a human life, [not just] a ready expedient and remedy in a moment of embarrassment'. And yet 'there are situations in which the killing of germinating life does not constitute murder but is in fact commanded'.[11] By this Barth means situations in which a choice must be made in order to protect life, because it is a matter of a life against a life. These are the situations we shall now look at in the context of various indications.

The Medical Indication. When it is question of one life against another, at the wish of the parents and with the support of the expert opinions of doctors, a pregnancy may be terminated through the killing of the embryo. More precisely defined, this situation arises when there is the a danger of death or of unacceptable damage to body or health. There is a severe damage of this kind if the injured woman is considerably mutilated, will be noticeably disfigured for a long period, will be considerably handicapped in the use of her body and senses, in her capacity for reproduction and her ability to work, or if as a result she becomes the victim of a life-threatening illness. According to these legal texts a medical indication is given not only in the borderline case of one life against another, but also when it is a case of 'life against health'. The term 'unacceptable' lays down a line which is hard to draw in the individual case, for it indicates the transition to the social indication.

The possibilities of prenatal and pre-implantation diagnosis opens up special problems inasmuch as they permit selection before birth. In China and India so many female embryos are aborted (because only a son can carry on the family tradition) that there is a male surplus in the population. Korean feminists say that traditional Confucianism is depopulating Korea.[12] In our society it is hard for children with disabilities to be born. A great number of embryos with Down Syndrome are aborted because, it is said, life with a child handicapped in this way cannot reasonably be expected of the pregnant woman in view of what the law describes as the effect on her 'mental health'. Leaving the individual aspect aside, this makes plain the devastating public opinion about disabled people.[13] By way of pre-implantation diagnosis, defective genes in embryos can be discovered before implantation in the womb and they can then be 'sorted out'. For this purpose, however, several embryos must be artificially produced, of which only one is going to survive. At this point I should like only to point out that in this way parents have imposed on them not only responsibility for the birth of their children but also responsibility for their constitution and genetic equipment. If nothing more is left to chance, no new life can come into being either. Human beings will become more and more alike.

The Ethical or Criminological Indication. This used to be the indication following rape. Here views diverge. According to the first view, rape constitutes an unacceptably severe damage to the woman's body and soul, her health and not least her liberty. Society cannot force any woman to let a pregnancy that results from rape go to term, and to live the rest of her life with an 'unwanted' child that has been forced on her. The assumption is that an unborn child in the mother's womb is still part of the mother, and that she therefore has the right to decide about its birth or non-birth. The second view assumes that this is not a matter of a threat to life, but a case of the deprival of personal liberty, so that the right to live of the child who has been imposed on her has to be harmonized with the right to live of the raped mother. The fact of brutal compulsion does not change the quality as person of the life that results, says the one argument. The ability to accept such a child has its limits, and these must be respected, says the other. For a child, its acceptance and affirmation is as important as its conception. But the state cannot by means of its laws force the woman concerned to provide this conscious affection, because it cannot provide the necessary strength of mind and heart. The solution to this insoluble dilemma is a compromise: because it is impermissible under criminal law to compel a woman to carry to term a child conceived in rape, abortion is not punishable in the case of an ethical indication, but the reproach of guilt remains. However, hardly any doctor will be found who, even though with the certainty of going unpunished, is held to be guilty in such a case. So what remains is solely the woman's decision: if she finds the strength to accept such a child as her own, well and good. If she does not find the strength, that is also well and good, in view of the unhappy circumstances. To release the child for adoption is probably the best solution. Anyone who rapes a woman must, if she has a child as a result, be condemned to pay lifelong for its support. It is unjust for a rapist to be free after three to five years, while the raped woman has to suffer all her life from his act of violence.

This discussion takes on a new quality when it is no longer a matter of individual rape but of the organized mass and repeated rape of women and girls in the wars of the alleged 'modern' world. What happened in 1945 in East Germany and in the recent Balkan wars bursts the bounds of all ethical concepts. Who would be prepared to give these women ethical advice, let alone reproach them morally, when their response to the trauma of those humiliations was abortion?

If the only way out of the hell is the death of the woman concerned or of the embryo, all that is left for other people is deep respect. God bears, he does not condemn.

The Social Indication. This is an intervention on the grounds of an extreme social situation: the parents are out of work; they already have a large number of children and very little living space; they are threatened with the loss of social status; the mother's youth and lack of means makes her incapable of accepting and bringing up a child. There are few objective criteria for these social situations. As a method of birth control, abortion is irresponsible towards the developing life. In my view it is also irresponsible to reject abortion and birth control too.

However, the other side must also be considered. The birth of a child involves not only engendering and conception, the carrying of the child and the giving birth; it also requires the attention of the whole person of mother and father, family and friends. That includes the affirmation of the child, joy in the child, and acceptance of the child in love. Rejected, unwanted children who are felt to be a burden become ill and grow up with severe psychological disorders. But the strength for such an acceptance is limited in every individual. So here too the rule obtains: *ultra posset nemo tenetur*—no one must do more than he can. On the other hand, this insight leaves open the freedom to allow the child to be adopted. These values of acceptance, affirmation and love necessarily belong to the birth of a child, but because the act of adoption also includes these values, they can also be exercised by others. Every child, whether it is one's own physically or is adopted, must feel that it is accepted and affirmed. It is therefore advisable that children who, with all the will in the world, cannot be affirmed and accepted should be made available for adoption, and that the adoption law in Germany should be made less rigorous, in order to make adoption easier.

All the indications listed here belong within the context of criminal law. They have, of course, no binding force for individual ethics. A mother can decide to sacrifice her own life for the life of her child. She can accept and love a child forced on her through rape because it is not the child's fault. Parents can later come to love very deeply a child whom they initially did not want. But these decisions are made freely, and in love. They cannot be enforced through accusations of guilt and threats of punishment. A Christian ethics will start from the really existing capacities and possibilities of the people concerned, and will say in cases of doubt: decide for life.

Unfortunately, fundamentalists and modern men and women often agree on the level of the soldier's morality which says, 'whatever is not punishable is permissible'. Consequently, the one side wants to have everything they disapprove of punished, and the other side wants everything they desire to be permitted. Both are wrong. Ethics is not a criminal code, and criminal law is not a substitute for ethics.

Is an Embryo a Human Being?

This question becomes the more pressing, ethically and legally, the easier it becomes to produce embryos in-vitro and thus to fertilize egg cells artificially outside the womb. In the case of an artificial implantation, several embryos are produced of which at best only one will survive. For stem cell research, embryos are produced solely for the purpose of extracting stem cells, and are therefore 'expended'. If an embryo is already a human person with the same dignity and the same right to protection as a life that has been born, then these embryos are not 'disposed of' or 'sorted out'; they are 'killed'. But if an embryo is not yet a human person what status does it then have, and what protection must be given to it?

Biographically speaking, we see the whole and say 'we are expecting a child', not 'a cell cluster'. But scientifically, the perspective is reduced to a single situation in the process of a developing life, the object is isolated from its natural relationships, and only the fertilized egg cell or the four-cell embryo is recognized. This is unavoidable for the purposes of scientific knowledge but it is not the picture of the whole; it is only a limited segment or extract.

An embryo has its own future, not just its present condition. It has its own potentiality, not just its actuality at the moment. It has its essential relationships and is not a *Ding an sich*, a thing-in-itself. An embryo has come into being out of the fusing of an egg cell of the mother's and a sperm from the father. It is abstract to isolate the mother's egg cell and the father's sperm and to treat the embryo as a 'thing-in-itself'. Whose sperm is it and whose egg cell? Not least, it is abstract to treat an embryo as a foreign body. Every researcher and every doctor and every one of us was once precisely this: an embryo. So someone who investigates an embryo is investigating something like himself. The person who calls it a ' cell cluster' is himself no different. Once the identification with human life is eliminated, whether from born or unborn life, whether from implanted life or life still in-vitro, inhumanity begins.

Embryos are called 'human material' or preliminary stages to human life, comparable with animal life. But these definitions of the embryo are definitions that serve the purpose of their application. They are not definitions of their life. We cannot take so easy a way out. It can very well be that a life has to be killed in order that a life can be saved. But then one should justify the act of killing, not disparage the object to such an extent that it is no longer a question of killing at all. We are not living in an unscathed world but in a world with defects. In this world one must try to do what is better under conditions which are unavoidably anything but good. Life often costs other life, not just in the case we are discussing. That is a tragic situation in which is surmounted neither by the cry of murder raised by the moral rigorists, nor by the demands for liberty made by the liberals, nor by the striving for profit of the capitalists.

Hope founded on the raising of the crucified Christ begins with the realities, not the illusions. It is only if we accept the tragic situation of having to act in the situations described that we shall work to change them, so that abortions and the killing of embryos are no longer necessary and no longer happen.

In the fight against the immune deficiency disease AIDS, every contraceptive method must be employed. To speak out publicly against them as the Vatican does is not merely irresponsible; it also means becoming coresponsible for the mass deaths of the poor. That is hostility towards life.

What Value and What Rights Does Developing Life Have?

I believe that every ethics has to be both defensive and progressive, because every ethics should preserve life and also further it. But the ethos of the scientific and technological civilization has become one-sidedly progressive, indeed aggressive. It is directed towards the seizure of power by human beings over natural processes, towards the increase of this power and the securing of it, so that the ethical reflection which follows often takes on a defensive character because it has to talk about the costs and the victims which result from the increase of scientific and technological power.

If the costs of the progress are pushed off on to nature, the Third World, or coming generations, the ethical reflection which follows the technological progress is bound to be defensive; that is to say, it must push for the preservation of life and try to find a balance between the empowering of human capacity and the preservation of life.

When we begin to think about the ethical implications of these questions, we must first eliminate the reductions which have developed, so that we can grasp the conditions as a whole. To be a human being means being a person in relationships. 'The individual' is an abstraction, and so is the concept 'species'. I am not an individual, but nor am I merely an example of my species; I am a son of my parents and the father of our children. That is to say, from the very outset I belong within these relationships. When I see myself as an individual, that is an abstraction from them, and so between individual human dignity and the dignity of the human species there is the dignity of the specific social relationships by virtue of which I am who I am, and each of us the one who he or she is. I believe that this is important, for in the relationships something takes place which is indispensible for the health of human life: the acceptance of a human child.

The acceptance opposes its rejection. Acceptance, affirmation, is a necessity of life. So it is not enough to engender, conceive and bear a human being. A human being is dependent on its acceptance, because otherwise it cannot develop self-confidence.

Becoming human is evidently a 'becoming' in the context of dependencies. If this is to be recognized, abstractions must once again be abolished. There has been much talk about sperm and egg cell and the fusion of sperm with egg cell to become an embryo. I am starting from the position that for the sperm there has to be a sperm-donor, and I am calling him the father. That sounds a little old-fashioned, I know, but it also brings out the relationship and the responsibility. The same is true of the egg cell. A donor belongs to it, that is to say, a mother. To whom does the embryo actually belong? Who is responsible for it?

People often talk as if there were unnumbered embryos which are apparently 'unclaimed property' so that they can be appropriated. But the legal position must be clarified so that the responsibility can be clarified too. In the case of donated sperm, who undertakes the fatherly responsibility for what this sperm brings into being, in and in conjunction with an egg cell? If sperm can be sold, the responsibility for the consequences of its action 'falls by the wayside', and the outcome is this 'unclaimed property'. If we view the embryo in its original relationships as well, we have to say that this embryo develops only in human surroundings which are responsible for its origin. It would be an abstraction and an isolation to see it solely in itself. It is human life, engendered and conceived, either naturally or artificially, by human beings. From this obligations towards the child result—obligations on the part of the sperm donor and the egg cell donor, i.e., the father and the mother—and rights on the part of the child towards father and mother, that is towards the relationships which are essential for the developing life, because they are essential for the acceptance of this human being.

Human dignity does not belong only to a human individual in his or her private sphere, nor only to the human species; it also belongs to the relationships in which people develop. I believe that an international consensus about human dignity has also meanwhile developed, a consensus very similar to the way the Anglo-Saxon traditions see it; the United States of America has also agreed to the Universal Declaration of Human Rights, in which Article 1 states that the human dignity and human rights of all are to be protected. So an international consensus has come into being which we can and, as I believe, must take as starting point. The relationships in which human beings develop also have human dignity. There are humane ways of dealing with embryos, and inhumane ways. Human dignity like values is a quality, and not quantifiable. There is no more human dignity or less; there is only an 'either-or'.

Human dignity is already defined in the Old Testament. The Abrahamic religions—Judaism, Christianity and Islam—are responsible for the religious background of Western civilization, and they have always seen this dignity as belonging to the human being as the image of God. For a long time this likeness to God was seen in the West as residing in his soul, not in his body. In this way the body ceased to be part of that likeness and became the material of the soul, which stood over against its body and could then make use of it. Later the likeness to God was seen as the conscious subjectivity of will and perception. If it were the soul or subjectivity which is like God, it would be sexless. But that is not in line with the primal history described in these three religions. It is the whole of the human being that is the image of God, body and soul, male and female. This image does not reside merely in a male and female soul, but in male and female existence and in the mutual relationship of male and female.

In the theological discussion there has come to be a consensus that this likeness to God should not be identified with a particular human condition, and to say the likeness to God awakens together with the consciousness. Instead we must say that the likeness to God is a relation, namely the relation in which God puts himself to the human being. The likeness to God therefore applies in all human conditions, whether the person is healthy or sick, old or young, disabled or not disabled, born or unborn. This relation, the relation of being in the image of God, if it is understood in the light of God, is true for the whole human person, body and soul, and for the whole person in all the forms that person takes in the course of time—and therefore it applies to the embryo too. It is hence impossible, as I believe, to ascribe differing values to the fertilized egg-cell, the embryo, the unborn child, the adult, the disabled person and the person who is dying. Human dignity is something different from a value, and if human dignity lies in this transcendent relationship of God's to the human person, it exists for that person in every condition.

If, then, human dignity and likeness to God and the right to life are already conceded to the embryo, then there are certainly conflicts between life and life, extreme situations. But these do not give us the right to deny in principle dignity to the weaker life. Every restriction of the right to life and respect for human dignity has to be justified. It is every denial of an embryo's right to life that must be justified, but not the embryo's right to life.

Human existence is a unity of person and nature. In our discussion we have had several definitions of nature. If we start from the assumption that there is such a thing as the human person and nature, then nature is what this person can stand over against objectively. One then arrives logically at a fissure into a non-personal nature—the fetus is 'human but not person'—and a nature-less person. But this fissure makes it impossible for the human being to identify himself in his nature. There is a cleft between person and nature, between determining subject and biological material. This gives rise to the interesting question: where then is the person localized in the human consti-tution—in the heart (but that can be transplanted), or in the brain? But if the brain can be transplanted too, is the person the same afterwards as before?

I believe we should start by interweaving or dovetailing this double con-cept of nature: on the one hand the human being is nature and has nature. According to Helmut Plessner this is reflected in the ambivalence that he is a body and has a body. But the human being must arrive at a harmonization in his life between the being and the having, because he would otherwise become his own double. At this point I would say: to be human is nature incorporated in person, and so the human being is also dependent on a con-tinuity, a harmony, with the nature surrounding him.

To be human is to be person in history. To be human has its temporal forms, which we can distinguish and must distinguish, but whose human identity we must preserve: embryo, child, adult, the person who is si(dying. Being a person is really the continuity of the human being course of these changing times and these temporal forms. The identification must be possible and must remain possible: 'That was I, and that is the one I shall be.' It is only if this identification can be preserved that there is a continuity. Otherwise the human being disintegrates. It seems to me that we often start from an ideal concept of what person is. It is the concept of the healthy, happy, successful, self-confident thirty-year-old man. Of course this concept cannot be applied to a newly born child, or to a child still unborn, let alone to an embryo. But neither is it still applicable when this thirty-year-old man one day begins to suffer from dementia, or if he is in a coma. So we must reckon with differing identities, or with the human being's identity in the alteration of his fundamental conditions, and must formulate the person's different rights to protection and liberty in the situation concerned; and we must do so in such a way that the human being can identify himself in these different situations. That presupposes the continual relation to transcendence. Otherwise the human being dissolves into the forms he takes in time.

The Strength to Live in Health and Sickness
Medicine for the Humanity of Life

'There is no such thing as illnesses per se. We only know sick people', wrote Ludolf von Krehl in his *Pathologische Physiologie*.[14] That is certainly true for the patients, but one has the impression that for the insurance companies today the exact opposite is the case: they know only illnesses; sick people are not part of the calculation. In this chapter we shall ask about the way life is experienced in health and illness.

The modern triumphal march of medicine is undoubtedly due to the application of scientific and technological methods. Right down to the middle of the nineteenth century, medicine was counted as belonging to the humanities. It was only later that it was ranged among the natural sciences. But medicine is really a medical art. To understand medicine as an applied science has its price. The patient's life as a whole, in the multiplicity of its relationships, is lost sight of, and in the process little regard is played to the personal dimension of the sick person. It is only when everything subjective is excluded that it is possible to gain a clear picture of the course of an illness. Many patients also see their illness as a physical defect to be put right through some repair. 'Illness in the age of the exact sciences is as dumb as the tissue in which it manifests itself.'[15]

Like all sciences, which aim to achieve precisely provable results, the appropriate medicine works by objectifying the illness, isolating the sick person from the world in which he lives, and excluding other perspectives. A specific therapy became possible to the degree in which it was possible to isolate the sick person's illness and to gain a grasp of the chain of cause and effect running from the causative agent to its typical effects in the process of the illness. The sick person is reduced to a collection of typical symptoms and treated as a 'case' of this illness. This procedure is both necessary and a matter of course. But it has only become possible during a laborious history in the self-understanding of the human being. The picture of the human being in the West begins with Plato's dualism of body and soul and leads to the detachment of the bodily existence which the human being *is* to the body he *has*; this can then be conceived of and treated as a bodily machine. The soul becomes the subject of reason and will, and the body is subjected to self-control. In cases of illness this shows itself in the fact that speech plays an increasingly small part in dealings with the sick person. Discussions between doctors and their sick patients are replaced by orientation towards measurable data. There is no longer very much talk in the doctor's surgery, and 'the hospital is largely speaking dumb'.[16] How many doctors can take the time to listen to a patient? In how many hospitals are there any conversations at the patient's bedside? If a doctor can afford these discussions, he is available only for a few; if he is available for many, he can hardly permit himself these discussions. How many insurance programmes pay for extensive discussions with the patient?

How do we experience life in illness and health? If we wake up one morning feeling ill, we say 'I don't feel well, I am ill.' It is only the reflection that follows on waking which isolates the pain and tells us: you have a pain in your stomach, or a temperature, or bronchitis. We begin with the experience of being ill and then push off this experience on to the 'having', so as to acquire detachment, and in order to say: I am not identical with my illness, I can rise above it and relate to it. It is a different matter after an illness has been cured. Then we say 'I am well', not 'I have health'. When we are well we are at one with ourselves; but not in illness.

In life as it is experienced and lived, bodily and mental functions harmonize and become the unity of the whole person. In the spontaneous impression made by experience and in the spontaneous expression of life, we exist physically with all our senses. In the reflection of the self-consciousness we acquire detachment from ourselves, and what we can confront over against ourselves in our bodiliness as our object is the body we have. Modern philosophical anthropology has called this the human being's 'excentric position': a human being lives in himself and transcends himself at the same time. That finds expression in his double role as Being and Having.[17] And here the 'being-body' is the primary experience in life, and 'having-body' the secondary one.

If this is true, then the experience of detachment must be followed by the experience of identity, so that the self-detachment does not become a schizophrenic doubling of our selves. The experiences of having-body will be integrated into the experience of being-body. Reflection will be caught up and absorbed into new spontaneity. Where it is a matter of illness and health, this means that the difficult process of the conscious objectification of the body into having-body, and the objectification of the sick person into the 'case' of an illness, also involves the no less difficult process of the subjectification of the body into the body of the person and the person's integration of the experience of illness into the process of the recovery of health.

The important thing on the way from isolation to integration is to reintegrate the order of the body into the order of the person, and once more to perceive in the illness the sick person's subjectivity. In the doctor's surgery, it must be clear to both the doctor who is being consulted and the patient who is being treated that the patient is a person; he is incidentally not merely a 'customer' either. The person is able to shape the processes of his illness through his bodily and mental influence on these very processes—to put it best, through his human influence. The sick person is not merely an object; he is always at the same time a determining subject.[18] But that requires 'the determining subject to be introduced' into the pathology.'[19] We should then learn to understand illness as something which sparks a question about the meaning of a lived life, and should direct the therapy towards a meaningful life, not just a life that once more functions. Medicine will then become not just an applied science but also an applied history. It will be aware that a medical history belongs within the wider framework of a life history, and will view this life history in the conditions of the cultural history which frames it. Medicine is then a critical study which starts with sick individuals and sees them in the conditions of society conducive to illness. Social medicine is moving in this direction. But conversely, it will also view a society's health system critically. Is it the repair workshop of a socioeconomic system conducive to illness or is it an approach to social therapy as well?

That brings us to the question: What is health? What can be called 'healthy' in the individual life? What is 'healthy' according to the cultural, economic and social standards of a given society? Aren't the standards for healthy life highly variable in the different cultures? Can the health standards in our modern achievement-orientated society be called 'healthy' in a humane sense? [20]

What Is Health?

Sigmund Freud and others defined health as 'the capacity for work and enjoyment'. If a person's capacity for work is reduced and his capacity for enjoyment is impeded, he counts as ill. Once both abilities are restored, he can be discharged as being well. This simple but commonly used definition of health exactly corresponds to the industrial achievement-orientated society, whose central values are directed towards production and consumption Pre-modern societies and non-European cultures cultivate different values and therefore have other concepts of health. This emerges particularly clearly in the spread of Western medicine in Africa and Asia. In the Western world too, this definition of health makes many people ill, stigmatizes them, and makes them 'valueless' and 'superfluous' when they are old.

The international World Health Organization has set up an extended definition: Health is a condition of complete physical, mental and social well-being, and not just the absence of illness and infirmity.[21] This maximum definition is good as far as its negation goes, but in its general position it reaches far beyond what is humanly possible. If only the person in a condition of complete and all-round well-being counts as healthy, then all human beings are more or less ill, since they are not living in paradise. Measured against the ideal of social well-being, there are no healthy societies which could guarantee anything of the kind. On the basis of this ideal, the demands made by human beings on the health systems rise immeasurably. The ideal of all-round well-being is a utopia, and not even a particularly humane utopia. It is the utopia of life without suffering, of happiness without pain, and of a society without conflicts. It is the utopia of life without death, for only an immortal life could provide 'complete well-being'.

Health and the freedom from both bodily and mental harm are certainly human rights which every human being can properly claim. But a 'condition' does not describe the healthy vital power to be a person. If health is described as an attainable condition, it awakens unrealizable claims of human beings on themselves, as we can see from the present trend in the wealthy countries to a fitness cult, diet fanaticism, anti-aging measures, and so forth, as well as from the claims people make on the health systems. It also absolves them from their own responsibility for their condition. Shouldn't a countermovement to salvage humanity begin by once more personalizing health and illness and by accepting ageing and dying as part of life? This proposal leads to different definitions of health.

If illness is seen merely as a functional disturbance to particular bodily organs, then health is a disturbance-free condition. But severe and prolonged illnesses affect the whole human being. In this perspective health doesn't mean 'the absence of disturbances but the strength to live with them'.[22] Here health is not a condition but 'the strength to be human' in conditions of health and of illness. This spiritual strength, as it used to be called, is shown in the capacity for happiness and for suffering, for joy and for sorrow—seen as a whole in the strength to accept life and to surrender life. To put it theologically, it is life and death within God's great Yes, the acceptance of life and death in the wide space of God's presence.

If, in contrast, health as a state of general well-being becomes a widespread human attitude, the result can be pathological attitudes towards health and illness, because then people are equated with their health. 'The main thing is to be well' is then the slogan, and illnesses should simply not exist. This can lead to the sick being pushed out of public life, and to illnesses being viewed as catastrophes, a view which robs the person of self-confidence and self-esteem. The modern health cult then produces precisely that which it wants to overcome—the fear of being ill. Instead of surmounting illness and infirmity it sets up an ideal of general well-being from which the sick and the infirm are excluded. When the healthy then turn away from the infirm and the disabled, the old and people unable to work, they condemn these people to social death. Relationships are broken off and the sick are pronounced useless. What is intended to minister to the health of life actually makes the people who are excluded ill. The definition of the World Health Organization is so open to misunderstanding because it talks about everything but not about death. But without the remembrance that people die, every definition of health is illusory.

Severe illnesses often lead to life crises. By life crises of this kind, we mean crises about the meaning and purpose of life. The sick person no longer understands his life, because illness has taken from him the confidence on which his life was previously based and on which he relied. He then reacts with anger against himself and aggression towards other people, and finally relapses into profound resignation and apathy. When one senses that one can no longer put one's trust in one's own health, competence or good looks, and can no longer base one's self-esteem on what one has achieved or enjoys, one either breaks down or finds the strength to live from a greater trust and a more profound self-respect. An existential crisis of this kind offers the opportunity to withdraw the trust of the heart from the good things that are now under threat or have been withdrawn and to set it instead on firm ground. The self-righteousness which is built up on the vanity of good works and pride in one's own achievement can also be found in the self-righteousness which springs from trust in one's own competence and leads to the anxious cult of one's own health. Human life is not a means to an end, life lives because it is lived. It is good in itself, because it is from eternity loved, affirmed and justified. It needs no self-justifications because there is no necessity for the great fear for oneself. The power to be human which we have talked about is God's great affirmation into which we can live and die. Human life is accepted, affirmed and loved life, so we can accept it even in its finitude, and love it in its infirmity. In this faith, men and women can find a great liberty towards the changes and chances of life. This is 'the sole comfort in life and in death' which the Heidelberg Catechism talks about. And from this we can deduce that nothing ministers to life which does not console in death.

The Strength to Live in Dying and in Death

'Thou shalt not kill', we read in the Decalogue. Does that mean one's own life too? My neighbour, a Catholic philosopher, once astonished me, as we were taking a walk, by asking: 'Must one really go on living as long as one can?' What bothered me was the word 'must'. Is life a duty we have to fulfil until we can no longer do so? Or is life a gift we give back when the power to hold on to it is quenched? Must we leave dying to nature, or can we decide on it ourselves, or at least the circumstances under which death takes place?

In this section we shall only discuss the questions about suicide, about active and passive euthanasia, and about the 'living will'.[23] The background is the Christian view of death and eternal life.

What determines whether a human being is alive or dead? In the course of the history of our civilization, ideas about the centre of the human being have undergone a remarkable shift. As long as the livingness of the human being was seen in his breathing in and breathing out, the centre of the person was localized in the diaphragm. In the rhythm of breathing, a person is alive. When he 'breathes his last', his life ends. Later, the livingness was seen in the great emotions, in the trust of the heart and in heartfelt love. Even

today, we talk about 'hearty' best wishes. So the centre of life was localized
in the heart. When the heart stops beating, the person is dead. But today the
human being is viewed as the subject of reason and will. So the idea about
the centre of life is migrating from the heart to the brain and is established
behind the two slits of the eyes. Today brain-death is considered to be the
true symbol of the death of the whole person, even if in a state of brain-
death the function of the heart can still be maintained and the lungs can be
artificially kept breathing.

What is considered the centre of life has now migrated from the centre
of the body to the head. Once it is the brain and no longer the respiratory
organ which is viewed as representing the whole human being, it is no
longer the breathing community between human beings and their natural
environment which is viewed as the human environment; that environment
is now 'the world', which human beings can make the object of a dominating
thinking and willing. Once the mind was given primacy, the de-sensorizing
of the inhabitants of the scientific and technological civilization began.
Consequently, many therapeutic approaches begin with the relearning of
deep breathing, so that the centre of life which has been abandoned can be
reawakened. Japanese and African doctors explain to us the many difficulties
their people have with the modern thesis about brain-death.

When I began to concern myself with these questions forty years ago, I
found the brain-death thesis immediately convincing: if no electrical cur-
rents in the brain can be detected for six to ten minutes, the brain is in
the irreversible process of dying. After that there is no longer any medical
obligation to keep the body alive, although it would be possible. Once the
possibility of reanimation has ended, the human being is dead. But at that
time I overlooked the fact that other interests played a part in the discussion
too. From what point can organs be removed from the dead person? Organ
transplantation is prompted by both noble and commercial motives. Consequently I was more cautious in what I said in the debate about brain-death.

Self-Destruction or Voluntary Death?

The purpose of the biblical prohibition of killing is to protect life. Does the
prohibition also serve to protect one's own life from one's own intervention? From the beginning, Christianity has viewed suicide as contravening
reverence for the life which no one has given himself and which therefore
no one is allowed to take away. But exceptions have always been respected,
for example in persecution and in martyrdom. The Christian churches have

condemned suicide as 'self-murder'; suicides were buried without the rites of the church, and their graves were at the edge of the graveyard. In the case of 'self-murder' the murderer escapes punishment because of his own death, but his reputation can nevertheless be damaged by the word 'suicide'. In the meantime, however, the Catholic Church too has moved away from the rigorous description of suicide as 'murder'. We do not call the Protestant writer Jochen Klepper a murderer although he committed suicide in 1942 together with his Jewish wife and her Jewish daughter because the daughter was threatened with deportation to a death camp. We did not call Hannelore Kohl, the wife of the German chancellor Helmut Kohl, a murderer when she took her own life because of incurable photosensitivity. When I was a young student pastor in Bremen, I had to take the funeral of two students who had taken their own lives. I did not bury them as 'murderers' or 'self-murderers', but I did not penetrate their motives either. Such a decision often brings us up against an insoluble riddle, and we must respect the mystery these people take with them into the grave, probably intentionally. But we must be all the more attentive to warning signs, which are often unconscious cries for help.

When we dispense with the term 'self-murder', as we must do, that does not mean that we have to view suicide as normal. Like all killing, it is directed against life, and life is in all circumstances deserving of protection. As Kant said, suicide is also directed against the dignity of a human being. We do not kill anyone because in his person we respect the image of God, in our own person too. So the description 'voluntary death' is not correct either. No one kills himself as a supreme act of freedom. Suicide is generally the outcome of a lack of freedom which sees no way out. The notion that it is the supreme act of freedom of an independent person comes from the ancient world. The Platonists saw death as the separation of the divine soul from the wearisome body, and celebrated it as 'the feast of freedom'. In the post-Christian world, this description of self-killing as 'freely chosen death' emerged again, and was considered to be the supreme act of a person's self-determination. But in the modern world as well the autonomous individual does not live solely in relation to himself, but in many social relationships too; so he does not belong merely to himself either. There are parents, wives and husbands, children and friends who are plunged into deep grief by a suicide.

How then do we experience death? 'One's own death one only dies./ With the death of others one has to live', wrote Mascha Kaléko in a poem, and it is true. We shall experience dying but not our death, for we shall not survive in order to experience it. But we do experience death in the people we love.[24] Their death leaves us behind, as those who have to come to terms with the loss. Life is good, but to be a survivor is hard. We receive our life out of love, and die into the mourning. Is suicide a 'voluntary death' if we view death in the real social relationships of a human being? Is 'voluntary death' the acquisition of freedom, if I lose that freedom immediately in the act of self-destruction?

If we cannot interpret suicide as either 'self-murder' or 'voluntary death' we can perhaps understand it in many cases as a matter of self-defence. In order to avert a calamity inflicted on his family, General Henning von Tresckow took his own life after the failed attempt to assassinate Hitler on July 20, 1944. Persons with depression take their own lives in order to avert unendurable psychological pressure from within, but in most cases we have to reckon with the 'impenetrable character of the final personal decision'[25] and must respect the person's decision to take his or her own life without reproaches and accusations.

Death on Demand

The desire to be killed can come from the person who seeks his own death, but it can also be suggested to him by other people. The focus usually lies only on the first group. Because people who ask for death are often no longer in a position to carry out their wish, they ask others to help them. Sometimes they even make other people promise to undertake the killing if they themselves are no longer in a position to do so. Sigmund Freud is a classic case of a killing on demand: he died of an overdose of morphine administered at his own wish. This rarely has to do with self-determination and liberty; in most cases it is an act of self-defence against some unbearable condition in which people find themselves, or a condition they imagine or experience to be unworthy. They can find themselves in such conditions because of incurable illnesses, or because of unreasonable life-prolonging measures.

To aid and abet a killing can consist of an act or the refraining from an act. If it is a matter of ending a dying life which is being extended merely through life-prolonging measures, e.g. in an intensive care unit, this is rather a matter of making oneself an accessory to the natural death, rather than a killing. If it is a matter of being an actual accessory, for example, through poison, then it means complicity in a killing. The first case, in my opinion, is an act at the service of life, of which dying is quite simply a part; the second case, in my view, is rather an act at the service of death. I consider the first case to be ethically justifiable, but not the second. But these are fundamentally speaking not 'cases' at all; every situation is different, and one does not know much in advance even about one's own future situation in the shadow of death.

It is another matter when it means killing in response to a demand made by other people, which today is driving old people to their deaths.[26] They are old, disabled, unsightly, only make work for us, are senile, and are taking a long time to die. They are superfluous. Why should they be a burden on other people? The ultimate way out is suicide. In Germany, the highest percentage of suicides is found among men and women over sixty. 'No one kills themselves unless someone else wants them dead', says Christine Swienek in her book *Letzter Ausweg Selbstmord* [*Suicide as a Last Resort*]. But the psychological pressure of believing oneself to be superfluous and feeling that one is only a burden for one's family is not only initiated by other people and the public interests of a society geared to performance and consumption; it also starts from old people themselves, who have thought this of others too before they themselves retired, and now relate these criteria to themselves in view of the disabilities of their age. When old people kill themselves so as no longer to be a burden on their nearest and dearest, it is not an 'altruistic suicide', which the philosopher Dagmar Fenner calls 'praiseworthy', for then this 'praiseworthy' suicide would have to be suggested to the old, who are more expensive than profitable. The demand that suicide should be suggested to the disabled, the incurably ill and the old is blameworthy because it is cynical. It relieves 'the healthy and competent' of solidarity, sympathy, and active neighbourly love.

Active and Passive Euthanasia

The ethical questions about euthanasia are directly connected with the questions about death on demand. Is there any such thing as 'a good death'? Who is supposed to decide? In Germany, we have had terrible experiences of active euthanasia practised on the disabled and the mentally ill at the order of the state. It already started after the First World War, when doctors thought about what was to happen to the most severely wounded and to the mentally ill soldier who had come back from the war. Some advised a state-ordered 'mercy killing' in order to put an end to their torment. Afterwards voices were added from the social medicine sector, which called disabled people 'idiots'[27] and viewed their disabilities as hereditary diseases in the body of the nation, this being a reason to recommend euthanasia for them. Not least, there was the social-Darwinist demand for the right of the stronger and the lack of rights of the weaker, with the familiar Nietzsche pronouncements.

But it was the Nazi ideology which from 1940 onwards led for the first time to the mass murder of the disabled and the mentally ill under the heading of 'euthanasia', on the grounds that they were condemned to 'valueless life'. This ceased only when Bishop Graf Galen in Münster and Bishop Wurm in Württemberg pointed to the severely wounded soldiers. The Nazis could not afford to rouse unrest among the population. Active euthanasia ordered by the state is mass murder and a crime against humanity.

What took place sixty years ago for political reasons is being attempted today for commercial ones: 'death on offer.'[28] This is 'active euthanasia' on demand, but only for 'customers' belonging to the relevant organizations. Since there are no 'noble motives' here, special caution is called for. It is true that every offer is a response to a demand, but every offer also initiates the demand. That is always the case in modern societies; otherwise they could not expand. The same ambiguities arise in the case of offers of active euthanasia as they do in the case of 'death on demand'. If it is a response to a person's own desire, that desire has to be respected; if it is active euthanasia at the demand of others, it means becoming an accessory to blackmail. I believe to make someone else bring about my death is asking him to bear a responsibility that can hardly be expected of him, for by doing so he is ministering not to my life but to my death. No man or woman should put anyone else at the service of death or let him or herself be put in that position by anyone else. Anyone who has to do so in an emergency situation, e.g. in war, has to bear a heavy burden. Active euthanasia on offer for commercial reasons I consider despicable.

If we once again draw on the distinction between doing and permitting, one can accept responsibility for a 'passive' or 'indirect' euthanasia which cuts short an artificial prolongation of life if the situation has no perspective or when pain-killing medication is given even though death is a possible result, for example, when the patient is given morphine, which can lead to an inflammation of the lungs. To 'let someone die' can be responsibly accepted. But part of this acceptance is the helpful accompaniment of the dying patient, so that he is comforted or can accept the end of his life.

The Living Will

Can I decide about the ending of my life in advance, in the case of the 'irreversible course of an illness in spite of medical treatment'? A persistent vegetative state and dementia are viewed as fatal illnesses of this kind, in which the sick person is no longer able to make his own decisions. Personally, I have to admit that I am uncertain. Can I decide now about myself in a future condition of this kind? Can I already pin myself down for conditions in the future? When I see other people in circumstances of that kind today, I am prepared to do so; but whether, if I am in such a condition, I should like to feel that I was bound by a declaration of intent given earlier, I don't know. For me it is also the question to whom I should entrust my 'living will',[29] surely only to someone I intimately and completely trust, not to an impersonal institution. I myself would also be prepared to implement such a living will only if it had been drawn up by someone I trust. Countries such as Belgium or Holland may lay down basic regulations for living wills, but in living and dying it is a matter of trust and intimacy. I personally have only been able to decide for such an ultimately binding declaration of intent at the age of eighty-four.

The Resurrection of the Body?

It may seem surprising to come upon a chapter about the resurrection of the body in a book about ethics. But in an ethics of hope, we also have to ask about hope for bodily life. The obvious answer is that after death the body dies and decays: 'earth to earth, dust to dust', we hear when we stand at graves. According to the view commonly held to be Platonic, the body is the outward mortal garment of the immortal soul. For Descartes, the thinking but non-spatial soul was only temporally linked with a spatial but non-thinking body. Modern people see the body as something they can form as they want: from high-performance sport to body building, from fitness to wellness, everyone can make something of his or her body, and do something on its behalf. But death is its end. Does it make any difference to the conduct of life whether we reckon with the end of bodily life or with its rebirth in the resurrection of the body?[30]

The patristic church inserted into the Apostles Creed the words about 'the resurrection of the flesh' (*resurrectio carnis*) although even at that time this idea ran completely counter to the general spiritualizing trend of Hellenistic-Roman culture. Why did the 'resurrection of the flesh' enter the orbit of the Christian hope, and make its way into the creed?

Many people have wracked their brains about how to translate *resurrectio carnis* in a comprehensible way. The translation 'flesh' seemed to many embarrassing, because it sounded like an echo of 'flesh and blood'. So they translated the phrase into English as 'the resurrection of the body', because that sounds more personal. Later on, the Catholic and the Protestant churches agreed on 'the resurrection of the dead', because that sounds personal in the same way as 'the living and the dead' in the second article of the Apostles Creed. This is the way it is now found in the creed. But do the two phrases mean the same thing? If we go back to the Hebrew root of 'all flesh', we find that what is meant is not simply the frailty and the transitoriness of human life; the Hebrew *kol' basar* means all the living as well. According to Isaiah 40.5, at the end 'the glory of the Lord shall be revealed, and all flesh shall see it together'.

This universal dimension of life is lost if what we have in view is only human beings in their individual bodiliness. In a 'resurrection of the flesh' human beings will be redeemed together with the whole fabric of the living, and together with the living space of the earth. Paul still knew this when he heard 'the groanings of creation' as it waits with us for 'the redemption of the body' (Rom. 8.22-23).

The Resurrection of Life

I would suggest that we talk about *the resurrection of life* instead of a resurrection of the dead, or of the body or the flesh. By the living body we don't mean the body without its soul, as an object; we mean the body as we experience it—the body with which I am subjectively identical: I am body, that is, my bodily form and my life history. In this respect life means the life that is lived, affirmed, loved and accepted. Real life is the bodiliness I am. How would it be if we were to talk in the creed about the resurrection of the lived life? We should then accept dying too as part of life and believe in the victory of life over death. We could then understand that eternal life will be lived in a glorified body. 'The body will rise, everything about the body, the identical body, the whole body', said Tertullian, emphatically, in his famed treatise *De Resurrectione Carnis* (written after 212): *Resurget igitur caro, et quidem omnis, et quidem ipsa, et quidem integra*. And he declared that 'the flesh' was the key of salvation: *Caro cardo salutis*. For God has 'appeared in the flesh' and in the lived life we encounter the living God. So how do we not encounter in death the God who raises?

But in saying this we come up against a difference between the sexes. How do men experience their body, and how do women? The woman's body, with its capacity for giving birth and its rhythms, was denigrated by the ancient world's notion that it was at times impure and was in general a source of temptation; it was assumed to be weaker than the male body, and unreliable. Right through the middle ages runs the idea that the human being's likeness to God begins only beyond the body, in the summit of the soul, *ubi sexus nullus est*—where there is no gender. But according to the creation story we must accept that we are made in the image of God as male and female, in our full bodiliness and should rejoice in the living God with body and soul (Psalm 84.2).

The Spirituality of the Body

That brings us to the relevance of the resurrection hope for bodily life here and now. The person who loves life in the light of the resurrection hope becomes capable of happiness. All the senses come alive, reason and heart are opened for the beauty of this life. But with this love for life we also become capable of suffering, and feel the pains, the disappointments and the sorrow of this mortal life. Ultimately speaking, the life of people who love comes alive from within and becomes vulnerable from without. Love lets us experience what life and death really are, because in love we go out of ourselves, become capable of happiness, and at the same time vulnerable. The opposite makes this plain. The person who loses the love for life becomes apathetic and indifferent. Nothing matters to him. He cannot rejoice and cannot shed tears. He bypasses the world as if it were nothing. This used to be called the death of the soul. Today we could perhaps talk about zombies, walking corpses, people who are spiritually turned to stone.

Rejected, unloved, negated life is life we have missed out on, dead life. What we experience in it is *death before life*. This comes out very well in the biblical image about the grain of wheat. Until it is sown and planted in the earth 'it remains alone' (John 12.24). It dries up and loses its vitality. This is denied, unlived and unfruitful life, a hopeless death.

Today we are learning a new *spirituality of the body and the senses*.[31] After the mysticism of the soul is now coming a mysticism of the body. The mystical turning away from the world of the senses is followed today by a new awakening of the senses and of attentive life. The Spirit which gives life to Jesus and to us does not only liberate the soul from its sadness. It also frees the body from tensions, and heals not only traumatic experiences but psychosomatic illnesses too. In a great sadness, after the loss of someone we have greatly loved, it is as if all our senses were snuffed out. We no longer see colours, the world around us becomes gray. We no longer hear melodies, everything seems monotonous. We no longer taste anything, everything is insipid. It is as if our feelings have died. We are cut off from the world around as if by a glass wall. We become apathetic and as if turned to stone although we are still alive. This is what the Spanish mystics called 'the dark night of the soul'. If in the divine Spirit we then again experience the unconditional love for life (it may be through other people or through a flowering tree—I am speaking of an experience of my own as a prisoner of war in 1945), then the joy in living awakens in us. We again perceive the beauties of the colourful world, we again hear the melodies of life, we can taste again, and our feelings draw us out into the world. We leave behind the snail's shell of our soul. Our senses awaken and we live life. This new sensuousness is part of the new spirituality of the body. In both senses and spirit we perceive the coming springtime of creation. In this way the hope of 'the resurrection of the body' has its effect on our bodily and sensory life here and now.

Forms Staged by the Body

The forms in which the body expresses itself (its *Gestalten*) are very malleable. They are moulded by experiences and can be deliberately formed. Our body language betrays much about our biography and our attitude to life. Forms of the body are not only 'given'. They always have a value as 'productions' too, because they are an answer to the questions: Who am I? How do we want to be? Human beings are born actors. They want to disguise themselves and to reveal themselves. 'Every profound spirit needs a mask', said Nietzsche. But that too is ambiguous. In its mask, every spirit also wants to present itself. For this, the way we present our bodies and the care we give to our appearance are important. We have really only 'had' experiences of life when we have brought them to an adequate expression. Every experience has its own expression, and every life the form it gives itself.

Human bodies are moulded by predisposition and biography. Illnesses, mental impressions and far-reaching experiences leave their traces behind. Work and suffering shape our bodies without our will. Job or profession moulds the form. Guessing people's job on the street and in the train is an amusing game. We recognize the labourer, the farmer, the civil servant, the secretary, the teacher, the boss from their walk and the way they stand, and from their facial expression. Their social position is often recognizable from a typical pose: the manager with folded arms, very much 'the master of the situation'; the banker, conscious of his success; the popular politician; the professor, aware of all the problems; the beauty, with her ingratiating charm. Let us look briefly at some consciously produced bodily positions.

1. In ancient Christian monasticism, there was an ascetic bodily behaviour. Through prayer and fasting, chastity and self-castigation, through an entry into the loneliness of the desert and into eternal silence, the body was crucified together with 'its passions and desires' (Gal. 5.24) 'so that the sinful

body might be destroyed, and we might no longer be enslaved to sin' (Rom. 6.6), as Paul had written. What this described in apocalyptic terms as the conflict between the body possessed by the evil powers of this transitory world time, and the body transfigured by the salvation of the future world-time, was given expression by the ascetics of the ancient world in a body-soul dualism. The body must be slain, so that the soul might be free from the ignominy of its imprisonment. The Christian ascetics sought to die with Christ so that with Christ they might rise again. In their asceticism they were imitating the Christian martyrs and preparing for their own sacrifice. The *imitatio Christi*, the imitation of Christ, was intended to make them like in form to Christ. That was why the physical expression of their faith in Christ was so important for them. Christian martyrdom and Christian asceticism were, and are, forms of becoming 'like in form' to Christ[32] in the visible world.

2. The 'soldierly' body could be much admired in the Prussian 'goose step', and something similar can be seen in the armies of all nations, in the American 'West Point body' too. The proper soldierly stance, the 'eyes right', the standing to attention—through strictly disciplined movements of this kind, armies are taught to react to commands like automatons. The purpose of the 'military bearing' was to achieve self-control to the point of self-sacrifice. In Prussia to this was added the breaking of the will, in order that all independent behaviour and all independent thinking might be excluded. In the soldierly body all the muscles are tensed, the soldier 'pulls himself together'. In the Chinese Buddha, in contrast, everything hangs loosely.

3. Ways of presenting the body through the methods of the modern world have as their presupposition the ascetic and military self-command of the human being over his body. Everyone can be the person he or she wants to be. The body drilled for performance and enjoyment must be 'fit for work, fit for fun'. If it no longer does what can be expected of it, it is of no more use and is set aside. So that the body is available at all times, one must keep fit, must jog, or visit the fitness centre. One must keep in good shape, 'toughen up', as used to be said in Germany. Nowadays the word is 'enhancement'—improvement.

Sport in its modern form has become the stage of modern society. High-performance sport counts as the model for enhanced achievement in normal professional life. Top sportsmen and sportswomen become lifestyle icons and publicity figures. To get higher, further and stronger is rewarded, and is an incentive for greater working intensity. Bodies are made fit for the performance demanded of them. Ski jumpers have to remain light, sumo wrestlers must become heavier. There probably is no longer any modern, high-performance sport without doping. The bio-technological possibilities and neuronal doping can hardly be controlled. The Olympic Games are no longer games; the fight for tenths of seconds is no longer sport.

Ways of enhancing bodily looks are no less widely developed and widespread. The individual body of a given time must be made to measure up to the timeless ideal body. In some sectors the beauty craze and the cult of 'the body beautiful' are already becoming a religion in which modern people find the meaning of life. Plastic and cosmetic surgery promise the person concerned that the result will be the body which they want to have, can assent to, and which is admired by other people. 'You have to suffer to be beautiful!' goes the saying, and what doesn't one do for the sake of recognition! Anti-aging programmes play an important part in the modern beauty craze. Only someone who stays young is beautiful, and people who stay beautiful count as young. They become in their way 'immortal'. A trained and beautiful body shows no traces of age, one might think. But are bodies 'styled' according to the ideal not strangely frozen and lifeless, impersonal and lacking character?

Must increased performance and the craze for beauty cures really be put down only to the justifiable free self-determination over one's own life? This is not the case. It is rather the compulsions of modern society which force people to be achievers and successful, good-looking and attractive. In the sports arenas of modern society, the compulsion is still given the noble-sounding name of competition. In the bourgeois society of everyday, it is a harder and colder term: the competitive struggle. In high-performance sport doping has become a systematic compulsion. The person who can't keep up is out. This is what the pharmaceutical industry tells us and profits from. In 2009, out of fear of not being able to produce the expected performance, Robert Emke, a well-known German soccer player, threw himself in front of a train. Out of fear of burn-out, teachers resort to neurological doping. The person who wants to keep up and to be counted among the winners has to work on himself and make sacrifices, in one way or another. The same is true of beauty. Being able to be more beautiful has long since given way to the having-to-be-beautiful. That is why beauties often give the impression of being so tense and so joyless. Their love for their bodies is no longer distinguishable from hate. Bodies in the modern world, highly competitive and beautifully styled, are often merely variations on the soldierly body and successors to the ascetic body. Max Weber talked about 'inner-worldly asceticism', meaning an asceticism in the interests of these worldly goals which are nevertheless so transitory.

4. The authentic Christian experience of the body is embedded in faith's experience of God's love.[33] People who feel that they are accepted and loved can also accept themselves and their bodies as they are, and as they become as time goes on. The experience of the divine love makes the believer not only 'just' but also beautiful. 'Sinners are beautiful because they are loved; they are not loved because they are beautiful', wrote Luther in the Heidelberg Disputation of 1518.[34] Human love also makes the beloved beautiful. Even on disfigured faces it evokes the radiance of beauty because it awakens joy. The 'body of love' is human life filled with the life that is divine.[35]

The incarnation of God has really already given us a counterimage to the modern 'human being as machine' and to the artificial products of 'performance' and 'beauty'. God became human so that we might turn from being proud and unhappy gods into true human beings,[36] human beings who can accept their youth and their age, and assent to the transitoriness of their bodies; human beings who know that life is more than performance, and that it is love which makes human beings beautiful.

Part 3
Earth Ethics

Before we turn to questions about ecological ethics, we must clarify what we really are talking about when we discuss ecological questions. Are we relating ourselves to the nature we confront, or to the environment belonging to us, or to a shared world which lives with us or to the earth on which we exist?

For us, the earth means two things: on the one hand, we mean the ground on which we stand; on the other, we mean the 'blue planet' on which we live, with its atmosphere and its biosphere. Satellite pictures show our planet earth with its thin atmospheric layer in which life develops. In this respect we live on the earth, which surrounds us on every side. How are we to understand as a whole the earth 'on' which we live? We shall first of all look at the Gaia hypothesis and then examine biblical perspectives.[1]

7

In the Space of the Earth, What Is the Earth?

The Gaia Theory

The astro-sciences have shown the interactions between the inhabited and the uninhabited parts of the planet. This has given rise to the idea that the biosphere of the earth together with the atmosphere, the oceans and the land areas constitute a related, complex system, which can also be grasped as being comparable with a unique 'organism', for it possesses the capacity to preserve this planet as a place suited for life. Through the continual absorption of solar energy, life is developed and sustained in a process of photosynthesis. This is James E. Lovelock's much discussed theory.[1] He really wanted to call the earth system so described as a 'universal biocybernetic system with a trend towards homeostasis'; but his neighbour, the writer William Golding, offered him the old Greek name for the earth goddess, Gaia. We understand our planet to be a feedback system seeking to create the best possible environmental conditions for the living things existing in it. We call the sustaining of relatively constant life-furthering conditions by means of active controls 'homeostasis'. In this way the theory came to be known as the Gaia hypothesis, and now, in its expanded form, the Gaia theory. This does not mean a remysticizing of the earth, let alone its deification, as conservative Christians fear.[2] But what it does do is to understand the earth not merely as a living space for many types of life, but as being itself 'living' and fruitful.

As Lovelock himself says, the Gaia theory offers an alternative to the modern view according to which nature presents only matter and forces, which have to be mastered and exploited. Gaia is neither blind nor dumb. The theory also offers an alternative to the depressing idea that the planet earth is a mindless spaceship which circles round the sun without meaning and purpose and will do so until one day it burns up or grows cold. Not least, the Gaia theory offers an alternative to the modern anthropocentrism, which perceives the earth only as the environment for human beings, and is conducive to thinking that what is human is orientated towards the earth.

The geosystem within which the human race exists together with other living things works like a planetary organism which develops complex forms of life from macromolecules and cells, and is in a position to keep them alive. There is a certain security system by means of which genetic combinations hostile to life are eliminated. There is a kind of Gaia language. The genetic code is used communicatively by all living things. In the course of millions of years, the world of the living on earth has accumulated a 'memory in nature', Gaia is awakening in us human beings and becomes conscious of itself in us.

Just as every cell is part of an organ, and organs are part of a body, in the same way the living things which Gaia brings forth are parts of the ecosystems in which they live and which live from them. We are right when we say that 'The whole is more than the sum of the parts', for in each case the whole is a new organization principle and hence different in quality from the individual parts, and these, again, will be changed when they are integrated into new wholes. In the world of life on earth, we can observe the build-up of ever more complex wholes, and can perceive in this a tendency of the planetary organism and a future for the earth.

Talking about human beings and their endowment with consciousness and reason, Lovelock says that Gaia must share with us our astonishment and pleasure, our capacity to think and to speculate, and our restless curiosity.[3] By this he means that Gaia is awakened by us human beings and becomes conscious of itself. But that is the old anthropocentric idea that human beings are the centre of creation.[4] At the same time, however, he prophesies that the earth will survive. But this 'optimistic' ecology suggested by the title of his book does not say that humanity will survive too.

The significance of the Gaia theory for the interpretation of the world, and hence for ecological ethics too, can hardly be overestimated:

1. It makes it possible to perceive the local and regional ecosystems in their global functions and not merely to relate them to the human life within them. Ecology is not an extension of the human world.

2. It turns the previous methods of the natural sciences upside down. The increasingly detailed knowledge of specialists is replaced by the co-operation between different sciences and their integration into geosciences. Natural sciences and the humanities become interlaced when it is a matter of investigating human connections with the organism of the earth.

3. Integrating knowledge is no less scientific than isolating detailed knowledge. Knowledge about the parts must rather be taken up and absorbed into our view of the whole. In the final analysis integrating knowledge is not a dominating knowledge that follows the method of *divide et impera*, 'divide and rule'; it springs from concern for the life we share and for our survival.

4. The Gaia theory forces us to break away from the anthropocentric self-understanding of modern men and women and their self-centred attitude towards nature. It serves what Lovelock describes as the democratic incorporation of the human race into the life of the geosystem as a whole.[5] Of course the earth cannot be viewed in isolation either. As a planet, it is part of the solar system, and the solar system is part of a greater galaxy, and so forth. For that reason, in the creed the Church Fathers already translated the Bible's 'heaven and earth' into 'things visible and invisible'.

5. The threatening nuclear catastrophe has taught us, following Carl Friedrich von Weizsäcker, to see that national foreign policy has to be grasped as part of a shared 'global home policy' and that political structures have to be constructed for the world-wide community of humanity. The threatening ecological catastrophe forces us to understand that the shared 'global home policies' which emerge are really 'earth policies', as Ernst von Weizsächer rightly concluded.[6] Today we are pursuing 'global' politics—world politics— without understanding our 'world' as 'earth', for what we mean is only the human world. We are pursuing globalized economics without paying any regard to the geosystem which has to bear the burden and the cost of these economics. We laud 'globalization' but where does that leave the globe? How much say in it do we allow the earth—or in other words the ecosystem, of which is the human world is a part, and on whose welfare we all depend? When shall we understand the human race as being one form of life on earth among many others, and as living together with these other forms?

Biblical Perspectives

As the first creation account already shows, in biblical language the earth is mentioned in two relationships: (a) heaven and earth, and (b) earth, sea and air.

'Heaven and earth' is the phrase used for the double form of the created world, for 'all things visible and invisible', as the Nicene Creed puts it.[7] Heaven is the term used for the sides of creation open to God; that is why 'the heavens' are conceived as a pluriverse, whereas 'the earth' is always named only in the singular: it is a universe. Although even the multiplicity of heavens cannot contain the infinite God, since they are finite creations, they are none the less imagined as God's dwelling place. 'Heaven is my throne, and earth my footstool. What house will you build for me, says the Lord, or what is the place of my rest?' That is what we read in Acts 7.49, as a quotation from Isaiah 66:1. The general view is that heaven and earth have been created in order to provide a dwelling place for the creatively living God. To put it without images, this is the theocentric view of creation which is in contradiction to modern anthropocentricism. It is not the human being who is 'the crown of creation'; God's Sabbath is the crown with which human beings are blessed, together with all other created beings. In that God already dwells there, heaven is the world which corresponds to God; the earth is the world that is in contradiction to God in that evil and death, and therefore the annihilation of what has been created, wreak their havoc there. That is why we pray that everything that is divine may come about 'on earth as it is in heaven'. The biblical hopes for the future are aligned towards heaven on earth, so that the sorely tried earth too may become the world that corresponds to God. This 'faithfulness to the earth' distinguishes the belief of Israel and Christianity from the Gnostic religion of redemption, where a yearning for the beyond goes together with contempt for the earth.

The Fruitful Earth

In its creation account, the Priestly Code uses the phrase 'earth, sea and air' to describe the living spaces for the living things which are going to exist in them.[8] It is ancient wisdom that the living spaces are created first of all, before there is any mention of living beings. For these living spaces themselves are not empty and passive; they are fertile, energy-laden and productive. According to Gen. 1.20: 'And God said, "Let the waters bring forth swarms of living creatures"...So God created the great sea monsters and every living creature that moves, with which the waters swarm.' The 'waters' and the sea creatures are linked by this energizing excitement. Gen. 1:24, 25: 'And God said, "Let the earth bring forth living creatures.... And God made the beasts of the earth.' Here the earth (*erez*) is granted the 'vital power to bring forth' together with which God 'makes' the animals. No other created thing is granted a creative power such as this. The earth possesses the energy for the evolution of life. Darwin was right. It is true that according to verse 25 God also 'made' the species, 'according to their kinds'. But that is not a biblical objection to Darwin's evolution theory, for 'kinds' means the evolutionary leaps to new forms of life, not unalterable orders of creation.

God's Covenant with the Earth

According to the Priestly Code, after the ecological catastrophe of the Flood God makes a covenant of life with the survivors: 'With you and your descendants after you, and with every living creature that is with you' (Gen. 9.9–10). This covenant is incorporated in the wider covenant with the earth:

'I set my bow in the cloud, and it shall be a sign of the covenant between me and the earth' (Gen. 9.13). God's covenant with the earth is not made via human beings, but puts the earth itself into a direct relationship to God. The 'bow', often and beautifully depicted as a rainbow, is a recollecting sign for God, not for human beings. For human beings, the knowledge that God has made a covenant with the earth means that its divine mystery has to be respected, and that its divine covenant-rights have to be preserved. These rights of the earth find expression in the Israelite Sabbath laws.

The Sabbath of the Earth

According to the Old Testament, the Sabbath of the earth is part of God's ecology. Modern men and women are aware of the earth and their own bodies preeminently in the framework of their concern with work and consumption.[9] They see only the instrumental side of their bodiliness, and only the utilitarian side of nature. But there is an ancient and simple Jewish wisdom as a way of understanding nature and ourselves as God's creation, and that is the celebration of the Sabbath, the day when men and women, their children, their servants, their animals, and the strangers among them too, come to rest and are intended to extol the wonder of their existence.[10] They are not just supposed to come to rest themselves, but to leave nature in peace as well. They are supposed to forget purpose and utility. Then they will know themselves just as they have been created to be, and will see nature as it exists simply for its own sake. The power for regeneration is to be found in this resting and 'leaving in peace'.

The commandment about the sabbath year, or year of jubilee, is focused on the earth, because it is fruitful, and is meant to remain productive. 'In the seventh year there shall be a Sabbath of solemn rest for the land, a Sabbath to the LORD', says Leviticus 25.4. For this Exodus 23.11 provides a social reason—'that the poor of your people may eat'—and Leviticus 25.4 an ecological one—'there shall be a Sabbath of solemn rest for the land.' According to the book of Leviticus 25, the Sabbath rest for the earth is of the greatest importance. All God's blessings are given to the obedient, but God will punish those who are disobedient. Leviticus 26.33–34: 'And I will scatter you among the nations, ... and your land shall be a desolation, and your cities shall be a waste.... Then the land shall enjoy its Sabbaths as long as it lies desolate, while you are in your enemies' land; then the land shall rest, and enjoy its Sabbaths.' This is a remarkable ecological interpretation of the Israel's Babylonian exile: God is going to save his land which has been so much exploited by his people that it threatens to become infertile. When God's land has recovered and has celebrated the Sabbaths withheld from it, the people can return—after 'seventy years' (Jer. 25.12).

All agricultural civilizations in the ancient world were familiar with the fallowing principle, as a way of preserving the soil's fertility. It was only the great empires which exploited their fertile regions without interruption, in order to feed their great cities and their armies, until the ground became a desert. Today too, this is the way most ecological conflicts arise between non-indigenous agrarian concerns and foreign powers, and the indigenous and native population. The people who live on the land and with the land must be given their right to provide for themselves before they produce for the world market. They have a right to nutritional sovereignty. It is only then that the fertility of the earth will also be safeguarded, and without that, humanity will disappear from the ravaged earth in the foreseeable future, just as Israel once did from God's land.

The Spirit of the Earth

The spirit of the earth is creative vital energy for everything that lives in it. When God's Spirit is 'poured out', it is poured out 'on all flesh'—that being the Hebrew expression for 'all the living'—so that 'all flesh' may become eternally living. But according to Isaiah 32.15–18, the Spirit is 'poured out' 'from on high' on the deserts and the fields too. Then 'the wilderness becomes a fruitful field, and the fruitful field is deemed a forest. Then justice will dwell in the wilderness, and righteousness abide in the fruitful field. And the effect of righteousness will be peace'. The 'Spirit from on high' will bring life to the earth. Everything that was benumbed will blossom, as it does in the spring. What the Romantics called 'frozen nature' will burst forth and the deserts, spread through human mismanagement, will become paradisal gardens. That is the resurrection of nature.[11] This is not a romantic wonder-world, but a realistic matter of right and justice.

When God comes, he will come 'to judge the earth'. The 'the sun of righteousness' will rise. It will lift up whatever has wilted and faded, and will awaken whatever is laid low.[12] With this righteousness and justice, God's judgment is not a punitive tribunal; it is the healing, rectifying, fruitful joy of the earth, a judgment that raises up: for the nations it means his truth—for the earth, his righteousness and justice. The expectation of God's coming is all-embracing and earthly. God comes with his righteousness to his earth and to all his earthly created beings, and that includes the nations too; but it does not apply preeminently to them but to the 'kingdom of the earth' in which they live. Perhaps in his solicitude for the earth God' concern is not human beings, but with human beings he is concerned about his beloved earth. The prayer 'on earth as it is in heaven' does really and truly mean the earth, and the peace of the Christmas message really and truly means the 'peace of the earth'. In the book of Isaiah, the earth is even ascribed a salvific efficacy:

> Shower, O heavens, from above,
> and let the skies rain down righteousness;
> let the earth open, that salvation may sprout forth,
> and let it cause righteousness to spring up also;
> I the LORD have created it (Isa. 45.8).

In Isaiah 4.2 the messiah is even called 'a fruit of the earth'. This salvific mystery of the earth also finds expression in a German Christmas carol which calls on the Saviour to 'spring from the earth'. The earth is not only the mother of all the living; in this perspective it is also 'the womb of God', that is to say the mother of the Saviour and of salvation. On Orthodox icons the birth of Jesus is depicted not in a human stable but in a natural cave in the earth.

The Splendor of the Earth

According to Old Testament ideas, God has evidently a special relationship to the earth. The creation story (Gen. 1.31) says that 'God saw everything that he had made' and found that it was 'very good'. God's pleasure is expressed in the 'shining face' he turns towards his creation. That their existence is rooted in 'the pleasure' of the creator is part of the joy in living of created things. In this pleasure, everything created senses that it is blessed. 'When thou sendest forth thy Spirit, they are created; and thou renewest the face of the ground' (Ps. 104.30).

All created beings are forms taken by God's creative Spirit. In the light of the creator's shining face, the whole earth with everything created comes to shine. The image used is the springtime sunrise: 'You are clothed with honor and majesty, wrapped in light as with a garment' (Ps. 104.1a–2).

'The LORD by wisdom founded the earth' (Prov. 3.19), so it will endure. The divine wisdom that shapes it can be perceived from the surviving existence of the earth and its interrelations. That is why the earth is 'full of the knowledge of the LORD' (Isa. 11.9). The foundation always given for this knowledge is that 'the heavens 'are glad' and that the earth 'rejoices' (1 Chron. 16.31; Isa. 49.13).

Just as in the beginning God takes pleasure in what he has created, and just as in the present the earth is full of the wisdom and knowledge of God, in the same way, in the ultimate future toward which everything draws 'the glory of God' will fill all the earth (Isa. 6.3). This is the conception of the future in which the creator himself will come so as to 'dwell' in his creation, and to fill everything with his eternal livingness.[13] 'God is coming': that testifies to the pleasure, the wisdom and the knowledge of God already filling the earth. This idea is portrayed in the image of the temple which the whole universe—heaven and earth—is to become. The ground of all being does not remain transcendent over against everything that exists, but enters into everything that is, becoming immanent in it. This cosmic hope is so bold that it can be viewed as a counter-image to the 'Big Bang' from which the universe has proceeded.

In the New Testament, this eschatology of the earth is carried further. Everything has been created through Christ, the Word and the wisdom of God. His death resembles the grain of wheat which falls into the earth in order to bring forth much fruit. Through Christ's resurrection, God 'reconciles to himself all things, whether on earth or in heaven' (Col. 1.20). This reconciliation of the 'universe' anticipates the future of the universe's glorification depicted in the image of 'a new heaven and a new earth' (Rev. 21; 2 Peter 3.13). With this, the cosmic Christ will become the redeemer of the earth as well. The earth goes to meet a glory far surpassing the glory of its origin. It will be ready to receive God himself and to become his eternal dwelling place.

The Christian spirituality of the earth has always had a special relationship to the kingdom of glory. It is not a kingdom of grace already fulfilling the expectations of the earth; that will be so only in the kingdom of the glory of the indwelling creator. For John Calvin, God has revealed himself 'in the whole edifice of the world, and thus still reveals himself today, so that men and women cannot open their eyes without necessarily descrying it. His Being is indeed incomprehensible, so that his Godhead is unattainable to all human understanding. But on each of his works he has put the evidential stamp of his glory ... Wherever we turn our eyes, there is around us no particle of the world in which at least some spark of his glory cannot be seen.' 'But', laments Calvin, 'all the flaming torches in the building of the world, provided for the glorification of the creator, shine for us in vain. From every side they flood us with their light, but we lack the eyes to see them, we are blind.'[14]

In this respect natural theology is an anticipated *theologia gloriae*, a theology of glory. It attempts to decipher and interpret 'the signs of his glory' in the forms and processes of nature. How is that possible? The immanence of the transcendent God brings all created things to their self-transcendence. Consequently, we can interpret the self-transcendence of all natural forms and processes as signs of the future of the coming God. 'The book of nature', together with the 'book of the promises', points toward the universal kingdom of glory.

The 'splendour of the earth' is the beauty of its natural forms and processes, and what Paul Tillich calls its 'dreaming innocence'. It points towards the beauty of the creator.

What Future Does the Earth Have?

If we go along with scientific predictions, the end of the earth is foreseeable. When the solar system collapses, the earth will burn up or grow cold, but the human race will already have died out millions of years before that, because the earth will have become uninhabitable. According to the prophetic promises of the Bible, a new creation, with a new heaven and a new earth, will take the place of this present world:

> For behold, I create new heavens and a new earth;
> and the former things shall not be remembered
> or come into mind.
> But be glad and rejoice for ever
> in that which I create (Isa. 65. 17–18).

What distinguishes the new earth from the old one? It is the righteousness which will enduringly dwell there. Even if the heavens pass away and the earth burns up, this hope endures:

> According to his promise
> we wait for new heavens and a new earth
> in which righteousness dwells (2 Peter 3.13).

For this hope is founded on God's faithfulness to his creative resolve, which no chaos and no annihilating power can make him set aside. God will shape the future of the earth 'according to his promise'. That is why the book of Revelation ends with the vision of 'a new heaven and a new earth' (Rev. 21.1). What is new about them, compared with creation 'in the beginning'? 'God will dwell with them and they shall be his people.' It is God's Shekinah

which will make the heavens and the earth new. By virtue of the indwelling
of the eternal and living God, heaven and earth and all created being will
become eternally living. The new creation will be an eternal creation: 'world
without end.'

"Brothers, Remain True to the Earth"

Friedrich Nietzsche wrote in *Thus Spake Zarathustra*:[15] 'I implore you, my
brothers, remain true to the earth and do not believe those who talk to you
about celestial hopes! They are poison peddlers…despisers of life…! Once
blasphemy against God was the greatest blasphemy…to blaspheme against
the earth is now the most frightful thing.'

In modern German theology it was really only the German pietist theologian Christoph Blumhardt and Dietrich Bonhoeffer who made the earth
the subject of theological thinking. Both understood the kingdom of God as
the 'kingdom of resurrection on earth', and brought the realism of bodiliness
and faithfulness to the earth into Protestant theology, which was generally
speaking idealistic and individualistic. Blumhardt wrote: 'The goal was an
earthly one first of all, not as we Christians think a heavenly one but a heavenly one on earth…so that on earth God's name may be sanctified, so that
on earth God's kingdom may exist, and so that on earth his will may be done
…The earth is the stage of God's kingdom…for the kingdom of God stands
in direct relationship to the earth, it lives now with the earth.'[16] 'Nature is
the womb of God. It is out of the earth that God will come to meet us.'[17]
Contrary to the neo-pietistic slogan 'salvation alone', with its reduction of
salvation to the salvation of the soul, the Blumhardt movement in Möttlin-
gen and Bad Böll put Jesus' saying: 'Seek first the kingdom of God and his
righteousness.' This movement began in the Black Forest village of Möttlin-
gen with healings of the sick, and in 1899 Christoph Blumhardt the younger
joined the Social Democratic party in order to stand beside 'the heavy laden'
and the people who had been deprived of their rights. The church thereupon
excluded him from its pastorate.

In 1932 Dietrich Bonhoeffer, then curate in Barcelona, held a lecture
under the heading 'Thy kingdom come', and followed Blumhardt: 'Only the
person who loves the earth and God in one can believe in the kingdom of
God.' Christ…does not lead people to a flight from the world into worlds
behind the world; he gives the earth back to them as their faithful sons.' 'In
the hour in which the church prays for the kingdom today, it pledges itself to
faithfulness to the earth, to misery, to hunger, to dying.' Bonhoeffer saw the

reason for this faithfulness to the earth in the resurrection of Christ: 'Here the law of death is shattered; here the kingdom of God itself comes to us, in our world.'[18] Whereas Christoph Blumhardt spoke out against the neo-pietistic individualist interpretation of salvation, Bonhoeffer protested against the liberal distortion of Christianity into a gnostic 'religion of redemption'. Both found their way into the biblical realism of the earth when they turned to the message of the Old Testament: 'Does the question of saving one's soul ever come up in the Old Testament? Isn't God's righteousness and kingdom on earth the center of everything?' asked Bonhoeffer when he was in prison.[19] Writing to Maria von Wedemeyer about their engagement, he wrote: 'May God give us [faith] daily. I don't mean the faith which flees the world but the one that endures in the world and which loves and remains true to the earth in spite of all the suffering which it contains for us. Our marriage is to be a Yes to God's earth, it is to strengthen our courage to do and accomplish something on earth.'[20] Bonhoeffer professed this Yes to the earth at the time when he was facing death because of his resistance to the Nazi dictatorship, at the time, 1944, when German cities had been razed to the ground, and the blood of the murdered Jews cried out to high heaven.

The important thing today is to live this faithfulness to the earth in the crises in which the manmade catastrophes to the earth are being heralded. The important thing is to prove this faithfulness in the face of the indifference and cynicism with which many people knowingly accept the destruction of the earth's organism and foster ecological death.

8

The Time of the Earth

The Doctrine of Creation and the Theory of Evolution

In this chapter I will not enter into models critical of evolution, such as creationism or theories about intelligent design, because I believe that both approaches are irrelevant. I shall follow a theological hermeneutics of nature and ask about an interpretation of natural phenomena sub specie aeternitatis. For this, we have to revise the traditional doctrine of creation, and to look at God's creative processes in the history of nature.[1] Having described the earth as creative space, we shall now consider the life-creating history of the earth and the evolution of life on earth. The Neolithic revolution to which we are indebted for our civilization took place only about twelve thousand years ago.

The biblical idea about God's creation took its impress from Israel's experience of God in history: the experience of the exodus from captivity through the wilderness into the promised land. Consequently, the idea about creation in the beginning is really the idea about the beginning of the divine creating. It is true that according to Hermann Hesse 'there is a magic deep in every beginning', but in creation the beginning holds within itself the promise of the goal and consummation of the divine creative activity. The creation Sabbath points toward the goal, which is the indwelling of God in the completed creation, the cosmic Shekinah.

Creation in the beginning initiates a divine creative process which will end in the new, eternal creation. We may therefore distinguish three stages in God's creative process:

1. The creating at the beginning: 'In the beginning God created the heavens and the earth' (Gen. 1.1).
2. The continuing creation of the new: 'Remember not the former things, nor consider the things of old. Behold I am doing a new thing; now it springs forth, do you not perceive it? (Isa. 43.18–19).
3. The completion of God's creating activity: 'Behold, I make all things new' (Rev. 21.5).

We are therefore talking about a unified creative process on God's part, with a beginning, a way and a goal, and we ourselves are in the midst of this creative process, together with the history of the cosmos and the evolution of life.

Creation in the Beginning

Why is there something and not nothing? This is the child's question under-lying all profound metaphysics, and inherent in it is the human being's astonishment over the wonder of being. The belief in creation is an answer to this 'Why?' question. Everything that is, doesn't have to be there, but that it is there, is good. It is a being that is threatened by non-being. It is an ordered being, which is threatened by chaos. The theological formula for this is creatio ex nihilo, 'creation out of nothing'. But the formula paraphrases in a merely negative sense the fact that all things have been created in an act of God's freedom. God did not have to create—God resolved for creation. Why? Out of love. Love drew God out of himself, so to speak, and drew him into the adventure of this creation. For love is the self-communication of the good. God could perhaps have sufficed for himself, but he wanted to have a counterpart who is not divine. So a reality is called to life which is not divine, but is not meaningless either, but is blessed—that is the world; and as God's good creation, the world is lovable and lovely.

The fact that the reality in which we too exist is God's creation emerges from the creator's self-distinction from his creation. The world is not divine, but as God's beloved creation it has its own dignity and its own right. A non-divine world coexists with God, a finite world coexists with the infinite God: that presupposes a kind of self-limitation on God's part: God with-draws himself in order to give those he has created space, time and a relative freedom, and he awaits their response, which the Bible calls their praise.[2] The meaning of everything created is 'to glorify God and enjoy him forever'.

The idea of creation out of chaos assumes that created things are different from chaos but are threatened by it. The cosmic powers 'sea' and 'night' reach into creation, but they are restricted by God's order: land and sea, day and night. If at this point we already turn our gaze toward the completion, we find that according to Revelation 21 these cosmic forces will be wholly excluded from creation. As Paul too says in 1 Corinthians 15.28, 'God will be all *in* all.'

The Continuing Creation Process

Throughout its history, tradition has talked about the finished creation and its preservation through God's providence. It has overlooked not only the future of creation still to come but, together with that, God's continuing creative process. But in the Old Testament the singular word for the divine creating, *barah*, is used more often for God's activity in history than for the creation 'in the beginning'. In God's creative world process, where the beginning is concerned it is a matter of preservation, but in respect of the goal it is a matter of innovation. 'Behold, I am doing a new thing; now it springs forth, do you not perceive it? ' (Isa. 43.19), and, 65.17–18, 'Behold, I create new heavens and a new earth ... and they will be glad and rejoice for ever in that which I create'.

What kind of creation is this? It is not a creation out of nothing. It is creation afresh out of what is old, a renewal and intensification, and the giving of new form to what has already been created and is already there.

God's creative process, therefore, has a double character: preservation and renewal. And in this we can detect another double character still: God's passion and his action. In order to preserve this world as his creation, God suffers and endures its contradictions, as the story of the Flood in Genesis 6:6 tells: when the earth was full of wickedness, 'The Lord was sorry that he had made man on the earth, and it grieved him to his heart.' God wipes out the wickedness by means of the Flood and with Noah begins a new creation, because he remains true to his creative resolve in spite of the wickedness of human beings. From early on this story was called 'the pain of God'.

God is a God who bears. He does not just rule from heaven with an unfathomable will, but carries and bears from below. The Exodus story describes this when it says: 'You have seen what I did to the Egyptians, and how I bore you on eagles' wings' (Ex. 19.4). There is a feminine image for this patient and purposeful 'carrying': 'As a nurse carries the suckling child' (Num. 11.12), and a masculine one, 'as a man bears his son' (Deut. 1.31).

In line with the New Testament, the passion of Christ is described similarly in the Agnus Dei of the eucharistic liturgy: 'Thou who bearest the sin of the world ...', and the passion story also allows us to say: 'Thou who bearest the suffering of the world'. The Suffering Servant of God (Isaiah 53) carries our sicknesses and shares in our sorrows. The Epistle to the Hebrews, finally, sums it up: 'who bears all things by his powerful word' (Heb. 1.3).

The God who 'bears' like this is not like Zeus, the father of the gods, in a far-off heaven; he is more like Atlas, who carries the world on his shoulders. He stands where according to Greek philosophy the *hypokeimenon* stands, 'that which underlies everything'.[3]

In our personal biographies, the God who bears is also important for trust in God: 'Even to your old age I am He, and to grey hairs I will carry you. I have made, and I will bear; I will carry and will save.' (Isa. 46.4).

A symbol for the sustaining foundation is the earth on which we can stand and lie; a symbol for the God who creates afresh is the morning sunrise: 'New every morning is the love'... We shall now turn to this new thing, and shall set the perceptions of evolutionary theory into the prophetic and apostolic category of the Novum, as Ernst Bloch presented it philosophically in his *Principle of Hope*.[4]

Evolution and Emergence

Darwin's researches are realistic and have been a hundred times confirmed by other research. What is in dispute is his interpretation of the results, that is to say his hermeneutics of nature.

In his own time Darwin did not attack the Christian religion's belief in creation. The target of his opposition was the divine-like position of the human being in the cosmos which has been maintained and justified by modern religion, modern atheism, and the modern natural sciences every since the beginning of modern times. 'Subdue the earth' was read in the biblical creation account, and Descartes declared that by means of science and technology human beings would become 'the lords and possessors of nature', for as Francis Bacon had said 'knowledge is power', and the more power the human being acquires over nature the more clearly his likeness to God will be restored. This is what H. E. Richter calls the 'God complex' of modern human beings. That is why so many people react with horror to the question: is the human being descended from the ape?

This became plain in the famous debate between Thomas Henry Huxley and Bishop Samuel Wilberforce in Oxford in 1860. Wilberforce opened the discussion with the impertinent question to Huxley: 'Was it on his father's or his mother's side that he was descended from an ape? ' Huxley answered indignantly that he would prefer to be descended from an ape rather than from a Church of England bishop who tried to make a subject of scientific research ridiculous.

If Darwin is right and human beings and apes have a common ancestry, this means the end of the human being's godlike position. As the Bible says, he is formed of the earth and can fulfil his specific human tasks only within the community of creation. Since we have come to realize that it is the religious-scientific anthropocentrism of modern times which has brought us to the present ecological crisis of nature and human civilization, we no longer see Darwin's evolutionary theory as an attack on Christian anthropology, but begin to understand that the human being belongs to the same family as other living things on this fruitful earth. That is ultimately also the substance of the covenant with Noah, with which creation begins afresh after the Flood. It is a covenant 'with you and your descendants after you, and with every living creature' (Gen. 9.9–10). So all living creatures are God's covenant partners and our covenant partners too.

Darwin used the word 'descent'. His pupils talked about 'evolution'. By that they meant a development of species through variations and selection of those who adapted best to changed circumstances for living ('the fittest'). But the term was conducive to a glance backwards: enquiry was directed only to the origin, for in a 'development' what emerges is only what was 'enveloped'. Consequently an evolution too only brings out what it presupposes. Consequently, only the variety of life forms which can be explained from the potential of the past is recognized. The concept of evolution lets us understand how whatever exists today has come about, but not how it might have been and can today possibly become. In the conceptual world of evolutionary theory, the past determines the present but not the future. Critically, it might be said that nothing new ever happens under the sun of evolution, Nature makes no leaps. I assume that this is the reason why historians have not applied the concept of evolution to human history.

The new emergence theories break down this frontier in the concept of evolution.[5] They tell us that in the history of nature something new does come into being which cannot be explained from the already given components. In the history of living forms there are not merely continuous developments but leaps in quality as well. An ant heap is something different from a sum total of ants. The whole is a new organisational principle, which makes parts out of particles and links the parts to the whole and to one another. The stages in the build-up of matter and life systems shows this: out of protons and neutrons there become atoms, from atoms develop molecules, from macromolecules cells, from cells organisms, from organisms living things, and so forth. And in each qualitative leap we cannot explain the new whole from the given parts. Let us take an example. A short time ago the famous genetic scientist Craig Venter analysed and published his own genome. We could wonder at it in the newspaper. Do we now know who Craig Venter is? After studying his genome we don't even know his name. Two years ago I met Craig Venter, person to person, so to speak. He told me that the Vietnam war had changed his life. From this I deduce that we don't understand the whole of his personality merely by investigating his genome, and generalizing from it. We don't understand the whole if we divide it up

and investigate only its parts. This scientific reduction is certainly essential
for our knowledge, but it is equally essential to put it aside so as once more
to gain a view of the whole. Reductionism by way of the phrase 'is nothing
other than' is not science.

This leads me to the conclusion that in the history of nature there is a build
up of systems of matter and forms of life, and that in this process ever new
wholes emerge. Nature is not after all blind. In the interplay of chance and
necessity, there is a trend toward increasingly complex forms of life and symbi-
otic networks. Nature plays with its forms and experiments with its mutations.

This trend has been called the 'self-organization of the universe' or
the self-organization of life.[6] The theological interpretation does not dispute this, on the contrary: it gives this idea new depth through the idea of
'self-transcendence' (Karl Rahner), on the basis of the immanence of the
transcendent divine Spirit. That is age-old idea of natural theology, which
has been current ever since Jakob Böhme. In his *Frühschriften*, Karl Marx
wrote: 'Among the innate characteristics of matter, movement is the first
and most excellent, not only in the form of mechanical and mathematical
movement, but even more as drive, vitality, tension, as the torment—to take
Jakob Böhme's word,—of matter.'[7] Embedded in this idea is the insight of
the apostle Paul into the 'eager longing' of creation (Rom. 8.19) which 'waits
with us' for liberation from transience. That is the hope of nature. What
follows from it for Marx is a non-materialistic, a dialectical materialism,
and for Ernst Bloch a natural philosophy of hope: *'experimentum mundi'*.
I myself interpret these signs of nature as the presence of the divine Spirit
which thrusts towards transcending, and which in the appearance of new
wholes anticipates the future of nature in the kingdom of God.[8] According
to human experience, the divine Spirit 'frees and unites' and anticipates the
new creation of all things. Consequently we can see in the history of nature
too the liberations and unifications and anticipations of the future which is
sought and longed for. We understand the present not merely as the presence of past evolution; we also understand the past as 'past future,'[9] because
we comprehend the present as the present of what is to come, and reach out
toward God's future.

The Struggle for Existence or Cooperation in Existence?

Are we right to start like Darwin from a 'war of nature' and a continual
'struggle for existence', or is it more appropriate to start from cooperation as the principle of evolution, and mutual recognition as the principle

of humanity? As we know, Darwin's 'struggle-for-existence' interpretation was exploited by the so-called social and racist Darwinists. But according to more recent research, in the build-up of complex systems of life in the evolution of nature, the principle of co-operation is more successful than the principle of competition. The Russian anarchist Pyotr Kropotkin already pointed this out as early as 1902 in his book *Mutual Aid. A Factor of Evolution* (1902), a book Gustav Landauer published in German in 1920 at the time of the Munich soviet republic (*Räterepublik*) under the title *Gegenseitige Hilfe in der Menschen- und Tierwelt*.[10] For the naturalist Jakob von Uexküll too in his research into animal environment, life-promoting relationship is the fundamental principle of life; and the well-known American biologist Lynn Margulis talks about 'symbiogenesis' instead of evolution through selection.

Where the development and unfolding of human beings is concerned, the new neurobiology of Joachim Bauer shows us that the genetic disposition of human beings is regulated by their motivation system.[11] But our motivation system is stimulated and enlivened by the acceptance, recognition, appreciation and esteem of other people. Rejection, depreciation, isolation and existential fears weakens it, and in the extreme cases eliminates it altogether. The fight of all against all makes human beings lonely. 'United we stand, divided we fall', said Patrick Henry during the American Revolution, and that is a general truth.

Giacomo Rizzolati's discovery of mirror neurons in 2003 proves that human beings already react unconsciously to signs and signals from outside, in the way that apes already do. Mirror neutrons are responsible for empathy, spontaneous participation and cognitive capabilities, which means for a large part of our inter-personal communication.

These new biological perceptions confirm in their own way the Christian doctrine of justification: 'receive one another as Christ has received you for the glory of God.' The unconditional acceptance by God—in spite of all unacceptability, as Paul Tillich added—is the heart of the Christian experience of God and is the eternal ground for self-respect and neighbourly love.

The Theory of Evolution and Belief in Progress

The theory of evolution often went hand in hand with a judgment. For Darwin, 'the semi-civilized' were better than 'the savages', and the 'civilized peoples' were better than the semi-civilized peoples. For him, the Victorian age in England was the peak of progress. If the theory of evolution is bound up with belief in progress of this kind, then every stage of development receives its value only through what proceeds from it, as the next higher stage. But

according to the theological viewpoint *sub specie aeternitatis*—more simply,
before God every form of life has its own value and rights. It is by no means
merely a stage on the ladder of progress. The historian Leopold von Ranke
was right when he said in opposition to Hegel: 'Every epoch is immediate
to God, and its value does not depend on that which proceeds from it, but
in its existence itself, in its own being.[12] So 'the savages' in Tierra del Fuego
from whom Darwin shrank back were not subhuman, and children are not
those who are not yet grown-up, and embryos are not human material. In
the transcendent perspective they are all immediate to God. The insight that
follows from this is that all forms of life have their own dignity in themselves
and belong to the same family of creation, whether they lived millions of
years ago or only came into being yesterday.

The particularly Jewish-Christian perspective which is added to this
transcendent perspective sees the history of nature in the light of the
coming of God, not merely in the light of his eternity.[13] It looks at the
self-transcendence of all living things and perceives that the human being
is aligned toward future. Human existence is open to the world, open to
the future, and open to God. In Greek antiquity, eternity was expressed by
saying that God is and was and always will be, that is to say, is simultaneous
to all three times. But the Christian experience of God interrupts time and
talks about the God 'who is and who was and who is to come' (Rev. 1.4). The
God 'who is to come' is 'the God of hope' (Rom. 15.13), whom Ernst Bloch
described as a God with future as his essential nature.

It follows from this for the self-understanding of human beings that they
are neither the final product of a development, nor are they always the same.
Rather, 'it does not yet appear what we shall be, but we know that when
he appears we shall be like him, for we shall see him as he is' (1 John 3.2).
Theologically this means that human beings in the present will be viewed as
an anticipation and beginning of a greater future. That is why they are born
with 'restless hearts' (Augustine).

The New Earth on Which Righteousness Dwells

Pronouncements about the future of history can be made only with the
guides of historical experience and hope. Otherwise they are speculative.
In the prophetic and apostolic visions of the future of creation we find two
formative principles: (1) the negation of the negative, and (2) the fulfilment
of the anticipations. In this double form, statements about the future are
simultaneously realistic and futurist.

The negation of the negative is: 'Death shall be no more, neither shall there be mourning nor crying nor pain any more' (Rev. 21.4). This delineates the open space for the positive. The fulfilment of the experiences of God in history will fill this space: 'Behold, the dwelling of God is with men. He will dwell with them, and they shall be his people' (Rev. 21.3). Heaven and earth, the visible and the invisible, will be created anew, so that they may become the cosmic temple in which God can dwell and come to rest. Then the presence of God will fill everything, and the powers of chaos and annihilation will be driven out of creation. That is the all-pervading cosmic indwelling of God, the Shekinah. Towards that indwelling God's creation Sabbath already pointed. Thus the new creation at the end will become the fulfilment of the creation in the beginning, and all the being God has created will become true promises of their own eternal future in the new creation. This hope also embraces 'a new earth' in which 'righteousness dwells' (2 Pet. 3.13). Righteousness is one of the names of God.

The true creation is not behind us but ahead of us.

9
Ecology

Ecological Sciences

Ecology (from the Greek οἶκος, 'house', 'housekeeping') was introduced into biology as a term in 1866 by Ernst Haeckel to describe 'the science of the relationships of the organism to the outward world surrounding it'. He was picking up an idea put forward by Charles Darwin, who had maintained in his theory of evolution (published in 1859) that in the long run changes in the environment act as factors in selection.[1] The interplay between plant and animal species and their specific environments had been known from time immemorial. The first listings are to be found in Aristotle's *Historia Animalium* and in Theophrastus's *Historia Plantarum*. But systematic research on the subject began only in the Enlightenment era.

Ever since Haeckel, a distinction has been made between autecology (the environmental field of individual organisms) and synecology (the environmental field of plant or animal communities). Successes in biological environmental research led to the expansion of the term to include human ecology, the biosphere and the global environment as a whole, so that today the term 'ecology' also takes in the changes in the conditions for life on earth brought about by human beings, and in general use means preeminently the human ecosystem.

In biology, the science of individual organisms and species was expanded to include the network of relationships in ecosystems. In the framework of the spread of human civilization and population, ecology led to the systematic research into environmental destructions on the regional and the global levels (for example through the World Watch Institute in Washington and other observation systems), and to applied ecology in environmental protection, environmental ethics and environmental politics.

Human ecology also has a root of its own in the development of psychosomatic medicine. In human beings themselves it is impossible to make a strict distinction between subject and object, spirit and nature. For himself, the human being is never entirely an object. Even as the carrier of an illness, as a human being he remains a subject. Psychosomatic medicine began by 'breaking the spell of scientific objectivity' through 'the introduction of the subject'—the sick person—into the pathology, and it developed holistic modes of observing the human person in his or her *Gestaltkreis* (Viktor von Weizsäcker)—*Gestaltkreis* being defined as 'the unity of perception and motion'.[2] The discovery of the body-soul totality of the human being and the reintegration of bodily and sensory experiences of the self into the life of the person and the community became approaches through which to heal the disturbed relationship of human beings to their own nature. The 'psychology of the environment' (Hellpach), 'psychological ecology' (Lewin) and 'Gestalt psychology' investigate human modes of behaviour in specific human-environmental fields, in particular living areas and living spaces.[3] A complete human ecology will link this ecological psychology with the human changes to the ecosystem of the earth as the inner and the outer sides of the same processes.

In the human ecosystem a distinction is made between the primary and the secondary environment. The biosphere is designated as primary, the technosphere as secondary. Rapid urbanization leads to the replacement of the biosphere by the technosphere in the outer perspective, and in the inner perspective to a suppression of human bodiliness and sensoriness. The wealth of secondary experiences available through the media replaces the primary experiences of life.

Human ecology, psychosomatic medicine and ecological psychology have called in question the anthropocentrism of modern anthropology. According to Pico della Mirandola's theses of 1486, animals are determined by nature, but human beings are created free.[4] Consequently, human beings have been set 'at the centre of the world'. According to Johann Gottfried Herder (1770), 'every animal has the sphere to which it belongs from birth', but the human being has 'a world of affairs and determinations'.[5] Toward every animal nature was a 'loving mother' but toward human beings 'the severest of step-mothers'. Hence the human being must compensate his natural deficiencies through the conscious creation of his own world, a world in which he himself is the centre. The theory that the human being is uniquely 'open to the world',[6] is scientifically untenable: animals and human beings are adaptable in varying degrees but a dependence on the environment is pre-given. Implicit in this modern anthropocentrism was not least an androcentrism equating the woman with nature and the body and subjecting her to a male culture.[7] Androcentrism founders on the simple requirements of humanity and modern anthropocentrism on the simple fact that although the human being is dependent on nature, nature is not dependent on human beings.

The Ecological Crisis

The spread of scientific and technological civilization as we have known it up to now leads to the annihilation of more and more plant and animal species. Carbon dioxide and methane gases produce the 'greenhouse effect' which is going to change the climate of the earth momentously in the next few decades. The ground is being poisoned by chemical fertilizers and diverse pesticides. The rain forests are being cut down, the pastures are being over-grazed, the deserts are growing. In the last sixty years, the population of the world has increased fourfold and in the year 2050 will total between eight and ten billion people. The required means of living (food, water, and so on), as well as the production of waste, will increase in proportion. The urbanization of humanity has grown from 29 percent in 1950 to over 50 percent today.[8] The human ecosystem has lost its equilibrium and is on the way to the destruction of the earth and hence to its own destruction. The slowly spreading crisis is given the name 'environmental pollution', and people are seeking technological solutions for it. But in my view it is in actual fact a crisis of the whole total project of modern civilization. Human destruction of nature is based on a disturbed human relationship to nature. Unless there is a fresh orientation of this society's fundamental values, we shall not succeed in finding a new practice in our dealings with nature; unless human beings arrive at a new way of understanding themselves, and at an alternative economic system—then an ecological collapse of the earth can easily be extrapolated from the facts and trends of the present crises. In earlier times, ecological catastrophes could be attributed to natural causes—for example, the annihilation of the dinosaurs. In those cases nature was able to restore the diversity of living things or develop it further. But the present ecological crisis is manmade, and whether, and how, life on earth can be restored after the 'ecological death' is uncertain; what is at all events certain is that the human race will not survive it.[9]

The living relationship of a human society to its natural environment is determined by the techniques by means of which human beings acquire from nature their means of living, and give back to it their waste products. This metabolism with nature is as natural as breathing in and breathing out. It is based on reciprocity. But since the beginning of modern times it has been determined more and more one-sidedly only by human beings, without consideration for nature. Nature counts on the one hand as the provider of the means for living and the reservoir of raw materials, and on the other hand as a rubbish dump. As a consequence of increased consumption in the countries of the First World, and of over-population in the Third, the non-regenerative sources of energy are dwindling and the natural foundations of human life are being used up.

In human technologies the natural sciences are involved. Technology is applied science. At some point all scientific discoveries come to be applied technologically, even if they are harmful, for as Francis Bacon proclaimed 'knowledge is power'. The sciences provide humanity with the knowledge of how to dispose over nature. That is the concern behind scientific investigation. The sciences are what Carl Friedrich von Weizsäcker called *machtförmig* —they are a form of violence not only in their application but already epistemologically: nature is constrained to provide an answer to human questions.

Technologies and sciences are always developed from particular human interests and concerns. They don't exist value-free. Interests precede them, guide them, and press their results into service. These human interests, for their part, are regulated by the society's fundamental values and convictions. These values and convictions are whatever the members of a particular society consider to be a matter of course, because in their system they are self-evident. If, in an ecosystem which links a human society with its natural environment, nature begins to die, the logical outcome is a crisis in the whole system, which cannot be confined to any one of its parts: crises in technologies, in the sciences, in attitudes to life and in the society's fundamental values.

What interests and values dominate modern civilization? It is manifestly the will to rule which drives modern people to seize power over nature—the nature of the earth and their own physical nature. The increase in human power and the securing of power is the driving force behind progress, which is always only measured quantitatively, economically, financially and in military terms, and the costs of which are pushed off on to nature. The modern civilization originating in Europe is a civilization of expansion, both towards other countries and towards nature. Lost is the wisdom of self-restraint and the preservation of an equilibrium between culture and nature, which was observed earlier in 'premodern' or non-European societies (nowadays called 'underdeveloped'). Today it is lost also among people who desire a Western standard of living. The expansion and spread of this culture of domination is accelerating, and in proportion to this acceleration ecological catastrophes in all countries are increasing.

This gives rise to the decisive questions of the present time. Is the industrial society unavoidably the 'end of nature', or must nature be protected against the industrial society? Is the biosphere the indispensible foundation of the human technosphere, or can the technosphere be expanded in such a way that the biosphere as we have known it hitherto becomes dispensable? Ought we to protect nature from us human beings for its own sake, or must we rebuild the earth into an artificial world like a spaceship, in which human beings who are then adapted to it by means of genetic manipulation can live?

Ecological Theology and Spirituality

The modern culture of expansion and the resulting ecological crisis have emerged from Christianity in its Western form. Is Christianity a factor in the ecological crisis? There are four points to be discussed in this connection:

1. The biblical requirement that the human being should rule over the earth (the *dominum terrae*) is often made responsible for human beings' seizure of power over nature, and for the boundlessness of their will to power: 'Be fruitful and multiply, and fill the earth and subdue it; and have dominion' (Gen. 1.28). True, this text is 2,500 years old, and the modern expansion culture came into being only four hundred years ago; but torn out of its context, this human destiny to rule has acted as a legitimation down to the present day.

2. The *dominum terrae* rests on the idea of the human being—and the human being alone—as being made in the image of God (Gen. 1.26). Whereas all other creatures display traces of God (*vestigia Dei*), human beings have been created to be God's image, representative and governor on earth (*imago Dei*). It is from this notion that Christian cultural history has moulded the concept of the human person. The human being is not just part of nature. He is also 'person', called forth by God and responsible to God. This lends him his human dignity, the dignity which distinguishes him from all other living things. This gives him an inalienable quality as determining subject. As the subject of perception and will, the human being is God's image on earth, and superior to all other created beings, which he can make the objects of that perception and will. Although according to the biblical traditions, this special human determination has validity only within the community of creation (so that it is only as a part of nature that the human being is 'person'), in Western cultural history this destiny has nevertheless legitimated the subjugation of nature and the instrumentalization of bodiliness.[10]

3. In spite of the whole primary theocentric thrust of the biblical traditions, the concepts of the *imago Dei* and the *dominium terrae* still reveal a secondary anthropocentrism. The creation of other beings on earth points towards the creation of the human being, according to Genesis 1, and according to Genesis

2–3 human beings are at the centre of the Garden of Eden, and are also the centre of the curse which falls on all flesh because of their guilt. Israel's experience of God is primarily the experience of God in the happenings of human history. At the centre of Christianity is faith in the becoming-human of God. In European cultural history Christian anthropocentrism slowly pushed out the cosmocentrism of the ancient world and prepared the way for the anthropocentric project of modern civilization.[11]

4. What had the greatest influence of all, however, was Jewish-Christian-Islamic monotheism. Through it, God and the world were divided. God was set over against the world as its transcendent creator and Lord, and the world was robbed of all the divine mysteries other religions revered in the nature of the earth. When monotheism robbed nature of its magic, it prepared the way for the world's secularization and its degradation into being the object of human beings.[12] 'Mother nature' became 'unclaimed property' which belonged to whoever first took possession of it.

In the history of European culture, the divine was seen for preference in the realm of what was spiritual over against what was material, in what was spiritual rather than what was bodily, in the historical rather than the natural, and not least in the male rather than the female. It follows from this that Christianity, viewed as a part of cultural history, is a factor in the ecological crisis into which the Western expansion culture is bringing the earth. What follows from this recognition is the need for Christianity, its spirituality and its theology, to be reformed, if we are to find Christian ways out of this crisis.

On the way to an ecologically responsible theology, what will be put in the forefront are the cosmological aspects of the doctrine of God and of anthropology.

The Immanence of the Transcendent Spirit of God

Modern monotheism has stressed God's transcendence. Panentheistic philosophy[13] tried with dialectical definitions to find the mediation between transcendentalism on the one hand and pantheism on the other. Alfred North Whitehead's process philosophy tried to grasp the transcendent immanence of God in the interplay between God's primordial nature and his consequent nature.[14] According to patristic and modern Trinitarian theology, creation is a Trinitarian process in which the Father creates the world through the Son in the Spirit.[15] Everything that is, is therefore from God the Father, through the Son, and in God the Spirit. Through his Spirit, God is present in each of the beings he has created and in their community of creation. Everything living lives from 'the source of life', the divine Spirit. The existence-sustaining and life-giving Spirit is poured out on the whole creation and forms the creation community.

Old Testament Wisdom literature already taught that the Spirit of God is to be perceived and revered in all things: 'The Spirit fills the world' (Wis. 1.7). 'Lord thou art the lover of life and thy immortal Spirit is in all things' (12.1). Medieval Christian mysticism also maintained this pneumatological view of creation, as we can see from the poetry of Hildegard of Bingen.[16] If the creative, life-giving divine Spirit is in all things, then the Spirit is also the soul of the world and extends over all material things, just as the soul extends throughout the whole body.[17] For the efficacy of God's Spirit in the world, perichoresis is an appropriate concept. This is a term in trinitarian theology for mutual indwelling and reciprocal interpenetration which brings out the unique unity of the triune God. The community of God with his creation corresponds to the inner community of the Father, the Son and the Spirit: God's Spirit is in creation, and 'creation lives and moves in him' (Acts 17.28). To this the community of created beings with one another also corresponds: they exist with one another, for one another, and in one another. Only the Spirit of God which sustains all things subsists from itself; created things do not exist from themselves but from one another and for one another. Unilateral rule is not the principle of life; it is mutuality in relationships. Everywhere life is communication in communion. 'The fellowship God', as the Holy Spirit was also called, creates the coming-to-community of created beings, as well as the differentiation between their own particular kinds. The words of creation differentiate and specify things, the creator Spirit binds them together, just as in human speech different words can be spoken in the same breath.

The Presence of God in All Things

The immanence of the transcendent divine Spirit means that it is possible and necessary to perceive God in all things. According to the tradition of natural theology, this is an indirect, mediated knowing of God.[18] It leads to fellowship with God by way of the fellowship of creation. It does not save, but it makes us wise. For a time, natural theology was considered to be a rival to revealed theology, and in the 1930s Karl Barth therefore fought against it. But natural theology is neither a rival to revealed theology nor its preliminary stage; it is its necessary consequence. The 'cognition' of God in all things can only be a 're-cognition' of the God who has first of all disclosed himself in his revelation. But on the basis of his revelation there must then come to be a recognition of God in all created things; otherwise God will not be perceived as God.

Earlier, in 'natural theology', people looked for a second way of access to God. Today people seek a new access to nature. If we understand nature as God's creation, all things have a transcendent inner side, and our experiences of them can become experiences of God, if we ask not only how they appear to us but also how they are in the eyes of God. They then acquire for us their divine dignity so that we respect and treat them as 'fellow creations'. 'Nothing created is so far from God as not to have Him in itself.'[19] Some people have talked about a 'sacramental presence' of God in the world and have declared the world to be the sacrament of God's presence. Others have talked about 'the world as parable' of God, so as to discover the 'traces of God' in things.[20] It is also helpful to decipher all realities as real symbols of their primal foundation and its future. In a transferred sense created things 'proclaim' to other created things their common creator.[21] According to the psalms, 'the heavens praise thy wonders, O Lord' (Ps. 89:5), all the natural elements and all living things 'praise the Lord' (Ps. 148), 'the heavens are telling the glory of God; and the firmament proclaims his handiwork' (Ps. 19:1, Job 26). 'To seek God in all things' is the one side of Christian cosmos spirituality, 'God awaits us in things' is the other side.[22] But this means that on the foundation of belief in God, God can be experienced in things with all the human senses. It is not only the direct human experience of the self which has the depths of self-transcendence; every objective and every social experience can become the experience of God. Over against the faith which 'comes from hearing', all the senses will then be sensitized to perceive the presence of God in all things, the senses of touch, feeling and taste as well. Christian mysticism, as its poems and songs show, was already always on the search for an ecological 'aesthetics of nature' of this kind.[23]

Cosmic Christology

Today the rediscovery of the cosmic dimensions of Christology is urgently required.[24] In a post-industrial society, ideas belonging to the pre-industrial world are returning in a different way. In the ancient world the theme of cosmic Christology was the conflict between 'Christ and the powers'. It was the world of feared and revered gods and demons. Into this world the cosmic Christ brought the freedom of faith. Today the conflict with which we have to do is Christ and the cosmic catastrophe. It is the world of ecological crises: Christ and the rubbish dumps. The theology of modern times reduced the relevance of Christ to the salvation of human beings and the salvation of human souls, and by doing so it delivered up everything else to a region outside the bounds of salvation. Cosmic Christology counted as a myth not open to existential interpretation. But if Jesus is the Christ of God, we must also think of him as the all-reconciling reality, as Paul did (1 Cor. 8.6) and, following him, the Epistles to the Ephesians and Colossians. Faith in the cosmic Christ discovers the reconciliation of all things in heaven and on earth (Col. 1.20), and accepts everything created as beings for which Christ died, and which he leads toward resurrection. The war of human beings against nature must be replaced by the reconciliation of human beings with nature, and of nature with human beings.

What follows from this is the cosmic orientation of the church of Christ. The church's restriction to the human world and the salvation of souls was a perilous abbreviation. The church has to represent the whole cosmos, so it must bring before God the 'groanings of creation' (Rom. 8.19ff.) as well as hope for the coming of God to everything created. The non-human creations are members of the church just as are the angels, so the church must bring human beings into community with both the non-human creation and with the angels. Consequently believers will draw reverence for all created being into their worship of God: 'I am the light which is over all,/ I am the universe, the universe has come from me/ and the universe returns to me again. / Cleave a piece of wood, I am there; lift up a stone and you will find me.'[25]

New Anthropology

Not least, the consequence of this is a non-anthropocentric anthropology. Behind the anthropocentrism of the modern world is a cosmology that has gone wrong, and a theology that has been surrendered.[26] As a result the human technosphere is supposed to replace the natural biosphere, and the human being is to become the God and lord of his world. The reversal in anthropology will once again see human beings and their world as embedded in the wider cosmic cohesions of the conditions for life on earth and in the evolution of all the living, and will stress that human existence is dependent on nature. We are indebted to modern feminist theology for dissipating the androcentrism inherent in most modern philosophical and theological anthropologies. Philosophical and theological process thinking offers a metaphysics and epistemology which are no longer subject-orientated. Finally, new cultural reform movements are leading to the rediscovery of the body and the senses in a world of subject-less information and secondary experiences acquired by way of the media. Many meditation and therapeutic centres are developing a new spirituality of nature and the body, and of the senses that mediate between the two.

Ecological Ethics

Ecological ethics is only in its beginnings, but at least four different approaches can be detected.

"Reverence for Life"

Albert Schweitzer coined this term in 1919, in affirmation of Tolstoy's ideas and in critical dissociation from Nietzsche's 'will to power'. In 'reverence for life', he found a term which, reaching beyond the relationships between human beings, was well-suited to describe the appropriate attitude of human beings to all the living. 'Through the ethics of reverence for life we arrive at a spiritual relationship to the universe.'[27] He believed that this ethics was an extended ethics of love and a philosophical insight into the ethics of Jesus, and that this was therefore the true ethics of peace. For him the foundation is the mystical experience of 'the great will for life' manifested in all living things. There is no 'less valuable' life, let alone valueless life. Experience teaches that 'I am the life that wants to live, in the midst of life that wants to live.' Schweitzer interprets this experience that there is life only at the expense of other life as 'the riddling self-dichotomy' of 'the great will to live'.[28] Human 'reverence for life' manifests the will 'which through us will do away with the self-dichotomy of the will to life'.[29] The love that is prepared for co-living and co-suffering heals the contradictions of life. Schweitzer's ethics of reverence for life in all living things is intended to overcome modern egocentricism, but it nevertheless maintains at the same time the fundamental ideas of modern anthropocentrism: only the human being knows reverence for life. 'Nature knows no reverence for life.' Through his love, the human being is to 'do away with' the self-dichotomy of the will for life in the conflict of living things among each other. The human being is destined to be the redeemer of nature: 'Wherever you are, there should be redemption, as far as this is within your capacity, redemption from the misery which the self-divided will for life has brought into the world.'[30] These ideas belong to the emotional elevation of humanity, a feature of the bourgeois world of the nineteenth century. They break down in the face of the need of human beings themselves for redemption, since human beings are much more the cause of the problem than they could be factors in its solution.

Environmental Ethics

In Germany, a detailed outline of environmental ethics was first provided by Alfons Auer.[31] It is an ecological ethics resting on a consciously anthropocentric basis. Auer considers the path from the ancient world's cosmocentrism to modern anthropocentrism irreversible and an inevitable consequence of Christianity. Nevertheless, his 'choice in favour of anthropocentrism' is directed against anthropocentrism in its modern boundless and unbridled form. His theological theocentrism justifies anthropocentrism but at the same time brings into play the limitations and constraints designed for the preservation of God's creation. The human being is rooted in nature and is a member of nature. But in the human being, and only in him, 'nature comes to itself and only in him is its meaning fulfilled'.[32] Consequently, the human being rightly knows himself to be 'the centre of nature' and its 'lord'. Only the human being has self-esteem and is 'his own purpose (*Selbstzweck*)'. That is why he has been given a claim to 'sole representation in the cosmos'. 'The whole of non-human nature must be integrated into the human orbit of meaning',[33] for the teleological world order points all things towards the human being, which they have to serve in order to arrive at the meaning of their existence. Auer rejects all postmodern attempts to find new cosmocentrism. Christianity seems for him so fused with the modern world that any criticism of that world has to be taken as a criticism of Christianity. Even nuclear energy was created by God, with the intention that human beings would discover it and apply it responsibly for the furtherance of their existence.[34]

Auer's apologetics neglect what he himself calls the 'rooting of the human being in nature'. His cosmic anthropocentrism breaks down because of the simple fact that nature was there before human beings, is there apart from human beings, and will still be there after them. The term 'environment', like the phrase 'our natural foundations of life', is anthropocentrically determined. It conduces to a destruction of the environments of all other living things and to a withdrawal from nature of its own value.

Ethics of a Shared World

We find a countering outline in Klaus Michael Meyer-Abich's physiocentric ethic of a shared world.[35] The human being is not the measure of all things; nature is. The misleading expression 'environment'—the world surrounding us—should therefore be replaced by the relativizing expression 'the shared world', for human beings are 'related' to the natural world they share, 'animals and plants, earth, water, air and fire', as a part of natural history. If human beings seek 'peace with nature', they must respect nature for its own sake, not for its usefulness to them themselves. That does not mean that nature should be conceded the same rights as human beings, for human beings are dependent on what they draw from nature, as is also the case with the food chain. But it does mean that we should recognize nature's own values and rights and then protect them in such a way that the civil state under law becomes a community under law with nature. Meyer-Abich seeks a physiocentric image of human beings which allows them to arrive at true humanity not just in the human community but already in the natural community with animals and plants. Experience of the self is found first not in social experience but in the experience of nature, through the 'local' senses of touch, taste and temperature, as we can see in every child. He therefore demands a new development of the senses which will further the perception of the natural surrounding world and also of a technology compatible with nature. For human beings to limit their use of energy is part of the minimization of violence towards nature. In the community under law between human beings and nature which we have to strive for, animals, plants, earth air and water have to be protected from the aggressive action of human beings. Every serious intervention in nature and its ecosystem must be justified. Nature is not 'unclaimed property'. What we do to nature, we do to ourselves. Yet Meyer-Abich himself breaks through his own physiocentrism with the anthropocentric thesis that in the human being 'nature comes to speak and hence comes to itself': 'It depends on us whether nature takes the chance for freedom which it has in the human being, or misses it.'[36] What Meyer-Abich maintains is not a naive concept of nature but a normative one, as the term is used colloquially in the words 'natural' and 'unnatural', in analogy to 'human' and 'inhuman'.

Creation Ethics

Finally, there are approaches to a theocentric creation ethics. Every theology starts from the assumption that neither the human being nor nature is the centre of the world; the centre is God, and the world is his creation. This decentralizes the relationship between human beings and nature. In recognizing their creator, human beings understand themselves and all other natural beings as being 'fellow creatures' in a community of creation.[37] This comes out best in the covenant with Noah: 'Behold, I establish my covenant with you and your descendants after you, and with every living creature' (Gen. 9.9-10). Fundamental human rights derive from the covenant 'with us'—the rights of coming generations derive from the covenant 'with us and our descendants

after us'—the fundamental rights of nature derive from the covenant 'with us
and our descendants after us and with every living creature'. Before God, the
creator and preserver of life, the present generation, the generations to come,
and every living creature—different though these all are—are partners in the
same divine covenant. They therefore enjoy the same dignity and have in
each case their own rights. Other living things are not human property, and
human beings are not just part of nature. All living things are God's partners
in the covenant, and in this covenant with God they must make a covenant
with each other for the reciprocal furtherance of life and the shared guarantee
of survival. In a creation covenant like this, it is a matter of balancing out the
different concerns in life in common responsibility before God. God's covenant with all living things constitutes the creation community, in which both
the fundamental rights of creation and human rights must be formulated.
Every human community is a community with nature too. Consequently, the
nature involved has a claim to the protection of its own rights in the framework of this human community. This federalist idea about the relationship
between human beings and nature says that anyone who destroys other living
things without a reason is destroying the covenant with God; anyone who
pushes off the costs of life on to coming generations is breaking the covenant
with God. The covenant with Noah, which is intended to guarantee life on
earth, requires codification of the contract with the society and the generation contract and also the codification of humanity's contract with nature.

Human Rights and the Rights of Nature

Human rights are always formulated and agreed upon in the face of threatening dangers. The individual human rights drawn up in 1948 were a response to
the question about the liberation of human beings from state oppression. The
social and economic human rights of 1966 pioneered ways for freeing human
beings from hunger and misery. Correspondingly, today the nations must
recognize and respect the rights of nature so that nature may be protected
from human oppression. Where nature is delivered over to human violence,
human laws must protect it.[38] The 'World Charter for Nature'—proclaimed
by the Central Assembly of the United Nations on October 29, 1982—was
a first step in this direction: 'Every form of life is unique, warranting respect,
regardless of its worth to man.'[39] Some politicians put the protection of nature
among the minimum guarantees of individual human rights: there is a right
to an intact environment just as there is a right to physical integrity. However,
this protects nature only for the sake of human beings, not for its own sake.

But the protection of nature—plant and animal species as well as the conditions for life and the equilibriums of the earth—must be given a rank among the goals of states and in international agreements equivalent to the protection of human dignity. The natural foundations of life must be put under the special protection of the state, which must protect them for their own sake from human exploitation.

According to the old anthropocentric idea, only human beings are persons or determining subjects; everything else is a thing or an object. But are animals 'things' for the human people who possess them and can make use of them? The German Animal Protection Act of August 18, 1986, has struck out a new path here: 'The purpose of this law is to protect the life and well-being of the animal as a fellow creature, out of human responsibility for it. No one may inflict pain, suffering or damage on an animal without sufficient cause.'[40] Here for the first time a theological framework—creature-fellow creature-creator—is used in a secular German statute. The expression "fellow-creature" indicates the creation community of human beings and animals, the word 'responsibility' appeals to the human being's special position in this community. The last sentence makes the author of any attack on an animal accountable. The next step logically is to apply this Animal Protection Act to other sectors of the natural world too, and to agree that:

1. Nature, whether animate or inanimate, has a right to existence, that is to say, to preservation and development.
2. Nature has a right to the protection of its ecosystems, species and populations in their interrelatedness.
3. Animate nature has a right to the preservation and development of its genetic inheritance.
4. Living things have a right to a species-appropriate life, including reproduction, in the appropriate ecosystem.
5. Interventions in nature must be justified. They are only permissible if the conditions for the intervention have been established in a democratically legitimated proceeding and with regard to the rights of nature, if the concern behind the intervention is weightier than the concern for an undiminished preservation of the rights of nature, and if the intervention is not excessive. After any damage, nature must be restored once more whenever possible.
6. Rare ecosystems, especially if they are especially rich in species, must be put under absolute protection. The extermination of species is forbidden.[41]

It is only if the declared and generally accepted human rights are no longer based solely on the dignity of human beings but on the dignity of all created beings that they will lose their anthropocentric character, which is conducive to the destruction of nature. It is only then that they can be related to nature's own rights and provide a framework under law for the community of the living shared by human civilization and the nature of this earth.

The community of creation is always a community under law. The biblical and Christian traditions stress the special position of human beings in creation and their special responsibility. But there was always the more comprehensive horizon of the community under law linking together human beings, other living things and the earth, and that is the rootedness of all things in the rights of the creator to his creation.

10

Earth Ethics

Benchmarks for Forming a Judgment
"The Preservation of Creation"?

The conciliar process for 'Justice, Peace and the Integrity of Creation' was set on foot at the General Assembly of the World Council of Churches in Vancouver in 1983.[1] What is at stake in the 'preservation of creation'? The ecological theme was not new in the ecumenical movement. As early as 1961 the American Lutheran theologian Joseph Sittler demanded a new 'Christology of nature' for the redemption of creation, on the basis of Colossians 1.20. In early Christianity the salient point of concern was Christ and the powers of nature, to which human beings felt they were delivered up. Today it is Christ and the human beings to whom nature is delivered up. In the ecumenical community, Orthodox theologians have always maintained a sacramental view of nature, because they hope for the eschatological deification of the cosmos. At the General Assembly of the WCC in Nairobi in 1975, in which I participated, the close connection between the social exploitation of human labour and the exploitation of the resources of nature was recognized and criticized. Because social and ecological justice correspond, 'a just, participatory and sustainable society' was formulated as a model for an ecumenical ethics.

Some people criticized the concept of 'the preservation of creation' because only God can preserve his creation; others rejected it because 'preservation' has a very conservative flavour and fails to indicate innovative connotations. The original English phrase was 'the integrity of creation'; but this is equally open to misunderstanding, because creation in its present condition is not 'integer' or untouched. It is not complete and intact. It is imperfect, in need of redemption, and open to the future. According to Gen. 3.17, a curse lies over the earth. So the earth together with human beings waits for its redeeming integrity.

If we take as a formula 'the preservation of creation', and if we look at it more closely, this can mean only the part of creation at the disposal of the human being, not the universe and not heaven. The earth is to be preserved from depredations by human beings. Is that 'conservative'? No, if progress leads to the annihilation of life on this earth, hope for the future of life lies in the preservation of the earth's sustainability. But this preservation has its own progress into the future of life, for it will further the earth's sustainability in order to anticipate the future of 'the new earth on which righteousness dwells'. In this sense 'the preservation of creation' must be called innovative through and through.

Economic growth and industrial development are thought of in terms of the linear temporal scheme of progress. There, past and future are in imbalance. But continuance can only be acquired if more and more equilibriums and cycles are introduced into the growth and development, in order to give them stability. It is only that which can be 'recycled' which does not disappear, and serves 'the preservation' of the earth's organism, the structure of which is itself cyclic and rhythmical. In order to further the earth's sustainability, we must first accept the divine promises which indwell in the earth. The consequence is acceptance of the life-furthering patience of the earth, with which down to the present day it endures the human race and its civilizations—and this acceptance must precede definition of the role of human beings as protectors and stewards of the earth. Not least, it means acting in harmony with the spirit of the earth, so that 'the wilderness becomes a fruitful field, and the fruitful field is deemed a forest. Then justice will dwell in the wilderness, and righteousness abide in the fruitful field' (Isa. 32.15-16).

I would formulate the motto for ecumenical ethics as follows: 'For freedom and justice; for freedom and the future of the earth'.

Protection of Nature

For our sake? For its own sake? For God's sake? Today many people are aware of nature only as the human 'environment', as if it were there solely for the sake of human beings. The egoism latent in the widely used term 'environment' already eliminates nature as a value of its own, even when the word is used in combination with the word 'protection', as in 'environmental protection'. The United Nations Earth Charter says: '[A]ll beings are interdependent and every form of life has value regardless of its worth to human beings'.

Consequently, the following declaration should be incorporated into the constitution of democratic states, as a national goal: 'The natural world stands under the protection of government. It must be protected for its own sake from exploitation and destruction by human beings'. Major industrial and economic projects must be compatible with nature; it is only then that they will be 'environmentally compatible' for human beings too.

Theological declarations about nature must go further than this. Nature must not just be respected and protected for its own sake. If God is believed in as its creator, it will then also be recognized as his possession (Psalm 24), and it is then as God's possession that nature must be respected. It follows from this that human beings together with other living things have a right of use over nature, but not the right of ownership. Whoever claims the right of use over nature (and that is just what we do as long as we live) must respect the owner's rights. He is not permitted to damage or destroy the owner's property. So if the creator is God, it is for God's sake that nature must be respected, cultivated and furthered.

This has direct relevance where the modern land seizure is concerned. Because in the future food is going to be scarce and therefore more expensive, what *Der Spiegel* described[2] as the great race for land has begun. Wealthy nations and societies buy up arable land and pastures in poor countries in order to secure future profits for themselves. To take an example: the Sudan has leased out 3.5 million acres of prime farmland to Saudi Arabia and the Gulf states for ninety-nine years, and is nevertheless at the same time the greatest recipient of international aid: millions of people are dependent on the provision of food from abroad, This modern land sale will lead to famines in the future. But the people's right to food sovereignty is a human right. No government has the right to sell or lease out the land of its people in order to enrich itself. Foreign investors are only interested in quick profits; once the soil has been exhausted they move on like locusts. Anyone who participates in predatory raids of this kind is guilty of a crime against humanity and against nature. The use of the land belongs to the person who looks after it, cultivates it and protects it.

In its preamble, the German Animal Protection Act of 1986 calls animals the human being's 'fellow creatures'. This definition does not apply only to animals, but also to the living space the fruitful earth provides for its living things. The earth is also a 'fellow creature', since it is the world created beforehand for the living, and it must be respected and protected like a mother. The person who protects the earth for God's sake protects it for its own sake too and, finally, for the sake of human beings. He is protecting the creature human being from self-destruction.

The worldwide acceptance of human rights has led to the international warrant for arrest and to international tribunals for the prosecution of crimes against humanity, such as genocide and war crimes. Crimes against nature will one day have to be similarly prosecuted. Crimes against humanity and crimes against nature are often connected—after all, war is the worst pollution of nature. But for this the rights of nature must be assigned the same rank as human rights. The catastrophes of the two world wars in the twentieth century were followed in 1948 by the recognition of universal human rights. So in the coming ecological catastrophes in nature there will have to be an obligatory declaration of the universal rights of nature. The right of nature to live must be put beside the political goals of political freedom and social justice. An ecological democracy will try to balance out these three objectives.

Instead of Ruling and Subduing, Let Live and Let Grow

A deeper intention is inherent in God's covenant with his people, humanity, with all living things and the earth: God makes the covenant with his people 'in order to dwell among the people of Israel' (Ex. 29.45; Jer. 7.2; Ezek. 37.27; 2 Cor. 6.16): God will in the end 'dwell among his peoples' (Rev. 21.3). He lives 'among those who are of a contrite and humble spirit' (Isa. 57.15). So he lives 'in the sanctuary', in the temple in Jerusalem (1 Chron. 24.25; Ps. 9.14; 74.2; Joel 3.21), and in an extended sense in the whole creation: 'Heaven is my throne and earth is my footstool' (Acts 7.48–50). In concrete terms this means 'You shall not defile the land in which you live, in the midst of which I dwell ' (Num. 35.34). Summing up, we can say that God's purpose in the creation of the world and in the covenant with Israel and the peoples is to make a cosmic temple in which he himself can live and come to rest. The 'Indwelling', the Shekinah, is the goal of all the creating, preserving, liberating and redeeming in history.

This is also the all-pervading motif in the way Christ and the Holy Spirit are presented in the New Testament: the Spirit descends on Jesus and 'dwells' in him (John 1.32); the Word becomes flesh and dwells among us (John 1.14); in the humiliated and exalted Christ the whole fullness of deity dwells bodily (Col. 2.9); the Holy Spirit dwells in the community of Christ's people (1 Cor. 6.19); that is his dwelling-place.

So if the goal of creation, the covenant, and the kingdom of God is his indwelling, this must also be the goal of the way his world is treated and ruled by his image, the human being. The purpose of the charge to 'subdue the earth' is that human beings may live and remain on this earth, and that all created things on earth should be cared for and allowed to grow. The deeper meaning of the scientific investigation of the world is not its domination, subjugation and exploitation, but the community between human beings and nature. Cognition means recognition—to know means to recognize, to accept. That is true for nature too. We only know in so far as we love, said Augustine. We do not know by way of subjugation and exploitation, for that is war with nature. We know through affection not through acquisition. Knowledge may be power, as Francis Bacon proclaimed so as to restore the god-like position of human beings in the world. But human beings will only arrive at wisdom when they come to rest, and let nature grow—if they live on the earth and want to remain there. The interest that is the driving power behind knowledge is then no longer to use and exploit the forces of nature. The driving concern will be to live together with nature—that is to say, peace with the earth.

This paradigm change in the interests motivating knowledge has far-reaching consequences for the hermeneutics of nature, for the meaning we give to the sciences and technologies, as well as for the civilizations and cultures of the nations and the economy of the earth.

Ecological Lifestyle

The ecological crisis is not just a catastrophe in nature; it is also a catastrophe of present-day human civilization, whether that civilization is organized socialistically or capitalistically. It does not have merely global consequences but personal ones too. 'Think globally—act locally!' Personal lifestyle has global consequences, and global changes reach into personal life. An 'earth ethics' therefore includes the way the earth's inhabitants shape their lives. By a lifestyle we mean the *façon de vivre*, the form which life acquires through the way it is led. This form is shaped by social demands as well as by personal decisions. In a lifestyle the ethos of a given society and the personal ethos of individuals overlap. If people adapt to the ethos of their society, there are no changes; if they withdraw into themselves the result is solitariness. In both cases we have to do with losses of freedom. A responsible lifestyle always develops out of debates with expectations from the side of society, and the expectations of a society are dependent on responses by the persons concerned. Adaptation and resistance peg out the debates individuals have to stand up to. The form a life takes will acquire its character in a field of relationships: the person and his or her bodiliness; the person and the community; older and younger generations.

An Alternative Lifestyle

If we ask about a new ecological lifestyle in the framework of an earth ethics, we come up against the need for an alternative lifestyle[3], for life as it has been practised up to now in the capitalist industrial societies is one of the main reasons for the ecological catastrophes threatening our world. If we don't succeed in finding an alternative lifestyle, then we shall not succeed in rebuilding industry and the economy ecologically, and we shall not be able to check or avert the climate catastrophe. Everyone living in the modern industrial societies is experiencing the ecological crises at first hand.

A new culture of moderation demands honest householding. If we live beyond our means, future generations, the so-called developing countries and nature will have the job of paying off our debts. Anyone who lives at the expense of others in this way is living unfairly. If the major nations are doing so because of their immense national debts, they have to be viewed as dictators. Economic growth, which the modern growth fetishists worship, has long ceased to be an indicator for the well-being of the people.

The suggestions I make here for a simple lifestyle belong to the context of my own world, and this has been moulded by the modern industrial society of the German Federal Republic, the European community and the Western world. They are not meant for the poor in countries of the Third World. In countries existing under the shadow of the industrial nations, an alternative lifestyle must be created in a different way. The criteria for humanity and the good life are not riches, success and private prosperity. But these are the unworthy dreams spread by the media through the agency of globally operating advertising. We have all heard the story about women in Kenya who walk for miles to sell their oranges to that they can drink Coca Cola. Christian congregations and communities are in a position to confront this with alternative pictures of good and just lives, because they have different standards. Part of this is the development of a culture of solidarity, which in Africa is called 'Ubuntu'.

We shall look at some of these personal distortions before turning to an alternative culture of solidarity.

Anxiety and Recognition

A society which takes the growth of its production of goods and services as the yardstick of its health is forced to increase consumption. In order to stimulate consumption, advertising must sell not only commodities but dreams as well—dreams of power and recognition. The market of unlimited possibilities elicits the feeling: 'I can afford everything' and 'I can have everything'. If I can afford something, I shall win recognition; if I can't afford it I feel excluded.

So what develop on the one hand are fears of a decline in the social scale, and on the other hand greed for more and more. Why do well-paid managers demand millions in bonus payments? The answer is simple: self-esteem and the admiration of one's own class increase together with income. Nothing motivates like recognition; nothing is so humiliating as disregard.[4] If that is the driving force behind progress, then behind the greed for life we can detect the shadow of the fear of death, and behind the life of luxury, nihilism.

The alternative facing us here is really the old alternative between justification through works and justification through faith. What was called 'justification' in theological tradition corresponds very well to recognition, acceptance, esteem—in short, the love which people despairingly seek. If people find this recognition through faith in God, they have no need to look for it in what other people see as their achievements or their luxury. For Christian faith, a person's value lies in that person himself, and his transcendent relationship to God is therefore more than the image which other people have of him or which he has of himself. For Christian faith a person's value lies in the nobility of that person's divine birth. So works do not make the person, nor do they give the person self-esteem. It is the sovereign person who makes the works. The human being as person is more than his achievement, more than his poverty, more than his own opinion of himself. A human being is more than his success in business and something other than his business failure. People who perceive this can cope unperturbed with successes and failures. Human relationships are more important for them than possessions and property. They will live more simply and confine themselves to what is necessary for life, and what furthers life. They are not interested in increasing what they can get, because their concern is not an increase in their consumption. I believe that alternatives in peoples' view of themselves provide the strongest incentives for an alternative lifestyle.

Awareness of the Body

The relationship of human beings to their own bodies 'within' always corresponds to their attitude to nature 'without', for human beings are part of nature. A man has learnt to control the drives and needs of his own body, and in the same way he tries he tries to control nature outside himself. Women are careful with their own bodies, and they act similarly toward nature outside. As we saw in part 2, the detachment of the human mind and spirit from the body developed in the course of the history of Western culture. The subjectification of the mind and spirit and the objectification of the body are cleaving ever more widely apart. The controlled body has been reduced to dumbness. Today the mind is detached from the limitations of its own body through the internet and is brought to an almost planetary omnipresence. In cyber space every one can be in several places at the same time, but in a bodiless and 'desensorized' form.[5]

An alternative lifestyle begins with the rediscovery of the body[6] and identification with one's own body, that is to say it begins with the overcoming of that laboriously learnt detachment through new spontaneity. A help here is the psychosomatic insight into the totality of the human being and into the unity of body and soul. This psychosomatic insight into the differentiated unity of body and soul, detachment and spontaneity, corresponds to the ecological insight into the differentiated unity of human beings and the earth. If we want to do justice to both nature and ourselves, the one-sided humanization of nature must be followed by the realistic counter-movement of the naturalization of human beings.

The Return of the Senses

The demands of the modern world lead to the 'de-sensorizing' of the people living in it. Of our five senses, we call touch, taste and smell the local ones, hearing and seeing the remote ones.[7] In the traffic and communications of modern mass cities, the remote senses are pressed into service to an undue extent while the local senses are neglected. Radio and television, telephone, fax and internet allow us to communicate globally, but only by way of the remote senses. The local senses are not merely neglected in the modern urbanized world; they are actually tormented: smell by exhaust fumes, taste by fast food, touch by synthetics. Even school children can hardly distinguish things through touch, smell and taste. Young people can play computer games all day long and live from pizza and popcorn. A return to a body-friendly lifestyle close to nature comes about through the return of the senses and the deliberate development of the neglected senses of touch, smell and taste. A new sensitivity in dealings with other people, with other living things and with the countryside reawakens the senses and diminishes the brutalities hurried people commit. For a new culture of the senses we must take time and allow ourselves time.

Time by the Clock and Experienced Time

Lewis Mumford called the clock 'the key machine of the industrial age',[8] and he was right, for through the clock, time as we experience it turns into rationally measured time. When I was young, one was given a watch at one's confirmation, and that meant that life was beginning in earnest. Through the clock, one is made to conform to the course of things as this is laid down. The clock regulates the planned day; one clocks into work and clocks out again, and one's wage is measured accordingly. The motto 'time is money' stimulates business. Punctuality is made the cardinal virtue. A waste of time is declared to be a sin. The clock dictates the time. In nature and our own bodies, time is certainly experienced, but in cycles and rhythms; but with the relentless ongoing clock, we conform to the linear sense of time which rules progress. Since time always 'moves on', as we say, we become short of time, and continually find that in fact we 'have no time'. If we get the impression that 'the march of time' is quickening, we become accelerated people. We feel that 'time is slipping by', and want to experience as much as we can. Why? Life is short.

Time measured by the clock is mechanically measured time. For this clock-time it is a matter of indifference whether the time is empty or full, whether we have been bored stiff or whether 'it has passed in a flash'—after sixty minutes the hour is at an end, and everything we experienced in it is past and gone, although we know in our heart of hearts that nothing which we have really experienced and nothing we have suffered is past. Mechanical time takes no account of experienced time; on the contrary, it makes all times the same. Measured time quantifies life, but experienced time is quality of life. When we are happy we have no sense of time. So it is important at times when we experience life intensely to lay our watch aside. Life comes alive when we break through the dictation of the clock. 'You have the clock', said a wise Indian as he took leave of an acquaintance who was interviewing him, 'but we have time'. An alternative lifestyle only becomes visible when we acquire a new relationship to time. Everything has its proper time. Life according to the clock 'has its time', experienced time 'has its time'. We shall learn how to distinguish and to limit ourselves.

In economic life and technology, competition is leading to an ever-increasing acceleration of the processes. Innovations demand it. In human development the accelerations do not further the maturing process; they actually hamper it. The pressures of high school or secondary education allow pupils no free time to develop their qualities outside the learning process. The bachelor's degree allows students no time to reflect, to discuss, and to get to know other subjects. Human development needs time.

In order to understand what one learns and to develop a reliable capacity for judgment one must be given time. And because we learn from mistakes and misjudgments, these must not be excluded by way of prefabricated learning material. In the sectors bearing on human development and education, we need a deceleration of the processes and more trust in the freedom of the people concerned. In industry and technology, the acceleration leads to an ever-shorter 'shelf life' of the products. That increases consumption and also the production of waste. Long-life products can be expected to be more reliable, more user-friendly, and kinder to nature. Why don't we allow ourselves more time?

The Simple Life: Doing without or Reaping the Benefits?

The necessary ecological restructuring of industry and the market today demands a new, ecological lifestyle. In negative terms, this can be described as an avoidance of extravagance, a restriction in the expenditure of energy, and reduction of the production of waste. Then the old ideal, 'produce more—consume more', will give way to the alternative ideal of 'the simple life' which the novelist Ernst Wiechert already invoked in Germany after the First World War. If people in the First World lived more simply, people in the Third World could simply survive: this was already said in ecumenical circles forty years ago. But a this-worldly asceticism does not appeal to everyone. And yet the renunciation of unhealthy profits always also embodies an increase in the wholesome quality of life. This must be kept in mind. The use of energy makes it clear. For a long time the expenditure of energy has counted as an indicator of the violence we inflict on nature. The reduction in its use, through saving and effective application, is at all events salutary both for tormented nature and for our own economic expenditure. But there is also the intelligent transition to renewable energy, such as solar, water and wind power. Once this transition has been made, we shall not absolutely need to restrict ourselves. Asceticism, fasting and 'doing without' are necessary when we are considering the violence done to nature, but they are only the preconditions for a richer life in ecological harmony with nature and its forces, and in harmony with our own selves. The natural life we look for when we put aside the lifestyle of the consumer age will be a healthier one. The happiness of a successful life depends on social relationships and the relationship to oneself, not on superfluity in material possessions.

Think Globally, Eat Locally

Changes in our eating habits also belong to an alternative lifestyle. In Germany we don't have to eat strawberries from Israel at Christmas time or fly in tulips from Kenya and cherries from Australia. When cheap apple-extract from China is on offer during the apple harvest in Germany, this competition ruins the regional fruit farming. The immense transport distances pollute the atmosphere and ruin the taste of what has been transported. Is it worth this, in order to feel 'globally' provided for, like a king? No, it makes more sense to eat local products, and to eat and drink in harmony with the seasons. This is part of the food sovereignty of the peoples of the world, and the sovereignty of one's own people as well.

The 'slow food' movement is a healthy reaction to the unhealthy fast-food chains and canteen food. Organic farming produces healthy foodstuffs and must be protected today against aggressive agrarian concerns and patented, exploitative, genetically manipulated products, until they can make their own way globally. An analogous healthy reaction is the new 'city farming' and the return to self-sufficiency through one's own foodstuffs. This creates new jobs at the same time.

It is also useful not to eat the foods which top the food chain but to move away from meat to vegetarian dishes. How much grain has to be used in order to produce one kilo of meat? It is not just cheaper to eat vegetarian food but fairer too, and healthier in addition. No one must suddenly become a vegetarian if his body cannot cope with the changeover to vegetarian food, but everyone can reduce his consumption of animal food to some extent, as long as this is not distasteful. The city of Bremen has declared Thursday to be a vegetarian day, following the example of some Belgian cities. That is no more than a sign or token, but it is a valuable one. Our food customs are either part of humanity's food crisis or will become part of its conquest.

A Culture of Solidarity
There Is Enough for Everyone

This is the message given to us by the first Christian community in the first Pentecostal event:[9] 'Now the company of those who believed were of one heart and soul, and no one said that any of the things which he possessed were his own, but they had everything in common. And with great power the apostles gave their testimony to the resurrection of the Lord Jesus, and great grace was upon them all. There was not a needy person among them…distribution was made to each as any had need' (Acts 4.32–35).

This community is the primal image of all Christian communities, and the origin of the fundamental idea of Christian social doctrine: solidarity. If we ask today about a new culture of solidarity in a world of individualization and globalization, we can begin here. We find three factors for the early Christian experience of the fullness of life and the overcoming of every need.

1. With great power the apostle proclaimed the resurrection of Christ. That is where it begins. In Christ's resurrection from the death the fullness of eternally living life is thrown open. Death's power over life has been taken away; threats of death no longer have any effect. To suffer need or want means being excluded from the enjoyment of life—not to have anything to eat and to drink; to be ill; to be lonely; and finally to lose one's life. The greatest want we suffer is in the death of life. Every other want in life is connected with death. That is why the fear of death is so threatening that we react with the greed for life. Because we know that we have to die, we cannot get enough of life. But if with Christ the resurrection is open, then we sense a life no death can kill. That is a life of which there is enough, more than enough, not just for the living but for the dead too.

2. 'The company of those who believed were of one heart and soul.' A throng of people who do not know each other become a community, and this community is immediately 'one heart and soul'. That is the experience of God's Spirit. The Spirit overcomes the barriers that divide people from people; the oppression of one person by others stops; the humiliating of one person by other people ends; the alienation of one person from another is overcome; masters and servants become brothers; men and women become friends. The privileges and discriminations on the basis of race, class and sex disappear. In the midst of a heartless world and a society of social frigidity people become 'one heart and soul': a community of trust. When something like this happens, what is experienced is nothing less than God's presence. Reciprocal recognition and mutual love overcome the fear of one another and the aggression toward each other. What the believers have in common is stronger than what divides them individually.

3. 'No one said that any of the things he possessed were his own.' In the Spirit of the resurrection and in the experience of the Spirit of life they share, no one needs to cling on to what he possesses any more. Anyone who lives a divinely filled life has no need for the ambiguous securities which possessions and property give him. So these things are there to be used by those who need them. Because they had 'everything in common…there was not a needy person among them'. In this little Jerusalem congregation, which was probably made up of poor people, 'there was enough for everyone'.

Is that 'early Christian communism? Is it an unrealistic ideal? No, it is a new, realistic experience of God we can make together at any time and in every place. This other world is possible! It is a counter-image to all the societies with social inequality and want. In these societies 'there is never enough for everyone', so they are dominated by a struggle of each against all for the means of living and the pleasures of living—to be more precise, by a struggle of the rich against the poor, of the strong against the weak, of the healthy against the sick, of the upper classes against the lower classes. The competitive struggles in the marketplace of modern society are explained in a social-Darwinian sense as being 'the natural rights of the stronger', but in actual fact they are driven by the fears of death and the greed for life. Where these rule, the result is a world of social frigidity, a dog-eats-dog society in which 'everyone is his own best friend'.

The opposite of poverty is not wealth, but community. In community individuals become rich, rich in friends who can be trusted, rich in mutual help, rich in ideas and powers, rich in the energies of solidarity. These energies simply lie fallow or are repressed. All helpful actions have come into being at the grass roots: kindergartens, neighbourhood help, care for the poor and the sick, and other citizens' action groups.

In the economic crisis of 2008, beneath the lamentations of the consumer culture a completely different culture of solidarity emerged. The misery of the unemployed and homeless, of the impoverished and excluded, released a wave of unexpected readiness to help in the major cities of the Western world. Free meals, co-operatives, and neighbourly help were set up in a way no one had expected.[10] This saved the lives of numberless people. So we should not overcome the present economic crisis by restoring the old consumer culture, but should surmount it by developing this culture of solidarity, and by drawing up guidelines for a post-capitalist society.

The energies of the people's solidarity also emerged in the terrorist catastrophes of 9/11, as well as after the mass murders by crazed pupils in German schools in Erfurt in 2002 and Winnenden in March of 2009. The families affected were not left alone. In the towns and villages a crowd of people unknown to each other came together to express their grief and thronged to spontaneous services in churches and in the market places in order to show their support, to participate in the mourning, and to comfort.

These forms of solidarity among people show a different culture from that of the consumer temples and the shopping malls.

What Is Human Liberty?

Article 1 of the Universal Declaration of Human Rights of 1948 says: 'All human beings are born free and equal in dignity and rights.' But how have liberty and equality been simultaneously realized today? It seems that the more liberty the less equality, and the more equality the less liberty.[11]

Possessive Individualism. The first definition of liberty familiar to us from political history interprets liberty as rule. Inasmuch as human history is a struggle for power, the person counts as free who acquires power and rules. The losers become un-free subjects of the free. The masters are free, the dependent are slaves, women and children are not free. The person who understands freedom as rule can only be free at the expense of other people; his freedom means dependence for others, his wealth makes others poor.

In the modern bourgeois world, freedom was made a function of ownership. Everyone has the right of disposal over his own person. Every man is his own master, every woman belongs to herself. Here freedom is understood as the autonomy of the individual over himself. C. B. Macpherson maintains that the essential nature of the human being is freedom and that freedom means the right to dispose over his own person and abilities.[12] Socially, this 'possessive individualism' has only one limit: the free right of disposal enjoyed by other people too. Everyone is free in himself and no one participates in other people. In the ideal case this means a society of lonely individuals who do not bother one another: 'the lonely crowd.'[13] In this way freedom becomes a universal human right, but is this really what human freedom is?

A human being is not an individual. According to the Latin derivation, an individual, like the Greek 'atom', is something finally indivisible. But a person, in contrast, is a human being in the social relationships of I-Thou— we, as Martin Buber, the founder of modern personalism, showed,[14] following Feuerbach, Hegel and Hölderlin. In the social network of taking and giving, listening and speaking, experiencing and touching, recognizing and being recognized, a human being becomes a person. Persons become persons only in community, and a human community exists only in personal relationships. If a person is individualized, he is atomized and turned into a being without relation. In Greek an 'idiot' was a private person, unconcerned with public affairs. It used to be considered an insult to describe someone as 'a certain individual'.

The freedom of human persons cannot be preserved through ever-greater individualization. It can only be preserved if people become capable of community, and are willing for community. That is the truth behind communitarianism and the 'communitarian network'.[15]

Where do I feel free in the human sense? In a supermarket, where I can buy everything as long as my money holds out, but where no one knows me and even the person at the check-out doesn't look me in the eye? Or in a local community or a congregation where people know me by name and look at me face to face, and affirm me? The freedom of the supermarket is the reality of individual freedom of choice; freedom in the community is the reality of communicative freedom. The first freedom is related to objects which can become my property; the second to persons who recognize and accept me. The first freedom is a function of my property, the second is a social function.

Communicative Freedom. The other definition we know from social history defines freedom as open community. Here freedom is not a function of property but a quality of inter-subjective relationships.[16]

The history of the German language shows that *Freundlichkeit* (friendliness) is the other root of *Freiheit* (freedom). The person who is free is friendly, gracious, open and gives freely. He lets other people share in his life and is interested in the well-being of others. Inter-subjective relationships are called free if they are marked by reciprocal recognition and mutual friendship. If I know that I am recognized and respected, I feel free and go out of myself and show myself as I am; if I feel disregarded, I withdraw into myself and defend myself. Recognition opens up a free space socially in which other people can develop freely. In a society like this the other person is not a restriction of my personal freedom; he complements it and enables it. The shared life develops out of the mutual participation in life. It is only a society of this kind that can be called a free society.

In the Christian community we call this 'love'—in Christian social doctrine 'solidarity'—in the political sphere 'equality', and, summing them up: community in solidarity. A free community is not a collection of private, free individuals, but a community in which people stand up for each other, and especially for the weak and the sick. Only the concept of communicative freedom is a concept of humane freedom.

The Multiplicity of Cultures and the Unified Global Culture

Today we often hear about the clash of civilizations and about the necessary dialogue between the different cultures.[17] That is valuable but it is already too late. The multiplicity of human cultures and the protean variety of cultural traditions has been overlaid and relativized by a global unified culture which looks the same everywhere. The high-rise buildings in Seoul and New York, Peking and Los Angeles, Moscow and London and wherever we go, look just the same everywhere, because everywhere they are built by the same star architects, with their global reputations. Transportation problems, traffic jams and pollution are the same wherever we go. Everywhere the big hotels have the same names because they belong to global hotel chains. Everywhere the big shops offer the same products from the same global firms—Gucci, Boss or Armani. Basic English is becoming the global unified language, and in television it is Hollywood that determines the pictures which make their impression on everyone. What we ought to look at in other cultures are turned into the objects of 'sightseeing' which are pointed out to visitors wherever they go. 'Global', universalized clothing has meanwhile been adapted for China too, and has pushed out the Mao-look. It is only in India, Africa and Arabia that local costumes still survive. The global unified culture is monotonous, uniform and tedious. What has happened to the different, brightly variegated cultures of the different peoples? They are reduced to 'folklore', to dance groups in the Hilton Hotel, to choral groups on cruise ships. The global culture debases the cultures into becoming the objects of World Heritage programmes.

This unified global culture is not a culture of solidarity. In destroying the multiplicity of the cultures it also destroys interest in other civilizations, languages, traditions and ways of living. It is not here that we can discover the hope for a favourable future for humanity. An ethics of hope for the fullness of life resists the unified global culture and preserves cultural multiplicity because it is in that that the potentialities for the future lie. It is multiplicity that is universal, not uniformity.

Part 4
Ethics of Just Peace

Initially, I wanted to call this part of the book 'Political Ethics', but that sounded too much like a textbook or a lecture promising to offer a survey. In this *Ethics of Hope*, I am not concerned with general surveys. My concern is concrete involvement in the face of the dangers threatening our world today. I have concentrated therefore on the substance of political ethics, which is called peace. Although real peace always has a multiplicity of components, I am assuming that, politically, peace consists of the present existence of righteousness and justice, not just the absence of violence. So I am beginning with a discussion of divine and human justice and righteousness.

A political ethics of peace is not an idealistic utopia of a paradisal peace. It is the realistic confrontation with the perils of a world which has no peace because it is unjust. The two world wars in the twentieth century demanded senseless millions of victims. In the twenty-first century, worldwide peace is vitally necessary and will demand voluntary victims in the face of the world's coming dangers and those already present, for peace already has its martyrs, of whom we may mention here only the familiar names of Mahatma Gandhi and Martin Luther King. Those who stand up for reconciliation and peace are not weaklings with subdued feelings and well-schooled wills but people who passionately love life. Their love for life stands up to hate, retaliation and other deadly violence because this love burns in them like a fire. It renounces power, but it is powerful and provides the readiness for risks and for sacrifice.

The foundation of a life in peace is righteousness. According to the Old Testament, righteousness is a name for God (Jer. 23.6); and according to the New Testament (2 Pet. 3.13), it is the quintessence of peace present on the new earth. What gives inner strength for the creation of righteousness are the love for life described in part 2, the respect for the earth explained in part 3, and the trust in God who has promised his future, as well as the corresponding trust between people and in the earth. So I shall begin by discussing the religious concepts of righteousness and shall pose the critical question: What human righteousness corresponds to God's righteousness, and furthers life and preserves the earth? The German word *Gerechtigkeit* covers both justice and righteousness, righteousness being the comprehensive and overriding term which embraces justice as well. The old saying, *Fiat justitia pereat mundi*—'let justice be done though the earth perish'—is assuming a deadly righteousness and justice. But if righteousness is supposed to create peace and life, the saying ought to run *Fiat justitia vivat mundi*—'let justice and righteousness be done so that the earth may live'. What righteousness is this?

11

Criteria for Forming a Judgment

We shall begin with the introductory question about the criteria for forming a political judgment in questions about a just peace.

Righteousness, Justice, and Equality

The first question in political decisions is whether they serve social equality in a society or promote the inequality of its citizens politically, socially and economically. The foundation of every democracy is the equality of its citizens. According to the tradition of democratic constitutions, equality comes before liberty, for there is liberty only on the basis of equality—only social equality can ensure a society's internal peace.

Between the nations too it is only justice which ensures peace, not the supremacy of a nation or an imperium. The military, ecological and terrorist perils have already become so great that if the human race is to survive, the concern for its survival must be given absolute precedence over and above the particular interests of nations, classes and races. Egoistic, particularist interests will bring about the world's downfall. It is only in a community of human beings that it can survive. Human rights are an initial outline for a universal basic law or constitution for humanity.

The Deficits of Politics in the Face of Global Problems

Every political decision and every political demand is made in the face of the fact that the problems of the modern world are becoming global, whereas the political institutions have remained local. The peoples of the earth are increasingly becoming the objects of man-made crises, but they must become the determining subjects of their own history if they want to overcome these crises. New nuclear powers are emerging which do not feel bound to any treaties about the non-proliferation or non-distribution of nuclear weapons. The financial markets have been deregulated and are leading the worldwide economy into catastrophes under which the poor countries have to suffer most. The ecological disasters do not come to a halt at national frontiers. The growth of the world population is uncontrollable. The nation states of the nineteenth century and the empires of the twentieth are becoming increasingly helpless. Out of their own self-interest, they are furthering the dangers instead of preventing them. Consequently, people are losing interest in their powerless policies and prefer to engage in citizens' initiatives locally and in global movements and non-governmental organizations (NGOs). These non-parliamentary global movements are driving beyond nationally limited policies. Greenpeace and the European Social Forum are the best examples. So the first task in the face of the global problems will be to overcome this deficit in politics.

Are Ethics Always Too Late on the Scene?

If we ask about ways out of the present worldwide dangers, we are always already too late. Politics then become a matter of crisis management, and ethics turn into damage limitation. What is ethically required is demanded only in case of need, and after it has become the subject of general agreement. But what we need is crisis prevention, and we must first surmount the ethics which are the cause of the crisis. We are not just looking for ways out of the dangers, but also for ways of preventing them. That is why it is important to look beyond the dangers themselves, and to anticipate a future in which all human beings will be able to live. Since the dangers are becoming global, what is required are not just system repairs but also a restructuring of the chaotic foundations of the world's previous political systems. It is only if we believe that 'another world is possible', as ATTAC says, and only if we hope that it will be better than the present one, that we can do what is necessary today. Erich Fried wrote forty years ago that:

> The man who wants the world to stay
> just as it is
> doesn't want it to stay at all.

This is even more apt today than it was then.

Is Trust the Substance of Democratic Politics?

Trust is the substance of democratic politics, said Konrad Adenauer, the first chancellor of the German Federal Republic (although his relationship to the truth was very much his own)—not power, not even the sovereignty of a government. Democratic politics is essentially speaking the self-government of the people, which means that it is peace politics, not power politics. Politics, as Althusius said long ago, is *ars consociandi*—the art of consociation. For a democratically elected government trust is the greatest good because, unlike authoritarian and autocratic forms of government, it has to be trust-worthy. Everyone must deal circumspectly with this general good and must not put it at risk through lies. People must do what they say they are going to do, and must say what they are doing. Anyone who replaces trust by controls sows mistrust and destroys his own basis. Without trust, nothing works in a democracy. Trust is won through truthfulness and is strengthened by honesty. Mistrust evokes fear, and leads to the struggle of each against all.

12

Divine and Human Righteousness and Justice

In the Reformation period this chapter would have been entitled: 'Of Divine and Human Righteousness', the frame of reference being that human righteousness should conform to the righteousness of God. But how was this correspondence viewed then, and how is it viewed now?

"Tit for Tat" Religion

Secular states are an achievement of the Enlightenment. Previously, and outside the modern world still, states were formed through their political religions and were under the sway, and subject to the retribution, of their gods.[1] According to the ancient doctrine of the state, worship of the gods of city, country and state is the state's supreme purpose (*finis principalis*).[2] The state's gods provide for its prosperity and peace, so the state's citizens must provide for their appropriate worship. The favour of these gods is won through public sacrifice, but if there are famines, pestilences, natural catastrophes and wars, these are signs that the gods are angry because of the blasphemy, insufficient cultic observance or the disobedience of the state's citizens. The people must do penance, as once in Nineveh, and must make special sacrifices, or they must slay the wicked who are in their midst. The book of Jonah tells of both reactions: the storm at sea, because one of God's prophets has taken flight, and the favour of this same God conferred on the repentant people in Nineveh. To ensure the favour of the gods was also the preeminent task of oriental rulers, for they were all priestly kings. The Roman caesar too was the *pontifex maximus* of Rome's state gods. The Chinese emperor certainly stood over against his subjects as 'Son of Heaven', but if he fell into disfavour with heaven and his country was visited by famine, plague, earthquakes and floods, he could be overthrown. The Moloch in Carthage demanded children as sacrifices, the Aztecs and Mayas offered their gods still quivering hearts.

Against the background of an interpretation like this, blasphemy is the worst of crimes. It is directed not against human beings but against the gods who protect them, and indirectly puts the life of the whole people in the greatest danger.[3] This crime against the gods calls forth their vengeance. The blasphemer has to die in order that the gods may be pacified and the people survive. In ancient Israel there was a legal regulation that 'He who blasphemes the name of the Lord shall be put to death: all the congregation shall stone him' (Lev. 24.16).

According to the early Christian testimonies, Jesus was condemned by the high priest as blasphemer, although he was executed by the Romans as a rebel against the imperium: 'Then the high priest tore his robes, and said, "He has uttered blasphemy. Why do we still need witnesses? You have now heard his blasphemy. What is your judgement?" They answered, "He deserves death"' (Matt. 26.65-66).

Jesus' 'blasphemy' was the revelation of his divine sonship.

In the pre-Constantinian period Christians in the Roman empire were accused of being 'atheists', and were persecuted on those grounds if they were not prepared to pay homage to the gods of state and nature and to the cult of the emperor, because they could not, as they said, get involved with 'demons'.[4] Justin Martyr called himself an 'atheist' in reference to these gods. Discipleship of the Christ crucified in the name of these gods freed Christians from this fear of the gods and instead made them in times of need 'enemies of the state' who had to be sacrificed to those gods. Tertullian writes, full of ironic bitterness: 'If the Tiber bursts its banks (setting Rome under water), if the Nile does not burst its banks (and the land of Egypt remains infertile), the cry is immediately: the Christians to the lions!'

Through the emperors Theodosius and Justinian, the Christian faith became the Roman imperial religion and thus took over the role that had been played by the ancient pagan state religion, without calling it in question. In Christian legislation, from then on the pagan cults counted as 'blasphemous'. The death of Jesus was laid at the door of the Jews in order that, with Pontius Pilate, the Romans might wash their hands in innocence. Christianity became one more 'tit for tat' religion.[5] As late as 1706 the law and theological faculties in the university of Tübingen declared jointly: 'That blasphemy was the most horrible and greatest of crimes, whereby God could easily be moved to wrath and could avenge the outrage on the whole land through famine, earthquake and pestilence.'[6]

In the German states, in times of emergency, the Protestant prince, as simultaneously the supreme bishop, would call for days of repentance so that God's wrath might be turned away. In Germany, the 'Day of Repentance and Prayer' was a public holiday held in Protestant regions until a few years ago;

it was thought of as a day observed by the state church in order to turn away the wrath of God.

The Catholic bishops of Portugal interpreted the famous Lisbon earthquake of 1755, with its more than 20,000 dead, as an educative punishment by God for the sinful inhabitants of the city, and thereby roused the protest atheism of Enlightenment thinkers such as Voltaire.

The Protestant fundamentalist Jerry Falwell interpreted the attack by Islamist terrorists on the World Trade Center in New York as God's punishment for 'homosexual New York', as if God were a terrorist God.

When the tsunami in the Indonesian province of Aceh left hundreds of thousands dead, fundamentalist mullahs interpreted this as the punishment of their God for the lax Islamic observance of the inhabitants. In Africa the theological pronouncement that AIDS is a divine punishment means death for women affected by the disease. They are stigmatized socially and are excluded and cast out. Today this 'tit for tat' religion has not disappeared either publicly or from the private life of many people. In the face of possible deadly perils, 'pacts' are always made with providence, and catastrophes are always followed by a search for scapegoats who have to be sacrificed.

In modern democratic constitutions blasphemy against the state's gods have been replaced by offensive behaviour towards religious communities. It is now no longer the gods who are protected; it is the religious sensibilities of men and women. In Prussia, a law of 1794 formulated the accepted standard. According to this, to offend religious sensibilities and insult religious communities was a punishable offence. The protection of peace, religion and peoples' sensibilities takes the place of blasphemy in the German constitution of 1919 and in the Basic Law of the German Federal Republic. For this three objective reasons can be given:

1. The theological reason

'For the Deity to be injured is impossible; that he should revenge himself on human beings because of an infringement of the respect due to Him is inconceivable; that it must be made good through the punishment of the offender is foolishness. But the church, as moral person, has a right to respect. Anyone who belittles its purposes belittles the society, anyone who disparages the object of religious worship ... disparages himself.'[7]

2. The moral reason

The good is not performed out of fear of punishment by the gods or out of expectation of a heavenly reward. That is religious slave morality. The good is done simply because it is the good.[8] That is the liberty of God's children.

3. The Christian reason

For believers, with Christ's giving of himself for the reconciliation of the
godless world, fear of the gods and sacrificial cults have been ended once
and for all. It is not the wrath of God that has to be reconciled but the
godless world: God was in Christ reconciling the world to himself' (2
Cor. 5.19). To put it in the old sacrificial language: God himself brings the
sacrifice, not for his own reconciliation but for ours. Natural catastrophes
and stroke of fate are not divine revelations; they are the outcome of a dis-
rupted nature for whose reconciliation and new creation Christians hope.

The Link between Acts and Consequences, and Karma

The ancient Indian doctrine of Karma transfers the divine justice from the
transcendent sphere to immanence.[9] Karma means the consequences of acts
which ensue with logical necessity: 'As one acts, so one will be after death'
or, to put it more simply: 'If you steal corn you will become a rat'. Or, as a
German proverb says: 'Life punishes latecomers.' The idea behind this is
an 'automatic retaliation causality linked to the acts committed'.[10] In India
what was thought of was a 'subtle potentiality' which adheres to the atman
(which is something like what in Greek thinking is the soul) and forms
its further forms of existence. Everyone forges his own destiny through
his good and evil acts. It is a cosmic law of retaliation, expressive of the
divine justice, which through the karma doctrine is applied to the individual
human subject. The law certainly affects everyone, but its foundation is the
inequality between human beings. Everyone is determined by the karma
of his ancestors and must try to alleviate or even to overcome the karmic
consequences of previous actions. With the reincarnation doctrine that goes
together with this, every individual life is embedded in the wider complex
of generations, and inasmuch as the reincarnation doctrine extends to the
animal realm, it can be seen in the wider context of all the living. 'Karma is
the fuel of the samsara, the cycle of rebirth, and all the efforts of the devout
person is directed towards producing no more karma at all, so that world
events in general may be brought to an end.'[11] That can only succeed if the
causes of the karma, such as desire and ignorance, are overcome through
renunciation and perception.

In the Old Testament this link between act and consequence is presented
in a very similar way. 'The deed returns to the doer.'[12] As the Old Testament
scholar Klaus Koch showed in his foundational essay, this is not a matter of
a so-called 'Old Testament retaliation dogma'.[13] He does not, however, go
into the proximity to the ancient Indian karma doctrine, although Hebrew

thinking starts from an analogous 'sphere of action which influences destiny'. 'The act forms an invisible sphere round the author of the act through which one day the corresponding fate will be brought about; the deity watches over this internal human order and continually puts it into force where it is in danger of being diminished.'[14]

Koch also calls this sphere a true reality belonging to the person as his property. It is a link between act and destiny of pure immanent causality, with a necessity resembling a natural law. Because he stresses this aspect of the link between act and destiny so emphatically, he ascribes to God only a spiritual function: God has created this law and watches over it, but he does not intervene because to do so would refute his own decree.

The connection between act and consequence can be seen individually. 'He who sows the wind will reap the whirlwind', 'You have made your bed, so you must lie on it', or—reaching over the generations—'the fathers have eaten sour grapes and the children's teeth are set on edge'.

Bernd Janowski has expanded Koch's view: no one is bound into an individual connection between act and consequence simply by himself. All human beings are incorporated into the social complexes of the corresponding retaliatory justice: 'Don't do to others what you don't want others to do to you.' He calls this the 'reciprocal solidarity' of a 'connective justice'.[15] On the other hand the divine justice and this immanent act-consequence law overlap, and are not as sharply divided as Koch thought. 'Retaliation' in both a good and a bad sense is always an intervention in history on God's part. If this were not the case, the God of Israel would not be a 'living God', living in historical relationships to his people and his creation; he would be a metaphysical principle.[16]

These ideas are questionable for two reasons. First, the problem on which the ancient Indian karma doctrine and the Old Testament teaching about the connection between act and consequence both break down is not the foreseeing promise of a good destiny or the warning of an evil one, but the retrospective search for an evil act which has to provide the reason for the present evil consequence. Who is guilty when a child is born with a disablement? Who is responsible for a severe illness? The dead in Auschwitz: For what guilt on the part of their forefathers are they supposed to have atoned? The dead of Hiroshima: what karmic retaliation are they supposed to have suffered for what evil acts? To what act does the consequence go back when in the Old Testament we find the question: why do the ungodly prosper, and the just suffer so greatly? There is of course a moral connection between act and consequence: the heavy smoker risks lung cancer, the heavy drinker destroys his

liver. But there is not an act-consequence *fate*. Dietrich Bonhoeffer did not
die an early death because he inherited an evil karma from his parents, as a
Christian Buddhist from Korea once maintained at a Bonhoeffer congress;
he died because he was murdered by the Nazis.

To talk about the link between act and consequence leads us to look only
in the direction from act to consequence, and to overlook the reverse way of
reading things. But the conclusion from the consequence to the causative
act in one's own life or in the history of earlier generations leads us astray. It
shows the untenability of this age-old mythical idea of justice in the Indian
karma teaching and in Old Testament Wisdom about a link between act and
consequence. No justice rules between act and consequence.

Second, the God of Israel is by no means the moral ground of all reality
and the positive power of this process of reality. Karma and the link between
act and consequence contradict the God who 'forgives all your iniquities and
heals all your diseases and redeems your life from the Pit (Ps. 103.3–4). This
God is himself the power of the new life, which overrules fate and cancels the
connection between act and consequence, and instead of endless retaliation
and consequences puts life's new beginning. The divine principle of compas-
sionate justice breaks through the curse of the evil act and repeals it: 'His
mercies are new every morning' (Lam. 3.23). This is the freedom of the new
beginning. There is no other freedom. This is the birth of life in the face of
mercy. This is the opening up of a new future in the midst of the compulsions
of guilt and the consequences of guilt. The Old Testament is more than the
book of fateful act-consequence assessments in ancient Wisdom sayings, it is
the book of the liberating promises of Israel's God, who is the creator of life.[17]

The Scales of Justice: *Justitia Distributiva*

Let us now look at righteousness and justice not as a personal virtue but as
social adjustment. An adjustment of this kind is made on the basis of mutuality and equality. It can be a matter of claims, property or chances. To repay
good with good and evil with evil has nothing to do with retaliation; it is an
equivalence aimed at a peaceful living together. This is expressed in the brilliant
definition of the Roman jurist Ulpian: *Justitia est constans et perpetua voluntas
jus suum unicuique tribuendi*[18]—justice is the constant and perpetual will to give
everyone that which is due to them. To everyone his or her own. This is called
'distributive justice'. It sounds as though all concerned should be equal, but it
does not have to presuppose this. In the Roman slave-holding society it could
also mean: to every master his own, to every slave what is his or hers: everyone
in his own place. But in an ideal society this justice would mean the unity of

equality and difference, as was later laid down in the Communist manifesto: 'To each according to his ability, to each according to his needs.' That would be difference without inequality, and an equality without uniformity.

If justice is the 'constant will', then what this means in modern words is the security of the law. If everyone is made content with what is his, the task of justice to achieve peace has been fulfilled. The 'perpetual will' indicates that the just equivalence never exists as a permanent state but always only as a continuing process. As the social ideal of an absolute harmony in a human society, this definition of justice can at most be the goal of overcoming the injustices which are always present and always emerge anew. As a description of the reality, it is inapplicable. It was therefore also considered to be a perfect heavenly world order to which the imperfect human world order was supposed to correspond.[19] God is the just judge. In just requital, he rewards the good act and punishes the evil one. God gives everyone what is his, in order to preserve his divine world order in peace. Anyone who infringes the human order of law through a crime, therefore also infringes the divine legal order. He must be punished, not merely in order to restore the just human equivalence, but also in order to restore the divine world order. This transcendent dimension is still always used as an argument in the discussion about the death penalty. The murderer must not be punished only by death but must also be sacrificed, in order to achieve an equivalence in heaven as well.

The concern behind the Old Testament rule 'an eye for an eye, a tooth for a tooth' is not retaliation but an abolition of never-ending retaliation through a just equivalence. Reward and punishment must be appropriate and reasonable if they are to create just peace in a society. *Justitia distributiva*—distributive justice—must always at the same time be a *justitia commutativa*—corrective justice—if it is to minister to life and not to death.[20] Distributive justice must be just and equitable.

That brings us to the other side of the principle of just requital: Confucius's 'golden rule'. For him too 'reciprocity' was already the foundation of his moral teaching—hence his formulation:

Don't do to others what you don't want them to do to you'.[21]

In positive terms this means: "Do as you would be done by."
In Matthew's Gospel (7.12) Jesus says:

"Whatever you wish that men would do to you, do so to them; for this is the law and the prophets."

But this 'golden rule' only works between equals and those who are equally strong. In a world where this does not obtain, it seems like a powerless ideal. What does the victor have to fear from the defeated, the strong from the helpless, the winner from the loser, the rich from the poor, the present generation from those still unborn? The strength of the stronger prevails against the rights of the weak. The golden rule does not prevent it. It does not give directions for a just life in an unjust and violent world. Without the liberation of the oppressed, the raising up of the weary and heavy-laden, and the rights of the humiliated and insulted, the golden rule cannot be realized.[22] A 'global ethics' based only on this is an ideal, even if a fine one.[23] A realistic global ethics in the face of the world's present conditions can only be an ethics of liberation on the side of the poor and the earth.

This idea of righteousness and justice has in my view two weaknesses:

First, *Justitia distributiva* is a justice which establishes what is; it is not a creative justice. The facts of the case are established and are appropriately adjusted in order to restore the order of the just peace. This justice does not act, it reacts. It is directed retrospectively towards what has already happened, so as to adjust it through reward and punishment. What is to each 'his own' must already be established in order for it to be distributed. The injustice that has been committed is punished according to the *ius talionis* ('an eye for an eye'). Crime and punishment must be balanced so that the adjustment can be made. But this does not help the victim of the evil deed, and the unjust does not as result become again just.

Second, the most surprising thing is that this justice is directed only towards the acts and the perpetrators, not the victims and their sufferings. It is a justice according to works, not suffering. It is a justice that is completely perpetrator-orientated, in line with the requital. But is a man or woman not more than the sum of his or her good and evil acts? Does a person go on living solely in the consequences of his works? Where is the person who is called by name? From the karma doctrine, via the act-consequence idea, down to the Roman doctrine of justice we can see this one-sided perpetrator-orientation, and the neglect of consideration for the victims. With this alone no justice can be brought into this unjust and violent world. Certainly, when we look at the sufferings and the victims we are recalled rather to the concept of compassion. But in unjust situations is compassion not a concrete form of justice?

The Sun of Righteousness: *Justitia Justificans*

Let us now turn to the other concept of justice, which is less familiar but highly efficacious: that is the creative, saving justice and righteousness which puts things to rights: *justitia justificans*—justifying justice. In Babylon, the king, as representative of the sun god Samas, was supposed to execute the divine righteousness and justice. With the sun, this righteousness rises in the morning and awakens everything to life. It leads the land and the people along the right paths. It cares for the land's fertility. Consequently, everything that heals and is healthful, and everything that has been put right and is upright, counts as just and righteous. Here 'to judge' has the positive sense of raising up, healing and giving life. As executor of this vital force, the king has to see to it that the strong does not harm the weak, that the widows and orphans are helped to their rights, that the country is protected from human exploitation and destruction. Here we have to do with a cosmological concept of justice and righteousness for which the sun is the symbol.[24]

Israel took up this creative and transforming concept of righteousness and justice from Babylon early on. YHWH is extolled as 'the sun of righteousness' (Mal. 4.2). According to the Sermon on the Mount too God 'makes his sun rise on the evil and the good' (Matt. 5.45) so that both may live. This is the reason for the love of our enemies which is to replace the repayment of enmity by enmity. True, YHWH does not like the sun merely stand in the cosmos as the power of life; as the creator of his creation he is also free towards it. But everywhere his righteousness is saving, healing and creative righteousness. It is not only manifested in the life-furthering cycles of the cosmos but in the contingent events of the people's salvation history too, and it is also experienced in the history of personal life. And when YHWH finally comes to live with his people on his earth, he will 'judge' the earth with righteousness and justice, which means that he will finally put right all things, all conditions, and all peoples. To this Psalm 96.11-13 is the most impressive testimony:

> Let the heavens be glad, and let the earth rejoice;
> let the sea roar and all that fills it;
> let the field exult, and everything in it!
> . . . For he comes to judge the earth.
> He will judge the world with righteousness,
> and the peoples with his truth.[25]

In Psalm 82 this justice-creating righteousness for the poor and the earth is even elevated as the standard for the gods:

> YHWH stands in the assembly of the gods,
> in the midst of the gods he pronounces judgment:
> 'How long will you judge unjustly
> and favour the wicked?
> Give justice to the weak and the orphans,
> uphold the rights of the wretched and the destitute,
> free the weak and the poor, deliver them from the power of the wicked!'
> They have neither understanding nor insight,
> they walk about in darkness.
> All the foundations of the earth are shaken.
> ....
> Arise, YHWH, judge the earth,
> for all the peoples belong to you.[26]

Here judging with righteousness does not mean judging good and evil acts; it embraces all aspects of saving and having compassion, helping and healing, justifying and putting right. It is not confined to human beings but actually applies first to the earth, with which human beings live and suffer. Where human beings are concerned, the acts are not weighed up without respect of persons, but the persons are perceived in their wretchedness and their suffering, so that they may be given their rights, be raised up and made just. This saving righteousness and justice has no bandages over its eyes, like the Roman Justitia, but looks very sharply. God 'judges' inasmuch as he saves and creates justice for those who suffer injustice and violence. 'In thy righteousness deliver me', prays the psalmist (71.2) and trusts to the time 'when God arose to establish judgment to save all the oppressed of the earth' (Ps. 76.9; 103.6). Saving, having compassion, healing and raising up are here the diverse life-furthering forms of God's creative righteousness. That is why righteousness comes to be one of God's names: 'And this is the name by which he will be called: "The Lord is our righteousness"' (Jer. 23.6).

Creating Justice in the World of Victims and Perpetrators

In a capitalist competitive society, things are not just, because new inequalities are continually created anew. That is why the cry for social justice never falls silent. According to the reports of the German parliament on poverty and wealth, the cleft between poor and rich is growing ever wider, even though every political effort is made to preserve the country's unity. In Germany, the difference in the chances in life open to the unemployed and those on social security, who are at the bottom of the ladder, and the super-rich elite with their million-dollar bonuses, who are at the top, is insupportable for a democracy. As the postwar years showed, one can live in poverty if everyone is in the same plight, but not if things are going undeservedly well for other people. It is not the poverty that hurts; it is the injustice. We shall first look at extreme cases where there are obvious perpetrators on the one side, and on the others clearly detectible victims; and we shall then go on to ask about just social contracts in times of growing inequality.[27]

The Cry for Justice

For the helpless and humiliated victims of injustice and violence, the cry for justice is the cry for God. Even the silence of the weary and heavy-laden is an expression of the cry for God and his justice. For it is not just the physical poverty, the hunger and thirst, which the unemployed and homeless suffer; it is even more the humiliations and disparagements. Their self-respect and self-esteem are degraded and turn into self- contempt and a feeling of being lost. The many legal and illegal migrants at the frontiers of the wealthy countries become people without civil rights, and whose human rights are ignored. Today the brutal fact of being without redress at the mercy of injustice and violence through persons and institutions is an experience for a majority of the human race.

Things are no better for the weaker, and hence misused, creatures of this earth, and the earth itself. The 'silent spring' and the threatening climate catastrophe are indictments enough. Anyone who still hears the echo of the cry of the Christ dying on the cross, hears today the cry out of the depths of God-forsakenness from the masses of the poor, and from the demolished forests and devastated landscapes of the earth. In the news, we take note only of the appalling figures of the starving and those facing premature death; but we know too that behind the figures human faces are looking at us.

The other cry for God and justice and righteousness is the silence of the perpetrators and their willing helpers. When they humiliated and exploited their victims, they became the assistants of evil. They let themselves be seduced by the greed for wealth and the lust for power, or they did only what was expected of them, or was commanded. They too became victims of evil, but unlike the suffering victims of evil they became its willing servants.

They strayed into a vicious circle of injustice and violence from which there is no way out. Out of their silence and their self-righteousness can we hear a cry for God and justice? No. But we recognize it in their blindness to what they have done knowingly or unknowingly, and in their hardness of heart towards the laments over the social frigidity they disseminate. In their cynical egotism there is a cry against God and against righteousness and justice. 'I hope there is no God and no higher justice', said a German army officer to my father in Russia in 1944, 'for if there is God and justice, a terrible fate is waiting for the German people at the end of the war, after these mass murders of Jews and Russians.'

Just as in their God-forsakenness the victims of injustice and violence cry out for God and justice, so the perpetrators of injustice and violence protest against God: there dare not be any justice to condemn what they have done and caused.

Yet we do not experience injustice and violence merely individually as victims or perpetrators, and not just socially in conflicts between perpetrators and victims. We experience it in highly organized societies as well, and generally speaking, systemically in the economic, social and political conditions. These are the systems in which we exist, and which regulate what we do and leave undone. Be it the low-wage sector or the unfairly bought up cheap products from Bangladesh, these are unjust structures and they are full of systemic acts of violence.

The economic laws of the market make many people poor and losers in the struggle for profits; the social structures stop many people from rising and keep them below the poverty level. People talk about the 'two-thirds society', in which two-thirds of the population exclude the other third and keep it down. We exist in political structures dividing the wealthy nations of the First World from the poor nations of the Third. We enjoy our present existence at the expense of future generations, which will have to pay off our debts. Finally, we eat and drink in a human world which plunders nature and diminishes the diversity of plant and animal species year after year.

Life at the expense of others is organized in the systems we have described. They make everyone who exists in them guilty towards the poor, the earth, and the children. In these systems it is not so much the evil we do which accuses us as the good we leave undone. It is true that the systems have become fixed in the form of objective powers which rule us through violence and fear, but they are man-made, so they can be changed by men. Like the dictatorship systems of the twentieth century, they can collapse like a pack of cards if men and women outside them and within them rise up and together demand righteousness and justice. The great financial systems built up on embezzlement and debts broke down in 2008. That shows how closely these objectified powers resemble those houses built on sand.

God's Righteousness in the World of Victims and Perpetrators

Christians see in the life and sufferings of Jesus Christ the revelation of God's righteousness in an unrighteous and violent world. In his discipleship, they turn to victims and perpetrators and press towards just and non-violent conditions. Let us look first at the victims, then the perpetrators, and finally the systemic powers.

Christ among the Victims. According to the Gospels, Jesus' gaze was directed first of all to the poor, the outcasts of his people—that is to say to the victims of injustice and violence, not to the perpetrators. His message brought the kingdom of God 'to the poor' (Luke 4.18), not the rich; his healing commitment was to the sick, not the healthy; his friendship embraced the outcasts, sinners and tax collectors; we see him among the lost, not 'the good people'.[28] Just as his gospel roused the humiliated, letting them stand upright in faith, so he brought the healing power of the divine Spirit to the sick, and divine justice to those without rights, and raised up the victims of violence.

Through the way he behaved, Jesus manifested to the victims God's compassion: God is beside them just as Jesus himself is beside them. He evidently saw the unimportant people as important, and the people who had been cast out by a self-righteous society as people called by God, as he says in the Beatitudes in the Sermon on the Mount. The lost are his first love. For the people to whom the society of the rich, healthy and righteous offered no future—the 'no future generation' of his time—he opened up the future of the kingdom of God on earth. In this way be pioneered a great 'reevaluation of values'. Now 'the devil doesn't take the hindmost'; with God they will now be the first. That is the great reversal in the world; it can also be called God's revolution.

So it is no wonder that the one who was beside the victims himself became the victim of the righteous and the powerful. The one group rejected him, the other crucified him. If God goes wherever Jesus goes, then Jesus brings God to the victims. And in his sufferings and dying he brings God close to the suffering and dying in this world. He himself entered into God-forsakenness on the cross in order to bring God to the forsaken, and so as to become their brother in their extremity. Talking about this great divine compassion in the passion of Jesus, Dietrich Bonhoeffer wrote in his death cell: 'Only the suffering God can help.'

The justice and righteousness of God manifested in Jesus is victim-orientated: God creates justice for those who suffer injustice and violence.

Christ for the Perpetrators. From early on, Christianity saw in the suffering and death of Christ the vicarious atonement for the guilt of the perpetrators. Following the pattern of the 'Suffering Servant' in Isaiah 53, they saw in the crucified Christ the one 'who bears the sins of the world'. Paul explains what Christ has done for us as being 'put to death for our trespasses and raised for our justification' (Rom. 4.25). In Christ's giving of himself for us is the forgiveness of guilt—in his resurrection our new righteousness.

Is an atonement of this kind necessary? I believe that no one who has become guilty can live with a clear view of his guilt. Once he recognizes it, he begins to hate himself. Consequently we ward off reproaches and suppress our unpleasant insights because they are unbearable. If we see ourselves through the eyes of the victims, the guilt debases us to the depths. In Germany we experienced this after Auschwitz, and rightly so.

Can guilt be 'forgiven' at all? What is 'forgiveness' supposed to mean? No one can ever undo what has once been done or 'make good' a wrong. All guilt fetters a human being to his past, and robs him of the freedom for his future. Even God cannot undo what has been done. Mass murder remains mass murder. But God can break the fetters of guilt for what has been done and make the past no longer a weight on the present, and in this way he can bring about a new beginning. That happens when God like Christ on the cross 'bears' the sins. When God takes our guilt on himself, he takes it away and we are free: 'With his stripes we are healed' (Isa. 53.5).[29]

For the perpetrators of injustice and violence this means nothing less than dying to the power of evil, whose servants they have been, and breaking with the systems of injustice, in order to live the new righteousness with the risen Christ. Anything else would be 'cheap grace' and without efficacy.

How is this possible? According to the ancient tested and tried sacrament of penance, a human being frees himself from the compulsions of guilt and arrives at a new beginning of life in righteousness in three steps:

1. Through recognition of the sufferings of the victims and confession of his own guilt towards them, that is through the step into the light of truth. Because perpetrators always have only short memories, they are dependent on

the long memories of the victims if they are to arrive at self-knowledge. They find themselves when they look at themselves through the eyes of their victims.

2. The second step is a change of mind and a reversal in the direction their lives take. That is bound up with the breaking of the ruling systems producing the injustice, so as no longer to live at the expense of the poor, of the earth and of children, but to live for them. It is a new orientation towards the shared life in righteousness and justice.

3. Finally, the perpetrators only arrive at a just community with their victims if they do everything to eliminate the damage they have caused. This is also called 'restitution'—'making good'—although we know that nothing that is done can be 'made good', and that nothing in the past is ever 'surmounted'. But *satisfactio operum*—or compensation through something performed—is the valuable beginning for the new community which must be sought and can also be found.[30]

For the perpetrators the churches have developed this sacrament of penance, or better: the sacrament of conversion—in German *Umkehr*, literally an about-turn. For sinners the Reformation proclaimed justifying faith. But both ways are orientated in a one-sided way towards the perpetrators. What about the victims? Do we not need a sacrament for the raising up of the victims, and a proclamation of the justification of the victims of the wrong?

After many discussions and experiences, I would make the following suggestion:

1. The victims of wrong, injustice and violence must first be brought out of their humiliation. They need a space of trust where they can cry out what has been done to them; they need ears that listen to what they have to say; they must rediscover their self-esteem. They must be able to utter their abuse and their shame. Priests have learnt to listen to the confessions of the perpetrators; we must all learn to listen to the cries of the victims, to loosen their tongues so as to free them from insupportable memories. Expressing what they have suffered is the first step to the truth which makes the victims free.

2. The second step is the lifting of their hearts to God and the rising up out of the humiliation, life with head held high. The victims also need conversion—a new direction. It is the resurrection to life and the experience of life loved after the sufferings over the ravages of their lives.

3. The third step may then lead on to a renunciation of retaliation for the evil experienced, in order not to be dominated by what has been suffered, but so as to repay evil with good (Rom. 12.21), first in oneself and then in the other person. Forgiveness is a medicine for one's own soul too, if it is to be

freed from bitterness and from the role of victim. The victims have ultimately the keys of heaven and hell in their hands. They can open the gates of hell for the perpetrators. The forgiveness of guilt is the divine right of the victims and an expression of their sovereignty towards the miserable perpetrators.[31] To forgive guilt frees the victims from helplessness and sadness, and frees those who have become guilty from the fetters of their guilt, and for both victims and the guilty it brings about the new beginning of a just community.

Righteousness and Right

Christianity brings the divine righteousness and justice for victims and perpetrators into society. The organized form of Christianity is the church, but in order to avoid a clerical misunderstanding, I prefer to talk about Christianity. How does Christianity witness to the divine righteousness and justice in what Karl Barth calls the *Bürgergemeinde*—'the civil community' or community of citizens?[32]

It witnesses through social service and prophecy, that is to say, through commitment to the victims and through criticism of the perpetrators. The connection between the two things is self-evident. The person who visits the sick and hears them complain that they have been left alone and forgotten by their families, goes to these families and appeals to their consciences. Through their congregational and organized social services the churches turn to the victims of this society and try to give them support, practically and spiritually. They surround the disabled with compassion and take in the unemployed and the homeless, and provide meals for the hungry. For this the churches are valued by many people, and in Germany are supported and furthered by the state. But they are also used by state and society in order to limit the damage caused by their systemic injustice. In order to prevent this, Christian service to the victims of this society must go hand in hand with public, prophetic criticism of the abuses resulting from the systems in force. Its service makes the church popular. This critical prophetic voice may in certain circumstances make it unpopular among many people. But what is at stake is the truth which alone can make free—societies too— and the righteousness and justice which is meant to give life to all. With its understanding of the justice and righteousness which justifies and sets things to rights, Christianity must push for the relevant legal enactments and legal reforms, for the Christian understanding of God's righteousness is not meant just for Christians but is intended to be an anticipation of the new earth for all human beings.

Some liberation theologians believe that the poor are called by God to bring about a truly human society, and that the oppressed are called to set up a humanely just society: 'The last shall be first.' This seems to me to be asking too much of the poor and the oppressed, whose 'preferential option' is quite certainly not poverty. The person who knows what poverty and oppression are does not yet know life and freedom. The social situation does not as yet create the right conviction. But it is true that the human emancipation of men and women begins when 'all the conditions are overturned in which the human being is a humiliated, an enslaved, a forsaken, a disdained being', as the young Karl Marx rightly maintained.[33] For this all human beings must be won, not just the poor and oppressed, who are often no longer in the position to act.

The humiliating conditions are certainly economic. Consequently the fulfilment of material requirements is the beginning of justice. Without liberation from hunger, homelessness and unemployment, equality in a society, which is the presupposition for social peace, will be lacking. But the circumstances to be overcome are more than economic. Their humiliating character also touches human self-esteem. Consequently the fulfilment of the right to freedom is the correlation of the material fulfilment. Human dignity is no more possible without economic liberation than, conversely, economic liberation is possible without the recognition of human dignity and the claiming of human rights. 'There is no human dignity without a stop to material distress any more than there is truly human happiness without a stop to old or new subservience'.[34] An inward raising of the consciousness of human dignity cannot be imposed from outside. It must come from within, so that people can cease to be the passive objects of distress and compulsions and can become the determining subjects of their own lives. People in the GDR offered a (literally) wonderful example in November 1989 when they rose up after forty years of political oppression and ideological paternalism and became the determining subjects of the 'peaceful revolution' with the cry 'We are the people'.

In Israel's history, the Exodus from slavery into freedom was followed on Sinai by the making of the covenant between the twelve tribes and God, and with each other. Symbolically, that means that the righteousness which puts things right for the victims and the justifying justice of God for the perpetrators aim at the covenant of the free and equal. The saving and transforming righteousness leads people to the righteousness which has also been termed faithfulness to the community or to the covenant.[35] In the covenant the equal partners pledge themselves to preserve their freedom, inwardly and outwardly. The twelve tribes of Israel swore a covenant with God and each other. Every later covenant made with a king was incorporated in this covenant between God and people. If a king broke the presupposed covenant with God, he counted as depraved.

In European political history, alliances such as the leagues between cities, or the Hanseatic League, or farmers' associations, were always concluded 'before God'. Israel's covenant counted down to modern times as a model for political popular sovereignty.[36] In the covenant (later called the constitution) politics became 'the self-government of the people, by the people, and for the people'.[37] Federal theology and federal politics became midwives for modern democracy, which overcame the absolutism of rulers 'by the grace of God' and for feudalism and—in principle—also surmounted class rule. Direct democracy is the foundation, representative democracy is the secondary offshoot, and is not a substitute for the former.

The fact that the popular sovereignty of modern state constitutions has a transcendent reference finds expression in the preamble to the Basic Law of the German Federal Republic as it does in the concept of American democracy as a 'nation under God'. German members of parliament are 'subject only to their consciences' (Basic Law, Article 38). The reference to Israel's covenant theology also makes the continually misused chapter 13 of Paul's Epistle to the Romans obsolete: 'Let every person be subject to the governing authorities. For there is no authority except from God, and those that exist have been instituted by God.' In the context of the early Christian period this must surely have been addressed by the apostle to Jewish-Christian anarchists in the Roman empire. A modern democratic state is not a 'governing authority' in this sense (in the 1611 Bible the phrase used is 'the powers that be').

In modern democracies Christianity works for the rights of the victims and for the conversion of the perpetrators, and supports justice in the covenant of the equal and free. They will give full support to just laws, secure justice, and the political and economic independence of court decisions.

However, in today's legal system as it stands the one-sided orientation towards the perpetrators must be subjected to criticism, and there should be a demand for an equivalent orientation towards the victims. The rapist gets away with a punishment of a few years' imprisonment, while the victim suffers all her life from her spiritual and mental humiliation, and often enough from physical damage too. But in Germany except for a few institutions (the Weisser Ring and 'Innocence in Danger') no one bothers much about the misery of the abandoned victims. The courts can order psychiatric help for the murderer, but psychiatric treatment for the family of his victim is not envisaged in our legal system. Christians are on the side of the victims, because Christ became a victim himself; but the traditional churches are still more interested in the justification of the sinner than in justice and righteousness for the victims.

Material social justice is the foundation sustaining the justice of the formal legal system. Without this presupposition, legal edicts can be as pointless as the famous old Paris regulation forbidding both poor and rich to sleep under the bridges over the Seine. Incidentally, the instructions in most public parks are similarly formulated, their aim being to keep the homeless from sleeping on the seats. Without detectible equality between people, equality before the law (in spite of all the differences which have to be respected) becomes abstract, and in borderline cases can become inhumane.

13

Dragon Slaying and Peacemaking in Christianity

The immediate occasion for the enduring discussion about peace in Germany was provided by the great peace movements in 1981, where people responded to the rearmament, with nuclear cruise missiles, of East and West Germany. Divided Germany had become the military focus of a world split into East and West. The protests of the peace movement were nonviolent. Christians who supported it felt themselves bound by Jesus' Sermon on the Mount—no violence—and perceived the sense for reality in what it taught. The Protestant churches in the GDR (East Germany) formally rejected 'the spirit, logic and practice of the system of nuclear deterrents'; the Reformed church proclaimed the *status confessionis* (which defines the point at which the confession of faith is at stake). For whatever reasons, in 1983 the nuclear missiles disappeared from the Federal Republic and the GDR, and the peace movement slowly dissolved. But something remained: the prayers for peace held every Monday in the Nikolaikirche in Leipzig. These sparked off the protest marches in October 1989 and the peaceful revolution which led to the demolition of the Berlin wall and to the downfall of the dictatorial system in the GDR.[1] Again the convincing motto was 'no violence'. The nonviolent overthrow of a despotic regime is not merely possible but has actually taken place all over the world since 1989, in the Balkan states as well as in South Africa.

With this convincing recollection in mind, we shall ask about a realistic politics of peace and an ethic for the fullness of life in that just peace.

Power and Violence

Violence is a diverse phenomenon. There is everyday violence in people's dealings with each other and with weaker creatures; there is violence of the stronger against women, children, the disabled and the sick; there is physical brutality and mental cruelty, and much more, which we feel to be inhumane and damaging to life. But concealed in acts of violence, there is always a force which can also become a power.

Power in itself is good. There is the power of love, the power to understand, the power of conviction and the forces for nonviolent communication.
We call God the Almighty Father, and in his proximity experience the life
forces of his creation.

With violence, we have to do with perversions of the powers of life into
destructive and ultimately deadly drives. Violence is an inhumane, degrad-
ing and destructive application of what are in themselves good forces.

Life itself distinguishes between violence and power. Power strengthens
and enhances life. Violence diminishes and destroys it.[2] If this distinction
between power and violence is correct, the main question that then arises is:
how can the violence of death be transformed into the power of life? How
can the energies invested in acts of violence be redeemed and formed anew
into forces for life? It is not only the sinners who must be redeemed, it is the
sins too, says the Staretz Zosima in Dostoevski's book *The Brothers Kara-
mazov*. Can the useless industrial military complexes be rebuilt into life-
furthering industries? Can a violent world be turned into a living world? In
asking these questions we are understanding peace as a turn away from death
into life, and are trying to follow the symbol of 'swords into ploughshares'.
Following Isa. 2.4, I am here understanding ploughshares as a symbol of
peace between the nations although through ploughshres violence can also
be inflicted on the earth, and is.

But there is a certain exception which delineates the main problem of
political ethics: the state's monopoly of force.

The Angel of Peace and the Dragon Slayer

What has Christianity got to do with force? If we go into a church, for
example the Stiftskirche in Tübingen, we hear the gospel of peace. And the
benediction wishes us the peace of God. We look upon the crucified One and
ask whether there can be any greater rejection of all force than that? When
we leave the church, if it is in Tübingen, we find ourselves in front of a pil-
lar, showing Saint George slaying a dragon with his lance. Dragon-slayers
like this can be seen all over Christendom in front of churches, especially
those dedicated to Saint George or the Archangel Michael. Either it is Saint
George, who is slaying the earthly dragon, or it is the Archangel Michael, who
is bringing about the downfall of the apocalyptic one. In the case of Saint
George, it is in addition a 'redeeming power' for the saving of the holy virgin
whom the dragon is holding prisoner, she being a symbol for the church. In
the West, other than in China, the dragon is the symbol of radical evil, of the

repulsively ugly, of what is stinkingly poisonous and unbearably horrible.[3] In the Holy Roman Empire from the fourth century on, the dragon was the symbol for the enemies of God and his holy realm. George was turned from being a Christian martyr into being the military imperial saint, and the Archangel Michael was turned from an angel of peace into the guardian angel of the Christian empire, armed with a sword. The one fought earthly wickedness, the other supernatural evil. From the frontiers of the empire on Mont Saint Michel in Normandy to Monte San Angelo on the Gargano peninsula in southern Italy, these places became places of pilgrimage in the Christian imperium. How did this contradiction between Jesus' message of peace and the dragon-slayers of the Christian empire come about?

Whatever else may be said historically about 'the Constantinian shift', it led to the transition from the defencelessly suffering church to the Christian imperial religion. The pax romana, which had begun under Augustus and which Constantine claimed to consummate, was baptised with the pax Christiana. With this the swords of the heathen were turned into Christian swords.

The Christian imperium also began with a cross but it was not the real cross of Christ but the dream cross of the Emperor Constantine, in whose sign he defeated his rival in 312 in the battle at the Milvian Bridge. The message of his dream was *In hoc signo vinces*—in this sign you will conquer. Constantine's cross of victory became the banner of the Christian imperium and its dissemination. With the standard of the cross and this cry, Hernan Cortes stormed the Aztec metropolis Tenochtitlan and subjugated the indigenous peoples of Central America. The crusaders, the Knights of St. George, the Templars and other conquerors carried this cross into the heathen lands. We find it on the flags and orders of almost all the Christian nations. These crosses of victory are empty, and know nothing of the One crucified: they have nothing in common with Golgotha—or have they? Are there no starting points in the original Christian message for Christianity's entry into political and military rule?

Sacrum Imperium—The Sacred Rule

The path from persecution to domination is not a long one. Paul already promised persecuted Christians that 'if we endure we shall also reign with him' (1 Cor. 6.2; 2 Tim. 2.12). In this way the 'Constantinian shift' could also be interpreted as the turn from martyrdom to millennium. If we look at the future of the helpless crucified Christ, we see the shift from humiliation to exaltation, and from helplessness to almighty power. For 'all power in heaven and on earth' has been given to the one 'who sits at the right hand of God'. Why should this rule of Christ take effect only in the church, and not in political rule as well?

In the domes of Byzantine churches we see Christ the Pantocrator standing above the Christian emperor, who is exercizing his sovereignty in the name of Christ. The nations do not find their salvation only through the faith of the church but through subjection to the sacrum imperium as well. This imperium was held to be the goal of the divine salvation history. According to early political theology in Byzantium, the emperor was God's representative on earth, and his rule was an *imitatio Dei*, an imitation of God, and an analogy to God's cosmic rule. The Byzantine court ceremonial was a visible presentation of this imperial liturgy.[4]

The biblical text on which this was based was the image of the monarchies in Daniel 7. Four bestial despotic empires rise up, one after another, out of the sea of chaos, lay waste the earth with their wickedness and disappear. But in 'the last days' comes 'the Son of man'. God gives him 'dominion and glory and kingdom, that all peoples, nations, and languages should serve him; his dominion is an everlasting dominion, which shall not pass away' (Dan. 7. 13-14). According to Christian interpretation, the fourth empire is the Roman one, for with its Christianization the End-time Thousand Years' Empire of Christ begins (Dan. 7.22; Rev. 20.6).[5] This political Messianism put an enduring stamp on the sense of mission in Christian imperialism.[6] In Europe it broke down only with the First World War, but in Russia, the 'third Rome', and the United States of the 'new world order' it is still alive.

The *sacrum imperium* was not the only solution. It is significant that with the Constantinian shift the Christianity of the monastic orders grew rapidly. On the one hand was worldwide Christianity, which took over responsibility for the exercise of political power; on the other hand was the Christianity of the monastic orders, which wanted to live without violence in radical discipleship of Christ. We shall come back to this twofold Christian existence in the final section of this chapter. With the establishment of Christianity as the religion of the Roman Empire, wide areas of Syrian Christianity remained outside the Roman borders. East Syrian Christianity reached beyond Mesopotomia as far as Persia, India and China, and was never imperial. Outside the Roman empire there grew up only the Christian realms of Armenia and Ethiopia. With the Constantinian shift Christianity lost its universalism; it became Rome-centred, and has remained so down to the present day.

What in the Long Run Was the Effect of the Christianization of Politics, and What in Christianity Was Capable of Being Political?

Two Jewish-Christian maxims broke in principle with 'the innocence of power' in the political sphere.

1. 'Render to Caesar the things that are Caesar's, and to God the things that are God's' (Matt. 22.21). With this Jewish distinction Jesus split the ancient world's cult of the God-emperor. The ruler is neither a God nor is he of divine origin; he is a man like other men. His office deserves respect, but he himself does not deserve worship. The church refused to conform to the Roman emperor cult, and replaced it by intercession for the emperor. In the long run, the separation of the religious dimension from the political one (in spite of the fact that the Christian emperor was emperor 'by the grace of God') stripped the political power of its magic and subjected it to the law. The exercise of political power became accountable to God and human beings. Only law justifies the exercise of political power. It is true that in history the might of the stronger always existed, but the stronger has no 'right'. Political power must be exercised in accordance with law if it is not to be despotism, and despotism has to be resisted in the name of the law.

2. The second principle is derived from the biblical account of creation. According to Jewish and Christian teaching, God did not appoint a ruler to be his image and representative on earth, but human beings: 'male and female he created them' (Gen.1.27). That oriental royal dignity belongs to every woman, every man, every age, every race and in all circumstances. This concept—that all human beings are made in the image of God—has exerted a revolutionary and democratizing influence down to the present day.

'When Adam delved and Eve span, who was then the gentleman?' 'All men are created equal' says the American Declaration of Independence. 'All human beings are born free and equal', begins the Universal Declaration of Human Rights of 1948. That is the democratic principle of equality. And something else is important here too. According to the biblical account of creation, Adam and Eve are not the first Jews or the first Christians; they are the first human beings. That means that Israel and Christianity are the historical bearers of hope for a shared world of all peoples, sexes, and races in accordance with humanity. In the new humanity, the historical vocations of both will be fulfilled.

Today, everyone finds it obvious that he is not merely man or woman, black or white, German or Chinese, Christian, Moslem or Buddhist, but first and foremost a human being, with certain indestructible and inalienable human rights. The recognition and implementation of these human rights will decide whether the peoples, races and religious communities grow together into a worldwide community or whether they will annihilate each other mutually, and destroy life on this earth.

Just Power: The Monopoly of Force and the Right of Resistance

The state's monopoly of force and the people's right of resistance are the presuppositions for a just exercise of political power. The monopoly of force in modern states has developed in the course of long struggles between the central and the local powers. In return for this monopoly, the government assumes the guarantee for public security. We see today on the one hand the disintegration of states no longer in a position to enforce their monopoly.[7] The result is then the terror of privately organized bands, which blackmail the people, as the Mafia does in Italy. But states also disintegrate if police are no longer able to guarantee peace and order in the slums of modern mass cities, so that the law of the jungle spreads there. In states that have disintegrated, international terror organizations spring up, as they have in Afghanistan, Pakistan, Somalia and Yemen. Today there is an international market where any amount of weapons and mercenaries can be bought. The political problem of the twentieth century was state terror from above. The problem in the twenty-first century is the international terror of criminal or religious bands which is directed against the civilized world.

The state's monopoly of force is, on the one hand, undermined by the rich who make 'security' a commodity, withdraw into gated communities and employ private security services.[8] In the United States and Brazil, there are more private security agents than there are members of the state police. In Sao Paulo the rich avoid the roads and fly by helicopter. In the long run these rich people destabilize their states more profoundly than terror bands can do. In situations like this the important thing is to defend the state's monopoly of force, or to restore it, and to guarantee public security for everyone. It is only if the state controls the violence that violence can be controlled by law. Without the state's monopoly of force, there are no ways of exercising power justly. The neoliberal privatization of security promotes terror, because it delivers people up to the criminal bands. It is nothing other than anarchy. If the state misuses its power, and if there is terror from above, the right to resistance steps in, and on three levels:

If—as is not infrequent in Latin America, for example—the police and the armed forces in a country contravene the country's laws, they must be made to answer for it before the courts, and the elected government is bound to ensure that they do so. If it does not, or cannot, do so, then the people and their representatives are not only justified in resisting but are also in duty bound to do so, so as to restore law and justice.

If a government passes laws contravening the country's constitution, it must be charged before that country's constitutional court. If this is impossible, then the people and its lawful representatives are in duty bound to resist, in order to restore the constitutional order.

If a government comes to power through an internal coup, or by way of occupation from outside, there is a right of resistance on all levels. What counts as tyranny or dictatorship are illegal seizures of power and a lasting misuse of power. According to Thomas Aquinas and Catholic tradition, passive and active resistance is then enjoined. According to Article 16 of the Lutheran Augsburg Confession, a Christian may obey the authorities only so long as they do not require anything that is sinful: *nisi cum jubent peccare*. Article 14 of the Reformed Scots Confession of 1560 states that Christian love of our neighbour requires us 'to save the lives of the innocent, to repress tyranny, to defend the oppressed.'[9] To claim the right of resistance in these cases is a civic duty; to refuse assistance is a punishable wrong. This right is also a Christian duty, for neighbourly love is more important than obedience to the powers that be.

As a result of the student protests of the 1970s and the peace movement of the 1980s, the following justification of civil disobedience was developed:

> Anyone who alone or with others, publicly, without violence, and for political and moral reasons contravenes a fundamental prohibition, acts in principle justifiably if he thereby protests against severe injustice, and if his protest is proportionate to the situation.[10]

Formally speaking, civil disobedience can neither be demanded nor forbidden. It only becomes legitimate if it is directed against unjust actions by governmental agencies, breaches of law by the government, and infringements of human rights. In these cases the law is broken in the name of legal justice, in order to enforce or restore it. Civil disobedience is illegitimate if it attempts to spread injustice, if it is a campaign against foreigners, is driven by racism or if its aim is the downfall of the democratic constitution through Fascist dictatorship. That was the difference between Martin Luther King and George Wallace, the Governor of Alabama at the time of American desegregation. The one called for civil disobedience against the segregation laws in the name of the American constitution, the other demanded civil disobedience in order to restore 'white supremacy' contrary to the constitution. In Germany we have experienced civil disobedience in the sit-down demonstrations by supporters of the peace movement and by nuclear power opponents; but we have seen it too in the riots of the autonomists, and the violence of the neo-Nazis. Consequently the courts cannot fall back on the letter of the law, on the grounds that the law is the law, and that law-breaking is law-breaking; it has to distinguish between legitimate and illegitimate civil disobedience.

The Doctrine of "Just War"

This doctrine is an astonishing achievement of Christian ethics in the *Corpus Christianum* of the empires and nations. Ever since Augustine, the church has tried to apply the concept of justice to the most unjust thing conceivable: the great murder, war. The motive was apparently that war was not God's will; the method, that unavoidable wars should at least be restricted by means of the concept of justice; the goal, if possible to avoid war; the outcome, there is no justification for war. So what was at stake was really not the justification of wars, but an attack on them. We can see this from the list of criteria for the *bellum iustum*, the just war, and for *ius in bello*, justice in war.

Ius ad Bellum—The Justification for War

1. A war must be publicly declared by a *legitima potestas*, a legitimate authority, which has a right to decide.
2. There must be a *causa iusta*, a just cause—for example defence in the case of an attack.
3. There must be an *ultima ratio*—war is permissible only as a last resort, after all peaceful methods to avoid it have been exhausted.
4. A just war can only be waged if it is backed by a *recta intentio*, a legitimate intention—for example the restoration of peace, or of a condition which is better than the existing one.

In the modern world three additions have been made:
1. The appropriateness of the means in respect of the consequences. The means must not be more harmful than the evil they are designed to overcome.
2. Consideration of the chances of success.
3. The exit strategy: war can only be begun if its end can be visualized, or the way in which it will be possible to escape from the warlike involvement.

Ius in Bello—Justice in War

1. The means employed must be appropriate and reasonable (landmines and uranium-enriched munitions, for example, being prohibited).
2. The civil population must be protected.
3. Prisoners of war have a right to life and a return home.

Ever since the rise of the European national states in the seventeenth century, the doctrine about the just war has been misused as a means for legitimating a state's sovereignty: war was considered to be the right of sovereign states. In this respect, national states have become obsolete. In order to judge whether wars are just or unjust, and whether the rights of the population and prisoners are being safeguarded, an international authority is necessary, such as was established for the first time in 1948 with UNO. The right to intervene by armed force in unjust situations such as genocide is only given if there is a UNO mandate. The criteria for the just war can be applied to interventions of this kind because their infringement is also indictable before the Security Council of the United Nations. But they have nevertheless failed to lead to the justification of these interventions, either in Vietnam or in Iraq, and as yet no proceedings have been taken against those who have demonstrably begun unjust wars, if they are the strong nations.

The result of the contemporary discussions about the doctrine of 'just wars' is for me that there is no such thing. The criteria can be applied in order to accuse the powers who are waging war, but not to justify their unjust acts of violence. The doctrine of the 'just war' does not provide any rules for beginning a war, although its does for ending one, if it has proved to be 'unjust', as we see from the examples of the United States' Vietnam war, or the Afghanistan war waged by what was then the USSR. The 'assymetrical' conflicts between military forces and 'terror' groups or 'freedom fighters' are outside those classic criteria, because these conflicts are not wars in the classic sense. Earlier they were more aptly termed 'partisan warfare'. A 'holy war' or a 'crusade' cannot be a just war, if it has as its goal the annihilation of unbelievers or the godless.

Under the Conditions of Nuclear Weapons?

Ever since Hiroshima in 1945, the human world has been subject to the threat of total annihilation through nuclear weapons. Does this mean an end to the doctrine about the just war, or is there a doctrine about a 'just nuclear war' or 'just nuclear armaments'?

A nuclear war restricted by justice will maintain, first the prohibition of preparations which will make a preventive strike possible; second the scaling down of nuclear weapons, so that they can be directed against specific military targets without annihilating huge numbers of the civilian population; and third, only if 'limited nuclear wars' can thereby replace 'massive retaliation in a global war of annihilation'.

The doctrine about just nuclear arming maintains that since 1945 the existence of these weapons has made peace more secure. The mutual 'believable deterrent' has prevented the bombs from being used. According to this doctrine, only the possession and threat of these weapons is legitimate, not their use. But if one is not prepared to implement what one threatens, where is the threat? The other argument introduces into the discussion the notion of gaining time: during the period of mutual deterrents an international order of peace must be found, and a security system without nuclear weapons. But is there ever an 'intermediate period' of this kind, since, as we know, the speed of the arms race is greater by far than the speed of disarmament talks?

The agreement between the nations possessing nuclear weapons about their non-proliferation has proved to be untenable: more and more nations are coming to possess the bombs, as we see at the moment in Iran and North Korea. Nor can we exclude possibility that terror organizations will come to possess dirty but easily constructible nuclear bombs with which they can blackmail major cities. And the suicide assassins cannot be deterred by nuclear means, because they have put themselves outside any such deterrent. Does a 'nuclear-free world' mean redemption from the nuclear dilemma? Certainly not without a new global security system, for nuclear weapons can certainly be done away with, but we cannot eliminate the knowledge of how to build them. To this extent humanity will have to live with this threat for all time.

These discussions were pursued in the 1970s and 1980s, and for me their outcome is that there can be neither a justification for the use of nuclear weapons nor for the threat of any such use. No one has any experience of a nuclear war and after a major nuclear war hardly anyone will be left who can become wise after the event. Fundamentally speaking, these are not military weapons at all; they are political status symbols of 'the nuclear powers' and the countries who want to become such.

A world of just peace is possible if a new political structure and culture comes into being globally.

1. The national foreign policy of individual states as it has existed hitherto is no longer capable of ensuring peace, because national states are not in a position to solve global problems. But nuclear bombs are a global problem. So for their control and for security, national foreign policy must be

turned into global internal policy, as Carl-Friedrich von Weizsäcker already demanded many years ago.

2. The terrorist threat has become trans-national, thanks to the new global media. If terror assumes these dimensions, international policing measures must be organized in which a distinction is no longer made between the armed forces for the preservation of security against danger from outside, and the police for the preservation of internal security. In the peacekeeping force of the United Nations in the Balkans, the two tasks already coincide.

3. The ecological catastrophes which are already making themselves felt in climate change do not stop at national borders. The Chernobyl nuclear disaster in White Russia in 1986 already poisoned the forests in Scandinavia and Bavaria. The catastrophe in the nuclear power stations in Fukushima, Japan, in 2011 had consequences which cannot yet be seen, not merely in Japan but also on life in the surrounding ocean and in the atmosphere. International 'earth politics' can only be realized through the joint efforts of the nations, the trade associations, and the growing number of non-governmental organizations.

4. For these new institutions we need a monopoly of force controlled by UNO, and this can only come into being at the cost of national sovereignties. We need trans-national courts, which have to ensure justice in the three sectors mentioned. For our legal systems are still largely speaking national, and are hence not equal to the task of coping with global crime. The international court of justice in The Hague, which punishes infringements of human rights, is only a beginning. New transnational, global bodies in global networks must be developed for a just peace on earth and with the earth.

"Creating Peace without Weapons"

This was a motto in the German peace movement of 1981 and describes very well the original Christian ethic of peace-giving: 'Blessed are the peacemakers'. It is not the peaceful who are meant but the people who create peace. But can they create peace in a hostile world of conflicts and wars, hate and violence?

In this unredeemed world we need the state, the state's monopoly of force, and its ties with law and justice. There is no other way of securing peace and repressing terror. What we have described hitherto is the responsibility for the world Christians share with all human beings. Even the disputed right of resistance is a Christian duty as a civic right, and is therefore not specifically Christian. Where does what is specifically Christian begin?

First of all, we recognize the limits of state force. Through the application of force, the state or a community of states can secure peace outwardly.

Through police measures and peace-securing interventions, state force can set up external frameworks and conditions for peace; but it cannot fill that framework with peaceful coexistence and with a life people can love and live gladly together with others. It cannot change the hearts of men and women, nor can it turn enemies into good neighbours. Men and women must do that for themselves. So the state is dependent on social peace internally and on peace initiatives of non-governmental organizations externally. A good example is the present situation in Sarajevo. The Eufor troops secure an outward peace and prevent deadly enemies from attacking each other; initiatives such as Doctors without Borders (Médecins Sans Frontières), the women's organization Amica, child-help organizations, and Christian and interreligious peace groups are trying to create an outward peace with inner life. There are situations where a forcible ending of violence has to create the presuppositions for the work for internal peace; there are also situations in which the peace movements must be the pioneers, for example in Israel and Palestine, in order to show that a shared life is possible in spite of murder and retaliation. But in such situations, how can deadly enmity be transformed into peaceful life, so that 'swords will be turned into ploughshares'?

Can one love one's enemies?

There are two ways of dealing with enmity once it has arisen and has come to affect us forcibly. Either we become the enemies of our enemies and try to annihilate them, our real enemies and all our potential enemies too—the latter by military means through pre-emptive strikes, following the strategy of President George W. Bush. We are then following the deadly friend-enemy thinking of 'He who is not for us is against us'. Or we try to overcome the enmity that has arisen and to turn our enemies into friends, or at least respectful neighbours. Then we must never become the enemies of our enemies, but must try to recognize and eliminate the reasons for their enmity.

The first method is the way taken by the violent. The fields of the dead throughout history witness to their madness. For it is madness. The person who becomes the enemy of his enemies may kill as many enemies as he likes; through his own enmity he creates ever new enmity. What comes into being through friend-enemy thinking is a world that is in principle hostile. Occasionally one discovers in the end—if one survives—that there is no peace if one becomes the enemy of one's enemies. One must first of all free oneself from the enmity. For enmity does not just destroy the life of the victims; it destroys the lives of the perpetrators too. So it is no more than consistent that the perpetrators of the school massacres should have finally killed themselves.

In Christian tradition there is a fine counter-image to George the dragon slayer, and that is Saint Martha.[11] According to the legend, Martha came by ship to southern France, accompanied by her sister Mary and her brother Lazarus, and missionized the Rhone valley. In Tarascon she was shown the bloodthirsty dragon to whom young girls had to be sacrificed every year. Martha tamed the monster, put her girdle round his neck, and sent him back to the Mediterranean, in whose depths he was at home. He had lost his way in the Rhone valley and had become wicked only for that reason.

Dragon slaying or dragon taming: Can the one be the male and the other the female way of dealing with evil? No, I believe that men can also turn evil to good. Men and women not only have to be delivered from evil; the criminal energies invested in evil must also be eliminated and turned to good. The powers of life can emerge out of the violence of killing.

Creative Love of Enemies

How is this possible in the very heart of a human being? If I suffer some injustice, if I am hurt by some insult, or am injured through an act of violence, I automatically feel the desire for retaliation, for I must pay back the evil done to me, so as to free myself from it. I cannot let the insult go unpunished, because what hurts me makes me ill. I have to restore my self-respect through retaliation. But if I succeed, am I then content, or do I feel empty and really no better than the enemy who has brought me to this point? Are we satisfied if the evildoer has suffered what we call his 'just' punishment? Is it quite right if the murderer receives the death penalty, and nothing more than that? We repay and punish, but no one changes as a result. Does everything become exactly what it was before the evil act, the injustice, or the pain I have felt? No.

In an ethics of reciprocity—a 'tit for tat' ethics—retaliation is the only way of reacting to an injustice that has been suffered. The other possibility is to suffer and endure, and to swallow what has been done to one. The results are depressions and self-contempt, or the stylization of one's own role as victim through self-pity and the search for the sympathy of other people. But that would be nothing other than an affirmation of the evil that has been done to one, and its deliberate prolongation in a process of self-destruction.

There is a third way. This leads to the overcoming of the revengeful feelings in oneself through the thirst for righteousness. I don't want the enmity I experience to be prolonged, either through retaliation or through self-destruction, but want to overcome it, first in myself and then in the enemy too. I want neither hate nor resignation, neither revenge nor depression. I want to transform these energies which have sprung up in me into the energies of a righteousness that creates peace and life. That is the transformation of enmity into love of the enemy. The person who has never felt the desire to pay back what the enemy has done is not capable of loving that enemy. But the person who through retaliation becomes his enemy's enemy, or subjects himself to the other's enmity, is conforming to that enmity and loses his freedom. Where do we find the freedom to transform enmity against life into the love for life?

We find the pointer to this transforming power of life in the reason why we are told in the Sermon on the Mount to love our enemies:

> But I say to you, Love your enemies, bless those who curse you and pray for those who persecute you, so that you may be children of your Father in heaven; for he makes his sun rise on the evil and one the good, and sends rain on the just and on the unjust (Matt. 5. 44-45).

Sun and rain are not just matriarchal symbols. They are also the real forces for all the living on this earth. They give life without distinguishing between evil and good, friends and enemies. Sun and rain are obviously not interested in our conflicts and enmities. Their concern is that we live together. So love of enemies too should also overcome enmity, and minister to the common life.

The hate of our enemies drives on the deadly spirals of violence set off by the law of retaliation. 'As you do to me, I will do to you', says the ethic of reciprocity. The golden rule of mutuality has this iron underside. This is not the role of the discipleship of Christ according to the Sermon on the Mount and Christ's own life. The ethic of the Sermon on the Mount and of Jesus' life is the ethic of going to meet the other, and of creativity, not reciprocity.

The first step in loving our enemies is not to let enmity be forced on us by the enemy, but to free ourselves from this compulsion, obvious though it always seems. Here our orientation is important. We are not the enemies of our enemies; we are 'the children of our Father in heaven', as we are told in Jesus' Sermon on the Mount. So we shall not respond to hate with hate and shall not pay back the evil things the enemy has done, but shall try to correspond to the God who loves life like the sun and the rain. If we do not react to enmity with enmity, we creatively make it possible for our enemies to turn away from their enmity and to enter into the life we share.

The second step in loving our enemies is to recognize the other person. According to Martin Buber's translation, the command to love our neighbour runs: 'Love your neighbour as yourself, for he is like you.' I see myself in the other, and the other in myself. He has the same human dignity and the same human rights I claim for myself. Recognition of the other person is important, for all enmity begins with the dehumanization of the enemies. They are sub-human, vermin, and scum, and must be rotted out. Dehumanizing words like this break down the normal inhibitions against killing. The war can begin. If the United States is 'the great Satan' and Israel 'the little Satan', then Americans and Israelis are the enemies of God and can be killed wherever they are met with. Enmity always begins with the demonization of the others.

The third step in love for our enemies must lead to an understanding of the reasons for enmity. Aggressions are generally the result of injuries that have been suffered, so it is helpful to listen to the histories of the sufferings of hostile people or nations, and then, together with them, to look for a way of healing these tormenting memories. What this demands is not an attitude of superior condescension, but compassion, co-suffering. A place for encounters of this kind is often the mass graves of people on the other side. Encounters like this are encounters in shared grief.

Love of our enemies does not work purely emotionally and only with the best of intentions. It must be intelligent as well. One motto of the peace movement of the 1980s was 'intelligent love of enemies'. This proceeds rationally. Love of enemies cannot lead to masochistic subjugation under the power of the enemy, for then the subject of the love of that enemy would be lost. A well-known psychological phenomenon in kidnapping is called the 'Stockholm Syndrome'. Here the victim develops positive feelings towards his kidnappers. But this is the result of fear, not love. With rational love of our enemies we shall also try to prevent our enemies from being drawn into the enmity ever more deeply. I imagine it being something like this: with one hand to ward off the aggression, and with the other hand to offer peace and a shared life. I love enemies not because they are enemies but because God has made them and wants their life, not their self-destruction through enmity.

Love of enemies is not a dispositional ethics as, in the wake of Max Weber, many so-called realistic politicians seem to assume. It is a realistic ethics of responsibility.[12] It calls for responsibility not only for one's own life and the life of one's nearest and dearest, but for the life of our enemies and their nearest and dearest too, just as the sun shines on the evil and the good, and gives life to all.

ory I heard after the Second World War, the story of a simple
_man who distributed bread to a train of German prisoners of war
as it passed through her village. When Russian soldiers wanted to stop her
from giving the enemies bread, she answered: 'I give bread to all the hungry.
When the German soldiers drove Russian prisoners of war through our village, I gave them food, and if one day you are driven through our village by
the secret police, I will give you bread too.'

That is love of the enemy, which is like the light of the sun and the power
of the rain for the life we share.

Christian Dual Strategy for a Just Peace

Responsible participation in the just order of things in industry, society,
culture and politics—or consistent undivided discipleship of Christ in economic, social, cultural and political decisions: that is the basic ethic question.
There are three options. To put it pictorially: to turn swords into Christian
swords, or to use only ploughshares without swords, or to make ploughshares out of swords. The time of 'Christian swords' in the Holy Roman
Empire is past, so only the other two options are left. Must we see these as
alternatives or can they also act together in a complementary way?

The peaceful Anabaptists of the Reformation movement described in
Chapter 1 decided for the ploughshares. They lived and died 'without arms'.
They rejected the *corpus Christianum* and wanted to live unresistingly and in
preparedness for suffering, like the pre-Constantinian church. At that time
they were persecuted as 'Enthusiasts'. Today we call them 'historical peace
churches'.[13]

'The sword is a divine order outside the perfection of Christ', say Article 6
of the Anabaptist Schleitheim Confession of 1527. The 'perfection of Christ'
is lived in undivided discipleship of Christ according to what is laid down in
the Sermon on the Mount. A Christian cannot commit acts of violence, not
even if these acts are designed to punish or prevent acts of violence. He cannot participate in any calling in society which makes use of the sword. The
perfection of Christ is lived in the voluntary fellowship of those baptized in
faith, where there is only admonition, no compulsion, only forgiveness, no
judgment, only love, no retaliation. It is Christ's contrast programme to the
existing society: 'It shall not be so among you' (Matt. 20.25). The community
of Christ is a community for living, such as we still see today among the fraternities of the Hutterites, the Amish and the Mennonites. Today's Catholic
movement in the base communities in Latin America, and the alternative

Christian land communes follow their example. These consistent Christian pacifists are not anarchists. They live a new, peaceful order and by doing so call this world of violence into question: another way is possible. This great alternative to 'this world' can admittedly lose its ardour and lead to a retreat from public life into a quiet corner of its own. Then the great alternative turns into total rejection, and 'the silent minority' no longer disturbs the mighty. If one rejects this whole wicked world, one is no longer capable of practical criticism of individual abuses. The person who is against war in any circumstances will no longer demonstrate against this particular war. But nevertheless, through his mere existence he is a reminder that, according to God's will, there ought to be no war.

'All government…and all established rule and laws were instituted and ordained by God', say Article 16 of the Augsburg Confession of 1530, countering the Schleithheim Confession. This sentence sums up Christian responsibility for the world: Christians can 'occupy civil offices' and so forth, 'in all that can be done without sin' They can 'render decisions and pass sentence…punish evildoers with the sword, engage in just wars…take required oaths, possess property…For the gospel teaches an inward and eternal…righteousness of the heart.' So the 'perfection of Christ' is not external as well, but solely inward, 'proper fear of God and real faith in God'. Consequently the gospel 'does not overthrow civil authority' but requires that the political order be kept 'as true orders of God' and that everyone 'manifest Christian love…in his station in life'. According to this idea, the Christian's duty is to cooperate responsibly in the given world orders. God is responsible for the orders, which he has conferred; the Christian has to obey them obediently and with love, but he is not commissioned to change them. There is no special Christian righteousness not is there a particular Christian wisdom. Consequently, no Christian ethics would deviate visibly from the ethics of the given society. In this way the contrasting ethic in the discipleship of Christ according to the precepts of the Sermon on the Mount is surrendered.

Whereas the Anabaptists were in danger of leaving the world silently and without criticism, the Protestants were in danger of going along with the fore-given orders of this world and of cooperating with them without criticism. The 'silent minority' and the piously conformist subjects of the state then also contributed little of their own to the development of righteousness and peace in politics and society.

I assume that in the radically lived discipleship of Christ according to the standards of the Sermon on the Mount and the precepts given by Jesus to his disciples, a great alternative to a violent and peaceless world is being built up which in its contrast offers a true confrontation. The Anabaptists of the Reformation period lived in such confrontation; otherwise they would not have been so massively persecuted and burnt at stake.

On the other hand I take seriously the Protestant idea of responsibility for the world and work in the structures of society, but turn it in the direction of a responsible changing of the world, so that unjust structures become just forms of life and so that swords are turned into ploughshares. That means that I do not recognize the social and political structures as God's ordinances—*tamquam ordinationes Dei*—But see them as human constructions for which human beings have to take the responsibility, and which can therefore also be changed by human beings.

Christian responsibility for the world requires an ethics for changing the world, based on the righteousness and peace which we believe in and try to live, in the discipleship of Christ. For that reason Catholic worldwide Christianity needs the Christianity of the monastic orders, and Protestant Christianity needs the historical peace churches as orientation for the far-off goal from which the immediate goals must take their direction. Without the great alternative, small steps in the direction of more justice and righteousness and more peace in the world will have no orientation, and will lose hope; but without practical changes in the world the great alternative will become irrelevant.

To put it in visual images, we need the peaceful world of pure ploughshares so that here and today we can re-forge into ploughshares the bloodstained swords.[14] Anyone who wishes to take his bearings from a person may be reminded of Dietrich Bonhoeffer, who at the conference in Fanö in 1934 called on the churches for a unequivocal intervention on behalf of peace, then in 1939 took up active resistance against Hitler's murderous dictatorship, and in 1945 paid for both with his life.

The more the Protestant churches cease to be state and established churches and become free churches, the clearer their witness for peace in the world can be. Before the development of a multireligious society turns our churches into free churches, we ourselves can grasp this freedom in order to intervene for greater justice and righteousness in society and clearer policies for peace in the state.[15]

14

Control Is Good—Trust Is Better

Liberty and Security in the "Free World"

Lenin: Trust Is Good—Control Is Better

In the sad old days of the Soviet Union, everyone was already amazed at the Socialist surveillance state as soon as they got to the frontier. If, after prolonged efforts, and with the submission of many documents, one had already acquired a visa, one had to present one's passport, not only to one frontier official but as a rule to four. The first checked whether the visa was correct and the passport was still valid, and stamped it. The second checked whether the first official had checked it properly. The third checked the second, and the fourth, finally, had to check the third, the second and the first official. Lenin's precept: 'trust is good, but control is better' was in full force.

But everyone who thinks clearly is bound to ask: where does this lead, and when does it stop? Karl Marx already foresaw this dilemma of the surveillance state a hundred years earlier, and raised the unanswerable question: 'Who controls the controllers?' It is the age-old question of the Roman satirist Juvenal, which has again become up to date: *Quis custodiet ipsos custodos?* The Soviet Union's answer was: controllers control the controllers. Consequently, the state security authorities in the USSR (the GPU, the KGB, the inland secret service and so forth) and in the East European, socialist countries grew monstrously. Like a cancer, the unfruitful cells, hostile to life, of the all-supervising state security organizations and their informers spread into every town, every village, and every factory, into schools, universities, even into every family, and disseminated not security but general mistrust. Never express your own opinion. The person who hears you could be a spy of the state security service. So stop forming your own judgment and say only what you are supposed to say. Never tell the truth but only what they want to hear from you. In this way not only confidence in the state is lost but self-confidence as well.

After Germany was reunited in 1989, we acquired access to the archives of the East German state security service, which were made generally available. The information gathered there was overwhelming. It reached from well-documented political comments on the street to the whisperings of

207

lovers in bed with each other. Spoken and written words were documented, telephone conversations were taped, letters were copied, bank business was recorded, and so on. The 'Stasi', the state security service, which oversaw security in the surveillance socialist states, was often compared with a many-tentacled octopus, a voracious Moloch, or a spreading cancerous growth, for the financial and personal expenditure, and the cost in personnel, for these unproductive activities was enormous, and expanded more and more. If the controllers have to control the controllers, the budget for the secret service has grown immeasurably before so much as one controller has controlled a single person among the people. Why? The answer is simple: because no controller can be trusted. Nowhere is corruption so widespread as in the secret police and the security services of totalitarian states.

Every escalating state security system leads inescapably to the security state. This is the total surveillance state, in other words the police state, the dictatorship, the Leviathan. It destroys itself because of two insoluble problems. First, security becomes more and more expensive the more security services and controllers have to be employed in order to delude those concerned that security exists. Second, no one in states of this kind tells the truth. Everyone says only what his superiors—in this case the party and the government—want to hear. So the production figures are falsified in order that progress can be reported. In the end the government no longer knows what and whom it really governs, and lives from imaginary figures.

We should not be wrong if we judged that the Soviet Union and the Socialist states in Eastern Europe destroyed themselves through these two factors: (1) through the phantom of total control of the people, and the control of its controllers; (2) through the state-required lies about the true conditions. The general insight to be gained from this failed experiment is that the question of trust is the question of truth. Controls spread mistrust and mistrust distorts the truth into lies. But the lie is the power which destroys life.

Unfortunately, the surveillance madness did not die with the breakdown of the Socialist surveillance states. On the contrary, it is spreading in democratic structures too.

Since the unexpected terror attack of 11 September 2001 in the United States, and the succeeding attacks in Madrid and London, the urge for general security has grown enormously in the Western world. The United States reduced trust and liberty through the Patriot Act, and the most extensive surveillance systems were built up. Through the justifiable defence against terrorism we are approaching the repressive surveillance state, and that raises the question: and who keeps the state itself under surveillance? Even in the plans for a rocket defence system under President Reagan, the goal of the security measures was already the 'invulnerability' of the state.[1] But since military measures can be circumvented by private terror, and since electronic measures always produce counter-measures, this goal is unattainable. Is it even desirable? The person who is invulnerable becomes apathetic too. He immures himself behind a protective bulwark which no one can penetrate but from which it is impossible to get out. If we want to live freely as human beings, we have to live with some degree of vulnerability. Without freedom there is no need for security, without freedom security is valueless. The fight against terrorists is pursued at airports and by way of surveillance cameras, but this fight will be won only in the minds of men and women through conviction, and in their hearts through a turn from death to life.

The new electronic surveillance methods have for some time also led major companies to control their employees. The scandals in Germany about the telephone company Telekom, the railway (the Deutsche Bahn) and the supermarket chain Lidl, to mention only a few, show the irrational wish of those responsible to destroy the working climate through controls. No firm becomes more efficient through electronic controls of its staff. On the contrary, the trust of its employees is its real human capital. Only trust creates interest and voluntary co-operation. These interhuman relations cannot be replaced by a computer.

In government ministries, offices, and the courts the same disease has spread. Working time is controlled through time clocks. More and more controllers are employed for the purpose of controls and checks, reports and feedbacks pile up in the control centres to such an extent that no one can analyse them any more. Everyone is roped in to evaluate his colleagues, and wastes the time he is being paid for in order to spread mistrust. Interest in one's work drops, personal initiative is paralysed. The results are 'working to rule', distrust by everyone of everyone, loss of self-confidence, decreasing pleasure in one's work, and less and less efficiency. Up to now we have not heard anything about the successes of 'goal-orientated quality controls'.

Behind this modern surveillance madness is a pessimistic view of the human being which paralyses the person and fails to mobilize his best powers. It is an inhumane and moreover an unrealistic view of the human being.

Who controls the new surveillance instruments? The data which are gathered everywhere can apparently be less and less protected. They are sold or stolen and used against our will. A 'surveillance mafia' has developed whose criminal machinations are becoming global through the internet, and can therefore hardly be traced or punished.[2]

Trust Creates Freedom

Without trust no controls work, but can one trust controllers? Without freedom there is no need for security, but what security guarantees our freedom? What is trust?

If we view trust psychologically, then we shall come upon what Erik Erikson called 'basic trust', the trust of a child which stems from its mother's loving commitment and care.[3] Astonishingly enough, this basic trust remains even if the mother turns away from the child, or if she is absent from it for a time. The child develops a trust in life which is stronger than the fears of life and mistrust of things that are alien to it. We might say that what develops is a capacity for trust with which even justifiable mistrust can be endured. Out of the commitment the parents, and especially the mother, bring to the child, the child slowly but surely develops self-trust, self-confidence. This self-confidence makes it possible to come to terms with the disappointments experienced if other people misuse our trust.

If we view trust ecologically, we understand it as an atmosphere in life without which there is no human life at all. Human life cannot merely be lived as animal life. It must also be affirmed, accepted and loved, for it can also be denied, rejected and hated. A human life that is denied, rejected and despised, withers, becomes ill and dies. That is not only the case with children who are turned into street children or made to become child soldiers. It is the same for adult people. Trust is freedom's essential living space. Where other people trust me, I can expand freely and go out of myself. Where I am met with mistrust and rejection, I feel forced into a corner, and withdraw into myself. Fish need water to swim in, birds need air in which to fly, and we human beings need trust if we are to develop our humanity and our powers. Trust is the element for human life.[4] In a trusted environment, I feel free; I enter into a strange environment with caution.

If we view trust sociologically, we discover that promise is the foundation of all stable relationships.[5] The free human being, thought Nietzsche, is 'the being who can promise' and, as every child will add, who must also keep his promises. If I keep my promises I am making myself reliable and trustworthy for other people. Through the promises I make I commit myself in my ambiguities, and become unequivocal for other people and for myself as well. In faithfulness to what he has promised a person acquires continuity in time, because when he is reminded of his promise he is reminded of himself. The free person who is not already fixed by traditions acquires identity in his promises: Anyone who breaks his promises loses himself; the person who keeps his promises remains true to himself. If we keep our promises as far as we can, we create trust; if we groundlessly break our promises we are mistrusted, and rightly so. The person who does not bother about what he has promised is a cheat, and ultimately no longer knows himself.

A person's identity in his life-history is called by his name. Through my name, I identify myself with the person I was in the past, and anticipate myself as the person who I shall be in the future. With my name I can be addressed, with my name I sign agreements and vouch for my commitments. The shared social life of free people is always a dense fabric of promises and dependabilities. In this social fabric of mutual relationships, trust acquires its familiar form.

If social dependability is the foundation of every free society, then we have the social consensus, or what Rousseau called the social contract. In every society, in our modern and highly complex 'pluralist' society too, there are fundamental agreements and understandings, basic laws, constitutions, and unquestionable matters of course. Anyone who breaks them must reckon with sanctions. They constitute the basis of trust for the dealings of men and women with each other in society. These are not eternal laws enforced under appeal to a divine authority, that is, to an authority that is unquestionable. This is a covenant made by free citizens with each other and with coming generations, and ultimately with the earth.[6] Here the principle is *pacta sunt servanda*—pacts must be observed. The person who offends against the society's covenant constitution excommunicates himself. Social trust is withdrawn from him.

In the political sphere, finally, this constitutive covenant is the constitution in which civil rights are laid down, so that they can be appealed to, and so that legal action can be taken to enforce them if they are infringed or withdrawn. A country's laws must conform to its constitution; otherwise they are illegitimate. The constitutional rights of the people can only be set aside in emergency situations, and then only for a time, if the general security requires it. In a country's constitution, civil rights will be formulated in accordance with generally accepted human rights.[7] The Universal Declaration of Human Rights of 1948 and the International Covenants on Social, Economic and Cultural Rights of 1966, as well as the Earth Charter of 1992, are the internationally accepted basis of trust for the community of peoples gathered together in the United Nations. The United Nations is at present the bond uniting the world community of peoples. Whoever leaves it because he trusts solely in his own power will be isolated. He will lose his trustworthiness among the other nations and peoples. He can spread fear and terror, but cannot win trust.

Truth Creates Trust

Having looked at the various dimensions of trust, we come to the question of how trust is acquired, created, and restored. The answer is simple both in private and in public life. It is: tell the truth, and you will be considered trustworthy. We all know the fable of the boy who for a joke cried 'wolf, wolf' so often that he was not believed when the wolf actually came.

Only truthfulness wins and creates trust, and restores it. The rule is quite clear. Gustav Heinemann, the third president of the German Federal Republic, put it like this for his colleagues in political life: 'Say what you are doing, and do what you say.' I would add: don't think that the people who have elected you are stupider than you are yourself. They can stand the truth, even the bitter truth, better than pious lies, or political excuses.

But curiously enough politicians of all people often have a defective relationship to truth. Do politics ruin the character? It probably depends less on the character of the people concerned than on the notion of politics as a struggle for power. In a struggle of that kind, speeches are not judged by their truth but by their effect. Then they are used for propaganda, and to deceive the speaker's enemies. We have experienced this especially drastically in times of war. In war, truth is always the first victim. In order to find reasons for going to war lies are spread and truths are suppressed. This was the case at the beginning of the Second World War in 1939, and it was also the case in the war against Iraq. Moreover, truth cannot be told during a war because it could be of use to the enemy and would shake the confidence of one's own people. Because in wartime the people must always stand behind their government, that government has no longer so much need to make sure of the people's trust. Martial law and states of emergency make government easy, but this is not so in conditions of freedom, and these things do not ensure trust.

How can trust be restored once it has been misused? Through an honest admission that one has lied, and the plea for forgiveness—that is to say, through a plea for new trust. If I tell the truth about my lie and my breach of trust, it is painful, and I shall be open to reproaches and attacks; but it is the first step into the light of truth and 'only truth will make you free'. Whether or not the others forgive the liar who admits his lie, or whether they continue to hold his lie against him, he is superior to them, because he is now true and has regained his self-respect. He has taken on responsibility for himself, and that elevates him far above all his accusers. One can trust a person who tells the truth about his faults more than someone who maintains that he has never done wrong. One disappointed trust is not a justification for doing away with all trust. Misused freedom is not a reason of dispensing with freedom altogether. *Abusus non tollit usum*—abuse is not a reason against proper use. Trust restored through forgiveness is strong, because it has passed through broken trust and mistrust, and trust that has become wise is able to endure the contradictions. Children have an inborn basic trust. Grown-ups have to find and learn a mature, realistic trust. Blind trust has to become clear-eyed trust. Nowadays, 'transparency' and 'predictability' are fashionable terms for trustworthiness, but these objectifications exclude the human and personal dimensions of trust and responsibility. Computers too are transparent and predictable. But they cannot be called to account for what they do.

Ways from Control to Trust

On the political levels, hostile conditions can be eliminated through 'confidence-building measures'. By virtue of trust in an alternative future of peace and cooperation, trust can take the place of mistrust. There are examples: from 1975 onwards, in the midst of the Cold War between the Eastern bloc and the Western world, Conferences on Security and Co-operation in Europe (CSCE) were held in Helsinki, in divided Europe. In these 'confidence-building measures' were agreed upon. They perforated the Iron curtain because they dissolved the mutual, ideological mistrust. Instead of deepening the divisions through propaganda, there was cooperation for the purpose of finding genuine common ground. Today's integration in the European community is the result of steady work to build up mutual trust.

On the political levels, in the last twenty years we have experienced the successful transformation of dictatorships into democracies. Is a corresponding democratization of conditions in the great industrial concerns and the state bureaucracies possible?

I believe it is possible to transform controls and controlled administrative processes into agreements with the people employed. Then the personal initiatives paralysed by controls will be aroused, and the potential—now suppressed through mistrust—of all members of staff for invention and improvement will be activated. Office parties and joint excursions do not improve the work atmosphere; this comes about only through human cooperation on the basis of mutual trust.

When 'disloyalty' in the management is punished, loyalty is after all assumed to be the norm. But loyalty exists only if there is mutual trust. Loyalty can be promised but not controlled, either privately or in wider contexts. Controls do not create reliability. The dignity of human beings is only respected through trust. The democratization of organizations in industry and management seems to me to be the right way. In Germany, in management sectors we still have the remains of the old military structure of command and obedience, and consequently the tricks of 'army morality' among employees too, as a way of safeguarding small liberties.

Recently, the logic of the market has made its way into many spheres of life where it has no place. Profitability is demanded by the sickness insurances but in hospitals it is not the main concern. Patients are sick persons, not customers. Medicine is there to help them, not in order to achieve profits. Education in schools and universities is also fighting against the capitalist logic of the market. Students are not the 'human capital' of a society. Their education through research and teaching is not profit-orientated. If it were, there would no longer be any pure research. Students are academic citizens, not attenders in vocational schools. In the academic sphere, only trust and reliability awaken mental potential. Without academic freedom in this atmosphere of trust there is no scholarly and scientific progress, but merely commissioned work orientated towards application. To replace trust by control means destroying creative life.

Are there reasons for trusting people, other people and oneself? According to experience with other people, we are told that the appropriate attitude is not trust but rather 'calculated mistrust'. Even biblical Wisdom literature counsels rather a general mistrust towards others. And when it is a matter of our own self-confidence, self-doubt leads to humility, while complete self-confidence easily become arrogance. 'It is better to take refuge in the Lord than to put confidence in man', advises Psalm 118.8. But trust in God belongs to the teachings of faith. Does it also have positive consequences for our dealings with ourselves, other people and the earth?

By divine trust we generally mean the human being's trust in God. 'In God we trust' appears on every one-dollar note. According to Luther, God and faith go together. 'The trust and faith of the heart alone make both

God and an idol. If your faith and trust are right, then your God is the true God. On the other hand, if your trust is false and wrong, then you have not the true God....That to which your heart clings and entrusts itself is really your God.'[8] What distinguishes God from an idol? 'To have a God properly means to have something in which the heart trusts completely.' Luther calls Mammon 'the most common idol on earth.' 'Complete trust' can be placed only in the creator of the universe.

But divine trust has another side too. It is not just human trust in God; it is also God's trust in the human beings whom he has created to be his image on earth. Trust is always mutual: we trust God because God trusts us. In spite of all disappointments and human faithlessness, God believes in his human beings, hopes for their humanity, and waits for them. That is the content of every experience of grace and mercy: God continues to think that human beings are worthy of trust and capable of covenant, in spite of all the contradictions. Even if we do not believe, 'he remains faithful—he cannot deny himself' (Tim. 2.13). Irenaeus even saw God's glory in every living person: *Gloria Dei est vivens homo*. God's trust in us is the firm foundation for a self-trust which frees us from arrogance and depression. God's trust in other people is the firm ground for trusting them, in spite of calculated mistrust, and for calling forth their reliability. God's trust in his earth is the firm foundation for accepting the earth as our trusted environment, in spite of all the frightful natural catastrophes, and the foundation for our hope for its future.

15
The Righteousness of God and Human and Civil Rights

The Discovery of Human Rights

Insight into the fundamental rights of human beings grew in many civilizations at the same time as the recognition of the humanity of human beings. Wherever the universal concept 'human being' was developed, instead of 'friend and enemy' or 'we and the others', the rights of human beings were formulated too, together with respect for the humanity of human beings.[1] This was not an exclusively Western idea, although rights formulated explicitly as 'human rights' made their way into the American and European constitutions at the time of the Western Enlightenment. They have acquired worldwide acceptance, formerly through the League of Nations and today through UNO. Like other universal ideas, human rights have detached themselves from their especially European development history, and are directly accepted as reasonable by all people who recognize that they are not just American or Chinese, black or white, men or women, Christians or Buddhists, but are human beings.

Consequently, no one in the West can claim to have patented human rights, nor is there any justifiable cultural or religious reason for rejecting human rights on the grounds of their being a Western idea.

The more different peoples, races and cultures enter a shared global history, because they are bringing deadly danger on one another through the nuclear threat and the ecological crises, the more important a consensus about human rights and the rights of nature becomes. In these rights it is possible to discern the contours of a global democracy in which humanity could one day become the determining subject of its survival history.

We find the declarations of human rights in force in the United Nations in the following:

1. The Universal Declaration of Human Rights of 1948.
2. The International Covenants on Human Rights (economic, social and cultural rights, civil and political rights, the optional protocol) of 1966,[2]
3. The Convention on the Rights of the Child of 1989.

The binding force of these declarations in international law was initially slight, for the Preamble of 1948 states only that they are 'an ideal to be attained together by all peoples and nations'. Nevertheless, in international conventions and transnational legal agreements they have shown an astonishing strength. A binding agreement against genocide was already passed by UNO in 1948. Right up to the end of the Second World War, it was internationally accepted that the question of how a country treated its own citizens was entirely a matter for that country's sovereign decision. Even though some countries today still reject 'interference in their internal affairs' on the grounds of human rights, the way a country treats its own people is also a legitimate matter for the United Nations too, for every one is also bound to observe internationally accepted human rights.

The subdivision and categories of human rights emerges from their history. In 1948 the North Atlantic states, following the crimes of the Fascist dictatorships, formulated individual human rights over against the state. The Eastern states, on the basis of their criticism of class rule and capitalism, introduced economic and social human rights into the International Covenants of 1966. Today demands by the impoverished people in the Third Word for the right to existence and the right to survive are being introduced into the discussion about human rights.

We can therefore distinguish between (1) protective rights to life, freedom and security; (2) rights to liberty, these covering freedom of opinion, freedom of association and freedom of religion; (3) social rights to work, to the means of subsistence, and to housing; (4) the rights to play a part in public life, and to participation in politics, industry and culture.

In the ecumenical discussions between the churches since 1945, interesting shifts of emphasis are emerging. Following the General Assembly of the World Council of Churches in Amsterdam in 1948, religious freedom was at the centre, until it was perceived that freedom of religion can be realized only in the framework of the other individual human rights. The importance of promoting individual freedom of religion and individual human rights, even after the collapse of the Soviet Union, is shown by those countries where Islam or Buddhism is the state religion. Since about 1960, the questions about economic, social and cultural human rights have moved into the foreground, because racism, colonialism and sexism are seen to be grave infringements of human rights. In a world with oppressions of this kind— where people oppress people—individual human rights can be realized only together with social, political and economic human rights. The ecumenical

consultation in St. Pölten in 1974 was a milestone in the history of the discussions in the Christian countries about human rights, because here for the
first time representatives from the Third World spoke and were listened to.

At the end of the 1970s we then saw the theological declarations on
human rights issued by the major churches. In 1974 the papal commission
Justitia et Pax presented its declaration on 'The Church and Human Rights'.
In 1976 'The Theological Basis for Human Rights' was published by the
World Alliance of Reformed Churches (WARC).[3] In 1977 the Lutheran
World Federation (LB) followed with 'Theological Perspectives on Human
Rights'.[4] Unfortunately, up to now there has been no joint Christian declara-
tion on human rights. At the moment a statement by the Russian Orthodox
Church, 'The Russian Orthodox Church's Basic Teaching on Human Dig-
nity, Freedom and Rights' (2008) is giving occasion to vehement discussions
in the Conference of European Churches (CEC).[5]

The Integration of Individual and Social Human Rights

'We hold these truths to be self-evident', says the American Declaration of
Independence, 'that all men are created equal.' This means all human beings,
irrespective of their age, their sex, their race, their religion, their disabilities.
In the Basic Law of the German Federal Republic too, Article I, 2 on the
rights to freedom enjoyed by the person is followed in Article I, 3 by a statement of the principle of equality and of equal rights. This means that all
democracies which have similar constitutional principles have the task of
combining, and of realizing, both individual and social human rights.

In the prophetic religions of Judaism, Christianity and Islam, the freedom and equality of all human beings is based on belief in creation. They
are grounded in the concept of the human being as being created in image
of God. Among many peoples, in their myths about rule, only the ruler is
God's image on earth; he is 'the Son of Heaven', over against the children
of earth. The Babylonian Mirror for Princes says that 'The shadow of God
is the ruler, and human beings are the shadow of the ruler'.[6] If, as Genesis
1.26 maintains, God created human beings to be his image on earth, this is
an early universalization and enduring 'democratization' of ancient oriental
ruler ideology. All human beings, just like queens and kings, are God's image
on earth, made in order to correspond to God's goodness and righteousness,
and to cultivate and preserve his earth. With this, the rule of one human
being over other human beings is in principle called into question: 'God
has created and formed men on the pattern of himself, and redeemed them

through his Martyr, the one like the other....According to my understanding, I am unable to comprehend that anyone [is the property] of another', we read in the mediaeval *Sachsenspiegel*.[7]

In European political history, this led to the development in principle of the democratization of all rule, because only then can the liberty and equality of all the members of a state be ensured. Equality before the law subjects rulers to the law as well. The sovereignty of the people is the modern political means of giving effect to the character of all human beings as the image of God.

However, the Western history of freedom was one-sided, because it stressed the individual rights of human beings where political rule was concerned, and neglected their social equality. Thus liberal democracy was increasingly developed, but social democracy was given a back seat. The liberty of individuals was protected but their solidarity was still neglected, Private property was sacrosanct, common property enjoyed only feeble protection.

Here we see an error in the history of Latin European belief. According to Augustine, the human being's likeness to God is seated at the summit of the soul.[8] It is in the subjectivity of the bodiless soul that the God-like dignity of the human being is supposed to lie. But that is not what the biblical account of creation says. It is not the bodiless individual soul that is the image of God and is supposed to correspond to God; it is the human being together with other human beings; for 'male and female he created them'. Nor does the Christian doctrine of the Trinity make the isolated individual soul the *imago trinitatis*, the image of the Trinity; the image is the community of the church in its mutual recognition and love.

If we take the relationship between the sexes as the primal image of human sociality, then human solidarity has the same divine dignity as human personhood. Neither is the person there 'before' the community, as Catholic social doctrine says, not is the community there 'before' the person, as socialism maintains. It is rather that person and community are equally primal and condition each other mutually, just as, in the context of development history, a human being's individuation and socialization come into being at the same time. This means that in principle individual human rights take no precedence over social human rights, although this is always assumed in the Western world because only the Universal Declaration of Human Rights of 1948 is read. The person's rights to liberty can only be realized within a just society living in solidarity, and a just society will only be realized in the rights of every person.

The 'free development of the person' (Basic Law 1,2) goes together with the free development of solidarity in the community. If this is correct, then an integration of the Universal Declaration of 1948 and the International Covenants of 1966 is urgently required.[9]

The Integration of Economic Human Rights and the Ecological Rights of Nature

Leading a life in dignity is part of human dignity in general. Minimum social and economic preconditions belong here, such as protection from hunger, illness and homelessness, as well as the right to work, the right to personal property and the right to have a say in public life. Just as in the political sphere to be permanently made the object of state power contravenes human dignity, it also contravenes a person's dignity if he is only regarded economically, as working and purchasing power. In order to live his 'quality as determining subject' in the economic sector too, human beings must be given a just share in the social product. The concentration of the means of production and living in the hands of a few, and the oppression and exploitation of the many, infringes human dignity. A worldwide economic condition in which millions go hungry is unworthy of humanity and, in Christian terms, is an offence against the glory of God, which can be found in the likeness to God shared by all human beings. Without more justice through a democratization of the world's economy there will be an economic, and then also an ecological, catastrophe to the human race, because growing exploitation and indebtedness will force the peoples of the Third World to cut down their rain forests, and to exploit their arable and grass lands immoderately, so that through the increase in steppes and deserts a large part of what provides the foundation for the life of humanity as a whole will be destroyed.

Ecological limits have been set to the fundamental economic rights of humanity. Economic growth is only possible within limits.[10] Consequently, social justice cannot be acquired either through more economic growth, even though today the growth we are promised will allegedly equalize injustices. That is growth fetishism. There is a negative correspondence between the social condition of human beings and their relationship to nature: if the exploitation of the work force is dominant in the social structure, then the relationship to nature will also be determined by exploitation of the earth's mineral resources. The exploitative relationship of the human being to nature will stop only if the exploitative relationship of people to one another stops too. Ecological justice will only be acquired at the same time as economic justice. Both begin with the ecological rebuilding of the industrial society and the social ethos which goes along with it. Because today the technical means of exploiting nature to the point of its destruction can be stepped up, it is a counsel of wisdom to say that it is stupid, because it is suicidal, to destroy the foundation of one's own life in the long run for the sake of short-term profits. That is a bankrupt's policy.

The ideology of modern civilization maintained that it is only the human being who exists for his own sake; everything else is there for the sake of the human being, and for his use. Cosmocentrism was the foundation of the pre-industrial agrarian society, but anthropomorphism is the foundation of its modern industrial counterpart. If the human being's dignity is seen only in his 'quality as determining subject' and if this quality is ascribed to the human being alone, human rights which are built up on that dignity are a threat to nature, and hence ultimately to the ability of human beings themselves to survive. The European concept of the determining subject stems from the division of the world into subject and object, and it was intended to secure the central ruling position of the human being himself.[11] But that means viewing human beings as bodiless subjects, and nature as an object without a soul. There is no community and no bond between the bodiless subject and the soulless body. Aristotle was still able to talk about 'the soul of plants', 'the soul of animals', and 'the soul of human beings', because for him a 'world soul' embraced and differentiated all the living. It was only the mechanistic world picture of the modern industrial society which drove out the 'world soul', so that nature might be subjugated.

Postmodern views, on the other hand, are now starting again from the body-soul totality of human beings, in order to develop the idea of a cosmic community into which human beings are integrated, out of the bodily needs and sensory relations of human beings with other living things. The modern split into soul and body, subject and object, person and thing, does justice neither to the totality of human beings, nor to their natural living community with the earth. If the modern fissure is rigorously pushed through, human bodiliness is destroyed and the natural community of life is ruined. Modern anthropocentrism is deadly for human beings themselves. Even though there can be no way back to agrarian economic cosmocentrism, it will nevertheless be possible to integrate a new ecological culture into nature. Remarkably enough, the Orthodox theology of the Eastern churches has never gone along with these Western European divisions, because it saw the human person not as standing over against objective nature, but as a hypostasis of nature.[12] In the human being, nature gathers itself together into a hypostasis; consequently the human being is dependent on nature. In his bodiliness the human being together with all other living things and with all material elements remains bound up with nature. Human beings have been created together with nature and together with nature will be redeemed.

It would be a great advantage if the different declarations on human rights and the Earth Charter of the United Nations were integrated. In 1990, in the World Alliance of Reformed Churches we expanded our theological declaration on human rights of 1976 by a section on 'The Rights of Nature'.[13]

Human Rights: International, Transnational, or Subsidiary?

The Universal Declaration of 1948 sees the human being as an individual belonging to the species human being. Does this mean the spread of urban individualism and Western cosmopolitanism, as is feared in Asia and Africa? If this were so, this declaration would be unrealistic, for it is not only in traditional societies that human beings have a strong social identity and only a weak individual one. They feel themselves to be members of their family, their clan, their people, their culture and their religious community, but they do not see themselves as individual examples of the human race; for their social security depends on their specific social ties, and these cannot be assumed by humanity as a whole. Nor do human rights exist in order to abolish or replace the specific, local and national civil rights. But they do bring a new dimension to the local ties and civil rights, which on the one hand are global and cosmopolitan and on the other hand affect the innermost being of every human being. In dictatorships, human rights groups fight not only for global concerns but also for the human right of every individual in his local ties and obligations. Specific civil rights can be called to account in the forum of human rights. To take a concrete example: the right to emigrate is a human right, but the former Socialist GDR (East Germany) punished emigration as 'flight from the republic', and thereby made itself guilty towards its citizens of severe breaches of human rights. Whoever stood up for his right to leave the country was standing up for a human right. The way a country treats its own people is no longer solely that country's own affair. It is also a matter for the community of states, and a matter of general human solidarity. In the question about the relation between civil and human rights, we advance a step if we ask about the goals of the declarations on human rights:

> Can we see in them the first outlines of a global, cosmopolitan democracy? Are human rights designed to be trans-national and hence also post-national rights?[14]

Or are these international legal agreements between sovereign national states—agreements, that is to say, based on the sovereignty of the national states and under their protection, because only these states are in a position to enforce them?

Ought the sovereignty of individual states to be restricted by way of human rights, so that they may one day be absorbed into the trans-national sovereignty of a world government? Or should they as trans-national rights merely further the interdependence of the now existing states? Through their realization, is something like the global governance of the community of states in sight?

In this political conflict between the advocates of a democratic cosmo-politanism and the supporters of national sovereignty, between internation-alism and trans-nationalism, it would seem obvious to remember the old principle of subsidiarity: it is only when smaller and limited social units are no longer in a position to solve the vital problems of their people that larger and more extensive social and political units are permitted to inter-vene. Today the particular states are faced with global challenges and have to build up transnational structures of law and authority in order to respond to them. So fundamentally speaking they do not surrender their existing sov-ereignty, but create new, transnational sovereignties in response to the global challenges. So the sovereignty argument is not really a weighty one. In 2009 an international climate summit was held in Copenhagen, but the neces-sary agreement about the reduction of carbon dioxide emissions failed to be reached, largely because of the egoism of the sovereign states. That shows on the one hand that transnational obligations must be built up, but also that the sovereign states must fulfil them.

There is some degree of agreement that severe infringements of human rights, such as genocide, must be punished on a global basis. The interna-tional arrest warrant and the international court of justice are first steps on the road to a trans-national institution. Severe injuries to nature, such as lasting damage to the earth's climate, correspond to infringements of human rights. Since wherever they begin locally these have global effects, they must also be punished on a global basis. But from this the international system of states is still far removed.

Can only sovereign states enforce human rights? No. Human rights do not offer only protection for the dignity of every human being, but also the right to participation, and hence chances for co-operation in the implementation of these rights.[15] More and more people are participating in civil non-governmental organizations (NGO) as a way of enforcing human rights and the rights of nature. To name only a few: Amnesty International, Greenpeace, Transparency International, Human Rights Watch, World Watch Institute, Villa Campesina.

Numerous private organizations concern themselves with global problems, such as Médicins sans Frontières, Reporters sans Frontières, ATTAC, the World Social Forum, and many others. These make it possible for individuals to participate in the solution of global problems. Non-governmental organizations of this kind are not powerless. Through publication—through 'name and shame'—they can effectively combat violations of human rights, the destruction of nature, and corruption. In some global questions they even drive the states forward and by so doing participate in world governance. Human rights are also the rights of everyone to share in the government of the world, and responsibility for the world. This is the sector in which a political ethics can be ecumenically developed; for after all the Christian churches when they join together ecumenically are global non-governmental organizations. It is also the sector where the churches work together with human rights groups and ecological organizations.

These civil and non-governmental initiatives probably do more to promote a global democracy than do the first political steps toward a worldwide state, whether in the form of an imperium or as a transnational superstructure. Both these concepts would lead to a Leviathan—a global surveillance state. Democratic initiatives, on the other hand, can pave the way for a global democracy, and can bring it about.

Human Rights and the Righteousness of God

The Christian churches have had an ambiguous relationship to the discovery and development of human rights. In the struggle for their own religious freedom and the freedom of their congregations from the fetters of the state church, the Reformed churches in France, Holland, England and America very early on became the upholders of human rights and of democratic civil rights,[16] whereas the Lutheran state churches on the continent stood aloof from them for a long time. From the French Revolution onwards, the Roman Catholic church was resistant to the atheistic—or to be more precise the laicist—ideas of democracy. The condemnations in the Syllabus of Errors of 1864 were only rescinded under the Second Vatican Council. Since then, the Catholic Church has been concerned to implement the human rights which had still been condemned in the Syllabus, including religious liberty. The Orthodox churches outside the Western world were prevented by religiously idealized Tsarism, and by the atheistic Stalinism that followed, from playing a part in the development of human rights. We shall therefore begin with the objections to human rights put forward by the Russian Orthodox Church in 2008.

Human Rights and Christian Morality

In 2008 the Russian Orthodox Church published their principle standpoints with regard to 'human dignity, freedom and rights'.[17] Here it was fundamentally a question of the theological interpretation of the basic concept of 'the dignity of the human being' as image of God. The declaration rightly starts from Genesis 1.26, and states that God has not merely created human nature but has also endowed it with the attributes of his image and his likeness. That is the general Christian approach. But then the declaration restricts itself to the 'likeness to God' and goes on: 'A human being preserves his God-given dignity and grows in it only if he lives in accordance with moral norms…Thus there is a direct link between human dignity and morality' (I, 5). In saying this, it transforms human dignity into a moral category. 'Moral acts give the human being dignity, immoral action withdraws it from him.' But this means that Christian morality precedes human rights. 'We must clearly define the Christian values with which human rights have to be harmonized (I, II, 1). Otherwise they can encourage 'abortion, suicide, incest, perversion, destruction of the family, the glorification of cruelty and violence' (II, 2). The Russian church is thinking of a moral misuse of human rights, but not their political violation. Nevertheless, Russia too has accepted the European Court of Human Rights in Strasbourg.

Ever since the biblical account of creation, however, a theological distinction has been made between *zelem* and *demuth*, *eikon* and *homoiosis*, *imago* and *similitudo*, being made in the image of God and possessing likeness to God. Imago expresses ontic participation (*metexis*), *similitudo* moral correspondence (*mimesis*). Human life is *imago Dei*, *similitudo* means a life in accordance with God. That was the view shared by the Latin and the Greek Fathers of the church. If we understand the two as both being attributes of human nature, the quantifying question arises: how much can be destroyed by sin, and what is indestructible? It is a different matter if we understand the two relationally. Then the image of God (*imago*) means God's relationship to human beings: God puts himself in such a relationship to the human being that the human being becomes his image on earth. Likeness to God (*similitudo*) then describes the human being's relationship to God. Sin is able to distort the human being's relationship to God in such a way that human beings in place of God make created things their idols, but it cannot destroy God relationship to human beings. Only God can rescind this, or withdraw it. Consequently the sinner remains God's image as long as God holds fast to it. The dignity of the human being is to be found in this objective relationship of God's to human beings; it is therefore non-disposable, inalienable, and indestructible. The child, the old man, the person suffering from dementia, even the criminal: all are God's image, and in this dignity have to be respected. To be made in the image of God is the universal dignity of every human being; similarity to God, on the other hand, is particular, the sanctification of the Christian life. Consequently universal human rights cannot be made subject to Christian morality; rather, Christian morality moves within this universal context. Nor can Christian ethics be reduced to a global ethic of universal human rights. Christian ethics has its identity in the community of Christ and in the discipleship of Christ, so that there it can manifest 'the better righteousness' (Matt. 5.20); but it finds its relevance in the problems and needs of its time. It has a particular point of departure, and aims at general acceptance.

Human Rights and the Hope for God's Just and Righteous World

As we have said, human rights were discovered and resolved upon in the actual injustices of a violent world. Inherent in them is their idealistic motivation. According to the preamble of 1948, they formulate 'ideals' which the peoples and nations are supposed to strive for. If we gather together all human rights and all the rights of nature, what emerges is indeed the wonderful picture of an ideal world.

Christian eschatology differs from this idealism through the realism of its hope. Its point of departure is the reality of Christ, and it discloses the future horizon of this reality; for this reality of Christ is of concrete universality. According to Colossians 1.15-20, in the crucified and risen Christ both the mystery of creation and the mystery of redemption become manifest in the midst of the history of this unredeemed world. The Epistle's first chapter encapsulates in a few sentences the heart of the Christian doctrine of creation and its doctrine of the future: 'In him all things were created, in heaven and on earth' (1.16). Just as in the prologue to the Gospel of John, the divine that is manifest in Christ is called the word of creation: 'All things were created through him and for him' (1.16). So through him God 'has reconciled to himself all things, whether on earth or in heaven, making peace by the blood of his cross' (1.20). From this reconciliation of the universe there follows the hope for the redemption of all things from the wreckage of the world, which they, and not only human beings, have brought about with their relative freedom.

Christian ethics moves in a world already reconciled by God, in spite of its deadly contradictions. It surmounts the violence of friend-enemy thinking and refuses to recognize the subject-object split between human beings and nature. But the future of this world, which objectively has already been reconciled in Christ, is the redeemed world, the world newly created in righteousness. Its symbols of hope are 'new creation', 'new earth', 'the indwelling of God and his righteousness in all things', 'the resurrection of the dead', and 'the bringing again of all things'. Orthodox theology calls the goal of creation and the future of all things 'the deification of everything created'[18] through the indwelling of God in them all. In this total concept of the world reconciled in Christ and of the future of the whole creation in the reconciling and redeeming righteousness of God which puts all things right and makes them live, human rights and the rights of nature fit together organically, as necessary and hopeful steps on a great path. They are immediate goals which correspond to the goals that are still far off.

Just as Christian ethics has to move in the framework of human rights if it wants to become relevant today, so Christian hope for the world integrates these rights into its total vision. On the one hand the Christian hope for the world, since it is at the service of reconciliation, is closer to reality than the idealism of human rights; but on the other hand it is wider in its vision of the future rise of the divine righteousness. In the service of reconciliation it takes over its own task in the world of perpetrators and victims; in its passion of hope it already anticipates today the hoped for future, according to what is possible and realizable, while relativizing at the same time all anticipations of the future. There is no 'end of history' before the resurrection of the dead and the annihilation of death in the presence of God, not in an ideal 'global state' either, or in a hegemonial imperium; for they themselves, after all, are in need of redemption.

Part 5
Joy in God
Aesthetic Counterpoints

Ever since the time of classic Greek philosophy, the Good and the Beautiful have belonged together and cannot be separated. Whatever is ugly cannot be good; whatever is evil has no beauty. Consequently, aesthetics is the reverse side of ethics, and every ethics of the Good issues from the aesthetics of the Beautiful and leads to these aesthetics. Christian ethics is the human reaction to the coming of Christ into this world and is an anticipation of his future in the new world.[1] That is why every good Christian ethics ends in doxology, so as with the praise of God to intensify the cry of hope, 'Amen, come Lord Jesus!' (Rev. 22.20). For in Christian ethics it must be clear that, we do not make use of God in order to change the world, but we change the world in order to enjoy God, as Augustine said.

In ethics too, God and faith in God cannot be measured by their utility. That would deprive both God and faith of their dignity. But the world is there so that we may use it and sanctify it for God's sake, and so that we may glorify God and enjoy his presence.

But how can I sing when I am in a strange land?[2] How can I laugh where it is grief and tears that reign? How can I praise the beauty when I am surrounded by hate and by so much that is hateful?

Is there really freedom in the midst of slavery? Is there a home in what is so alien? Is there 'joy in every sorrow', as Paul Gerhardt says in one of his hymns—hope where fear overwhelms us, and praise of the creator even in the sighs of those he has created?

I believe that there is already a true life in the midst of false life, otherwise we would not feel the falsity of life at all. How could we feel the humiliations of captivity if we knew nothing about freedom? How could our suffering become conscious pain if there were nothing in which to rejoice? And why should we sigh over our own fragility and the transitoriness of our fellow creatures if we did not already have the praise of the creator in our ears?

Where Freedom Is Near, Chains Begin to Chafe

It is only when the kingdom of God 'is near' that we make an about turn. In the dawn of the day, we sense the darkness of the night and get up. It is only when we experience the nearness of God with all our senses that we come alive and resist the powers of death. The people who are oppressed politically and socially do not surrender to their oppressors but mock them, unmasking them in jokes about their miserably pompous rulers, and 'the laughter of the oppressed'[3] echoes the laughter of God. 'He who sits in the heaven laughs; the Lord has them in derision' (Psalm 2.4). The revolt of the humiliated begins with the mocking exposure of the powerful: 'Let us tear their bonds asunder and cast away their ropes.'

Every ethics of being-able-to-act and of having-to-act needs counterpoints of this kind. According to the Chinese Tao te Ching, this is the 'wuwei', the not-doing in doing; according to Israel's Torah this is the Sabbath rest; this, according to the gospel, is the Easter jubilation of Christ's raising into the kingdom of God. The peace of God is not an ideal—beautiful, but for us mortal and fallible human beings unfortunately unattainable. Nor is it some far-off future at the end of our laborious days on earth. It is the immediate present in our hearts and in the mystery of the world, and we discover, as Friedrich Hölderlin says, that 'All that are sundered find back to each other / And there is peace in the midst of strife'.[4]

In this final part of the *Ethics of Hope* let us find a taste for peace, and think about

1. God's Sabbath rest,
2. The Easter jubilation over the raising of Christ,
3. The 'peace in the midst of strife'.

16

Sabbath—The Feast of Creation

According to the first creation account in the Bible, the creation of the world *ends* on the sixth day: 'And God looked at everything that he had made, and behold, it was very good' (1.31). And yet 'on the seventh day God *finished* his work which he had done' (Gen. 2.2).[1] What did God add to his finished creation on the seventh day? What was still lacking in his creation? What did its completion consist of?

The answer is a surprising one: the completion of the creation consists of the coming to rest of its creator, and from the creator's rest spring the blessing and sanctification of the seventh day of creation. According to Exodus 31.17, God 'was refreshed'—he 'heaved a sigh of satisfaction.' The creator withdraws himself and frees himself from his work; he detaches himself from what he has made and leaves what he has created in peace. The first step in this detachment is that 'God looked at everything he had made' (Gen. 1.31). In order to look at it he needed space, for seeing is a remote sense. The second step in the detachment was that 'God rested on the seventh day from all his work which he had done' (2.2). This resting in himself brings peace to what he has created.

This is a strange way of 'completing' his works. Today, when we retire, start drawing a pension and have to leave our job or professional life, we ask: Are we still of any use? What will I do now? We talk about 'active retirement' or 'happy non-retirement'. One surely can't just stop going! One surely doesn't belong on the scrap heap of ageing, passive, useless senior citizens! Christians especially feel that they are 'always at the service' of an unceasingly active God. *Deus non est otiosus*, ran a mediaeval saying—'God is never unoccupied'. So we have become what Goethe describes Faust as being, 'a monster without rest and peace.' To go faster is not a problem, but to leave everything aside certainly is, and to reduce our speed is almost impossible. Yet 'power lies only in rest'.

On the seventh day of creation, God encounters us in a very different way: he is at leisure, so to speak. God comes to rest. God detaches himself from his works. God puts aside his being as creator. God comes to himself again, after he had creatively gone out of himself. As their creator, God is wholly with those he has created, but now he detaches himself from them and becomes free from his works and withdraws into himself. God comes to rest in the face of all those he has created, and with his being, resting within itself, is wholly present among them. His pleasure in his creation becomes the joy of those he has created. God is not just active, he is passive too; not only creative but also at rest; not just speaking but also listening; not merely giving but also receiving. In the beginning God created, and at the end God rests: that is the marvellous divine dialectic.

Perhaps artists can understand best how one can 'complete' a creation by coming to rest. A painter puts his whole soul into his painting. When it is finished, he stands back in order to come to himself again and to let his work of art make its own way. Without this withdrawal, no work of art is ever 'completed'.

Only in one respect was the physico-theology of the eighteenth-century Enlightenment (Deism) represented by the notion of God as the 'watch-maker' behind the machinery of the world who became unemployed after the creation of this law-regulated world because he had arranged everything splendidly and no longer could intervene without contradicting himself. In another respect, this physico-theology was part of the baroque 'theology of glory', which perceives and extols the creator of the world in his Sabbath rest.[2] The much-abused Deism was also Sabbath theology.

'So God blessed the seventh day and hallowed it.' What he blesses, he endorses. His blessing gives self-confidence and strength. God blesses his living things with fertility (Gen. 1.22, 28). But on the Sabbath what he blesses is not any living thing; he blesses a time, the seventh day of crea-tion. This is remarkable, because time is not an object. Time is invisible and flowing; we cannot hold time fast. How ought we to understand this divine blessing of a time for all God's creatures? God blesses this day not through an action but through his rest, not through something he does but through his being. He blesses those he has created through this day of his resting presence on which they too are supposed to arrive at their rest.

'Thou hast made us for thyself and our hearts are restless within us until they find rest in Thee', wrote Augustine.[3] This restlessness is not limited to human beings; it torments all living things which want to live and have to die. Where is the harbour of happiness, the home of identity, the place of rest? It is not far off in 'the seventh heaven'; nor is it in the innermost part of the human being—in the seventh chamber of 'the castle of his soul', as the mystics Theresa of Avila and Thomas Merton have described. It is on earth and easy to find in time: on the Sabbath day the eternal one is present in his rest, and those he has created can find him if they themselves come to rest.

God's first blessing was not conferred on his chosen people, nor on the promised land, but on the universal Sabbath day of creation. This was the way Israel understood the Sabbath from the time of the Babylonian exile. God dwells in time.[4] The Sabbath is the Jewish cathedral.[5] On the Sabbath, time and eternity touch. The Sabbath is the mystical moment, the 'present' of eternity.

That means that the weekly day of rest is not merely a making-present of creation in the beginning; it is also a making-present of redemption at the end, a time of remembrance and a time of hope. Beginning and end are present on this day on which time and eternity touch. On the Sabbath, transitory time is abolished, the time of death is forgotten and the time of eternal life is perceived. It is the liberating interruption of transient time through eternity.[6] And if we then look at the weekly succession of Sabbath days, we perceive a rhythm that belongs to eternity: the times oscillate in the dance of eternity. On every Sabbath, time is born anew.

The Sabbath is not only the day of rest but also the day of no longer intervening in nature. In the Sabbath stillness, people no longer intervene in the natural environment through their work. With this the view of the world changes: things are no longer valued for their utility and practical value. They are perceived with astonishment in their value as being. Things appear as they are in themselves. With this, the environment as it is related to human beings becomes the world as it proceeded from God's creation. There is no proper understanding of the world as God's creation without this way of perceiving it in the Sabbath stillness.[7] In pure pleasure, without reason or purpose, things display their creaturely beauty. The world becomes more lovable when we no longer weigh it up according to the criteria of utility and practical value. We shall then also become aware of ourselves—body and soul—as God's creations and as his image on earth. We are then entirely without utility—we are quite useless—but we are wholly there and know ourselves in the splendour of the shining face of God. The fearful questions about the meaning of life and our usefulness vanish: existence itself is good, and to be here is glorious. On the feast day of creation, we come to ourselves and to God, who surrounds us from every side. But we cannot purchase the peace of this day; it cannot be earned. We must seek this leisure, and then it will suddenly find us.

The Jewish Sabbath corresponds to God's creation Sabbath and as the 'seventh day' is a day of ending and completing. It is the day of rest after six working days. It is like the quiet evening after a laborious day. When 'Queen Sabbath' enters Jewish houses, a completed week is crowned. The Jewish Sabbath with its rituals teaches us joy in existence and the wisdom of age.

Consequently, this celebration is full of gratitude for the works of creation and for safe-keeping in the history of the world and is an echo of the creator's judgment: 'And God saw that it was good.' And yet, or just because of that, hidden in the Sabbath lies a hope that embraces the world. All the days of creation have an evening, when night falls, but the seventh day knows no night. It is like a day without end, and because of that it points beyond itself to the day of God's coming, the day when he will come to dwell eternally in his creation. That is why the rabbis often said, 'If Israel were only to keep one single Sabbath, the Messiah would come immediately'. The experiences of the Sabbath were always used as a way of describing the happiness of the messianic time.

The Jewish wisdom of the Sabbath is the completing: 'All's well that ends well.' That is why the origin of the world is not celebrated on the first day of creation, as it is in the creation myths of the different peoples, but on the last.[8]

The Christian churches, on the other hand, moved the weekly feast day from the seventh day to the first. That has a profound symbolic meaning. It celebrates the feast of Christ's resurrection on 'the eighth day', as it was called in the patristic church—that is, on the day following the Jewish Sabbath. The Jewish Sabbath passes over into the Christian Sunday: out of the resting comes the resurrection jubilation; out of the end, the new beginning. The Christian Sunday too is a feast of creation. It is with Christ's resurrection the beginning of the new creation of all things. It is the consummation towards which creation at the beginning points. That is why the first creation account is read as part of the Catholic liturgy for the Easter vigil. The whole creation is drawn into the happening of the resurrection, which begins with Christ. With this the Christian Sunday becomes entirely 'the feast of the beginning'.[9] Franz Rosenzweig characterized the Christian very well from Jewish eyes: 'The Christian is the eternal beginner; completion is not for him: all's well that begins well. That is the eternal youth of the Christian; every Christian lives his Christianity every day as though it were the first.'[10]

17

The Jubilation of Christ's Resurrection

Sunday as an officially decreed day of rest is not really a Christian feast day at all. The birth of Sunday can be viewed as having occurred on 3 March 312: 'The Emperor Constantine to A. Helpidius: 'All judges, the people of the cities, and all forms of trading are to be free to rest on the worshipful day of the sun'.[1] What has the day of the Roman sun god, *sol invictus optimus*, got to do with the Christian feast day?

The Christian feast day was celebrated by the Jewish Christians on what according to the Jewish calendar was 'the first day of the week' (Acts 20.7; 1 Cor. 16.2). The expression 'the Lord's day' (Rev. 1.10) was then added, coming from Syria. In the second century, the curious phrase about 'the eighth day' came into use. These terms presuppose the Jewish Sabbath and do not replace it. The Christian feast day is not the Christian Sabbath. Consequently, Sabbath laws cannot be applied to the Christian feast day either, although all the Christian catechisms do so. When we look at the events celebrated, we find rather that there is a close *factual* connection between the celebration of the Jewish Sabbath and the Christian feast day.[2] On the Christian feast day, Christians celebrate the raising of Christ from the dead into eternal life and with that the annihilation of death through the beginning of a new creation in which death will be no more. They celebrate God's uprising against the powers of destruction in order to complete his creation. Historically speaking, this goes back to the first appearances of the risen Christ at the empty tomb, without which we would know nothing at all about Jesus. But in the content of its truth, it is of the most tremendous explosive power, so that men and women break out into terror and jubilation.

On the day of the resurrection, Christians perceive the beginning of the new creation of all things into their true and abiding form. Whereas Israel's Sabbath lets us look back to creation in the beginning, the Christian feast day points forward to creation's future. Whereas the Sabbath lets men and women share in God's rest, the feast of the resurrection confers a share in God's life-awakening power. The Sabbath holds within itself the wisdom of the ending—the Christian feast, the joy of the beginning. Remembering and thanking on the one hand, and hoping and beginning on the other, belong substantially together. It is necessary to be clear once more about the connection between the Sabbath and the Christian feast day, because the Christian feast became pagan when it coincided with the Roman day of the sun. In actual fact the Christian 'first day of the week' is already hidden in the Jewish Sabbath, since although for God the creation Sabbath is certainly 'the seventh day' for the human beings created on the sixth day it was the first day they experienced.

Among the Christian churches, one has radically detached itself from the Sunday of the Constantinian Christian imperium and celebrates the Jewish Sabbath in a Christian way—the Seventh-Day Adventist Church. For the post-Constantinian church, this is an important signal, but does it not mean surrendering the special Christian day of resurrection?

My own suggestion, which I try to live by, is this: why don't we on Saturday evening let the week merge into the Sabbath stillness and begin the new week on the following day with the feast of the resurrection and the new beginning? Why don't we celebrate from Saturday midday until Sunday midday? The 'Sunday' will again become the authentic day of the Christian resurrection if we succeed in celebrating a Sabbath the evening before. From Saturday midday onwards, I should like to let the week draw to a close, finish work or lay the work aside, and love and marvel over the created things round about me, then on 'Sunday' morning begin afresh with Christ's resurrection and anticipate the new creation. In the creation story too we read that from the evening and the morning came the new day. The modern, worldwide way of counting time, which counts from Monday ('1') to Sunday ('7'), is not Christian. It was established by the churches without its being noticed. Anyone who has flexible working hours is forced to see his days of rest as movable holidays and has to incorporate them deliberately into his timetable. These days do not only contribute to one's health, as people say today; they are holy too, as used to be said.

The piety and devotion of the Western churches stresses Christ's resurrection from the dead and the assurance of eternal life; [3] in the Orthodox church, on the other hand, emphasis lies on the annihilation of death and the new creation of all things. In the West, stress lies on redemption from sin through Christ's giving of himself and the vanquishing of death through his resurrection; but in the East, the transformation of creation is emphasized. In the Lutheran church, Good Friday counts as the greatest of the feast days; if we want to encounter the original Christian Easter jubilation, we must go into an Orthodox church, for the Eastern churches are churches of the resurrection. All things are caught up in the resurrection joy, so that the Easter jubilation of us human beings embraces the whole cosmos. In order to draw this ecological dimension once more into the Christian feast day, and especially into the Easter festival, we can pick up thoughts from the 'Sacred Hymns of the Eastern Church' and follow the canon of John Damascene for the feast of Easter.[4]

> Rejoice ye heavens in worthy wise!
> Earth too shout for joy!
> Exult greatly, O cosmos,
> the visible and the invisible both.
> Christ has awoken, He the joy of the aeons.

> Therefore we celebrate the slaying of death
> and the binding of Hades—
> the beginning of a new life
> which will endure eternally.

> Day of resurrection,
> Yes, let us be light on the people's feast,
> we will embrace one another!
> We shall call brothers those who hate us!
> And the resurrection lets us forgive all things.
> So we shall cry:
> Christ has risen from the dead,
> defeating death through death,
> and giving life to those who lie in graves.

It is good to react with such cosmic resurrection jubilation to the catastrophes in the human world, and to the terrors of the coming climate changes and to natural disasters. The ethics of life, of the earth and of righteousness and justice follow from this jubilation. The exuberance of the Easter joy carries over into the continuing hope for God's future. This answer to the question, 'what may we hope for?' makes the hope greater than anything we have to fear, for its takes our fear away.

18

"And Peace in the Midst of Strife"

On the Sabbath, a peace becomes possible in the unrest of transitory time. The nearness of God resting in himself radiates an atmosphere of tranquillity. In the festival of Christ's resurrection, we too experience resurrection into life, in spite of all the violence of death. In the presence of the risen one, we are seized by the fullness of life in many dimensions, and an atmosphere of hilarity spreads abroad which I should like to call Easter jubilation, compared with the Sabbath stillness. In addition to tranquillity and to jubilation, we may add as third gift *peace*—not already the peace which ends all strife but as yet only the peace which makes it possible for us, in the midst of strife, to bring the conflict to a just end. Theologically, this is called 'reconciliation'; this ends the enmity and is the beginning of a peaceful community.

According to Ephesians 2 and Colossians 1, through Christ's giving of himself God has created 'peace' between Gentiles and Jews, since he 'brings the hostility to an end' though himself (Eph. 2.16) and proclaims peace to those who were near and those who were far off. In the Epistle to the Colossians, the cosmic dimension is added to this concrete peace between Jews and Gentiles, since through Christ God 'has reconciled to himself all things, whether on earth or in heaven, making peace by the blood of his cross' (1.20). In the human dimension as well as in this cosmic one, it is important to perceive that peace has already been made by God; so for human beings the one thing necessary is to perceive and accept what is objectively already existent *sub specie aeternitatis,* whether in human conflicts or in the cosmos. 'God was in Christ and reconciled the cosmos with himself' (2 Cor. 5.19).

This is the 'peace in the midst of strife.' In the depths of the paralysing and often deadly conflicts between the peoples, this *divine peace* already reigns. In the divine depths of the universe, everything is already reconciled. The person who perceives this views his enemies as 'already reconciled' and will try to turn the conflict into just community with them. The universe, which to some scientists seems so meaningless and pointless, also holds in its transcendent depths this divine peace and appears meaningful in itself. The person who perceives this will not fear the universe as silently alien but will know himself to be reconciled with all things. These two things may seem contrary to appearances, but the certainty of human and cosmic peace transcends the visible contradiction; 'peace in the midst of strife' goes beyond the strife.

Just as the peace of God already dwells in the midst of the world, it is already present in the depths of human existence as well. 'Contemplation in a world of action' is the way Thomas Merton described the spirituality in which we find this peace in the resting point of one's own soul. On the one hand this peace of God is 'above' all understanding, and yet on the other hand it 'keeps our hearts and minds' and senses within us. Why? The reason Paul gives in Philippians 4.5 is that 'the Lord is near'. How near? As near as Christ is in us. According to Augustine, God is closer to us than we can be to ourselves. According to the Qur'an, God is closer to us than our jugular vein. Consequently, Augustine told us to 'withdraw into yourself. Truth dwells in the inner man.'[1]

We 'withdraw into ourselves' when in a quiet hour, or in conscious meditation, or in a momentary insight, we let all actions, interests, burdens and projects fall away and ourselves become calm. We do not then fall into vacancy but are gathered up by the divine peace which dwells in us in the depths of our being. We then attain the soul's hidden resting point, where we can gain a foothold and stand. In Christian contemplation we call this mystery: God, who dwells within us, Christ who lives in us, the divine Spirit, out of whom we are born anew. This hidden resting point of the soul is also the point from which our livingness springs. The closer we come to this point the more the peace within us grows, and, more than that, an immeasurable joy lays hold of us.

It is not only our 'restless heart' that will be 'kept' but our five senses too: feeling, tasting, smelling, hearing and seeing. If through Christ in the peace of God they are preserved within us, they become aware, attentive, and curious for God's future. Ancient Christian mysticism turned away from the world and told us: 'Close the gateway of thy senses and seek God deep within' (G. Tersteegen).

The new Christian mysticism is turned towards the future, and with its hope for God awakens all the senses for the future of God's world. Those who have found God in their innermost being can forget themselves, go out of themselves, and do their utmost without losing themselves. The person who senses in himself the nearness of the risen Christ will be filled with a joy that embraces the world. He sees this disputed and suffering world as already in the daybreak glory of its eternal beauty.

Notes

Preface

1. Konrad Raiser, 'Globalisierung in der ökumenisch-ethischen Diskussion', in *Verkündigung und Forschung* 54, no. 1 (2009): 6–33.

2. Michael Haspel, 'Globalisierung—Theologisch-ethisch', in *Verkündigung und Forschung* 54, no. 1 (2009): 34–44.

3. Matthias Schreiber, ed., *Wer hofft, kann handeln: Johannes Rau—Gott und die Welt ins Gespräch bringen* (Holzgerlingen: Hänssler, 2006). The title was contributed by his wife, Christina Rau.

Introduction

1. Jürgen Moltmann and Carmen Rivuzumwami, eds., *Hoffnung auf Gott—Zukunft des Lebens* (Gütersloh: Gütersloher, 2004).

2. Søren Kierkegaard, *The Concept of Anxiety: A Simple Psychologically Orienting Deliberation on the Dogmatic Issue of Hereditary Sin*, Kierkegaard's Writings VIII, ed. Reidar Thomto and Albert B. Anderson (Princeton: Princeton University Press, 1981).

3. Hans Jonas, *The Imperative of Responsibility: In Search of an Ethics for the Technological Age*, trans. Hans Jonas and D. Herr (Chicago: Chicago University Press, 1984). For a comparison of Bloch and Jonas, see Bames E. B. Bleyer, 'Die unbedingte Pflicht der Menschheit zum Dasein', *Orientierung* 73 (2009): 203–6. Bloch was well aware that the reverse side of hope is fear: 'Where there is danger, deliverance also grows, that is the best hope; but where there is deliverance, danger grows too; that belongs equally to the end, and constitutes tried and tested hope, which by no means has its sights set on what is already guaranteed but, militantly, is directed in hostility towards Nothingness and, equally, towards whatever aims at whatever is radically related to the Universe', *Experimentum Mundi* (Frankfurt: Suhrkamp, 1975), 238.

4. Friedrich Hölderlin, *Werke*, vol. 1, ed. Emil Staiger (Zurich: Atlantis, 1944), 334.

5. For more detail, see Jürgen Moltmann, 'What Are We Doing When We Pray?' in *The Source of Life: The Holy Spirit and the Theology of Life*, trans. Margaret Kohl (Minneapolis: Fortress Press and London: SCM Press, 1997), 125–44.

6. Jürgen Moltmann, 'The Spirituality of the Wakeful Senses', in *In the End—the Beginning: The Life of Hope*, trans. Margaret Kohl (Minneapolis: Fortress Press and London: SCM Press, 2004), 79–86; Jürgen Moltmann, *Spiritualità dei sensi vigili*, (Modena: Fondazione Collegio San Carlo di Modena, 2006).

7. See Ernst Käsemann, 'Theologischer Rückblick' in Jens Adam, Hans-Joachim Eckstein and Hermann Lichtenberger, *Dienst in Freiheit: Ernst Käsemann zum 100. Geburtstag* (Neukirchen: Neukirchener, 2008), 101.

1. Apocalyptic Eschatology

1. Heiko A. Oberman, *Luther: Man between God and the Devil*, trans. Eileen Walliser-Schwarzbart (New Haven: Yale University Press and London: SCM Press, 1989).

2. Ulrich Duchrow, *Christenheit und Weltverantwortung: Traditionsgeschichte und systematische Struktur der Zwei-Reiche-Lehre* (Stuttgart: Klett, 1970).

3. 'Interim (scil. evangelium) non dissipat politiam aut oeconomiam, sed maxime postulat conservare tanquam ordinationes Dei et in talibus ordinationibus exercere caritatem'.

4. This is particularly emphasized by Ernst Wolf, 'Politia Christi', in *Peregrinatio I: Studien zur reformatorischen Theologie und Kirchenproblem* (Munich: Kaiser, 1954), 214ff.

5. Dietrich Bonhoeffer, *Ethics*, in Dietrich Bonhoeffer Works, vol. 6, Clifford J. Green, ed. (Minneapolis: Fortress Press, 2004), 131–32.

6. Ibid.

7. Here I am following Heinrich Meier's thorough account, *Die Lehre Carl Schmitts: Vier Kapitel zur Unterscheidung Politischer Theologie und Politischer Philosophie* (Stuttgart: Metzler, 1994).

8. Ibid., 109–10.

9. Ibid., 245.

10. Ibid., quotation on 249. For the history of catechon interpretation see Wolfgang Trilling, *Der Zweite Brief an die Thessalonicher*, EKK zum NT XIV (Neukirchen: Neukirchener, 1980), Excursus: Die 'aufhaltende Macht', 94–104.

11. Mary Kaldor, *New and Old Wars: Organized Violence in a Global Era* (Palo Alto: Stanford University Press, 1999).

12. Wilhelm Bousset, *Die Offenbarung Johannis* (1906) (Göttingen: Vandenhoeck & Ruprecht, 1966), 399.

13. The dualistic eschatology goes back to John Foxe, *Acts and Monuments* (1550), ed. G. Townsend and G.R. Cattley, 8 vols, London 1837–41.

14. See Richard Bauckham, *The Theology of the Book of Revelation* (Cambridge: Cambridge University Press, 1993).

15. Avihu Zakai, *Exile and Kingdom: History and Apocalypse in the Puritan Migration to America* (Cambridge: Cambridge University Press, 1992).

16. Stephen Sizer, *Christian Zionism: Road-Map to Armageddon?* (Downers Grove: Intervarsity, 2004). See the earlier work by Peter Toon, ed., *Puritans, the Millennium, and the Future of Israel: Puritan Eschatology, 1600 to 1660* (Cambridge: James Clark, 1970).

17. Avihu Zakai, 'From Judgment to Salvation: The Image of the Jews in the English Renaissance', *WTJ* 59 (1997): 213–30.

18. New York, 1970; more than forty million copies.

19. *Time Magazine*, 'Armageddon and the End Time', November 5, 1984.

20. Geiko Müller-Fahrenholz, *America's Battle for God: A European Christian Looks at Civil Religion* (Grand Rapids: Eerdmans, 2007).

2. Christological Eschatology

1. For more detail cf. Jürgen Moltmann, *Politische Theologie–Politische Ethik* (Munich and Mainz: Christian Kaiser, 1984) 137–51; partial trans. by M. Douglas Meeks in *On Human Dignity: Political Theology and Ethics* (Philadelphia: Fortress Press, 1984, 2007).

2. Walther Köhler, *Huldrych Zwingli* (Leipzig: Koehler & Amelang, 1943).

3. Josef Bohatec, *England und die Geschichte der Menschen- und Bürgerrechte: Drei nachgelassene Aufsätze*, ed. Otto Weber (Graz: Böhlaus Nachfolger Weimer, 1956); Jürgen Moltmann, 'Covenant or Leviathan? Political Theology at the Beginning of Modern Times', in *God for a Secular Society: The Public Relevance of Theology*, trans. Margaret Kohl (Minneapolis: Fortress Press and London: SCM Press, 1999), 24–45.

4. Rudolf Weth, *'Barmen' als Herausforderung der Kirche: Beiträge zu Kirchenverständnis im Licht der Barmer Theologischen Erklärung*, Theologische Existenz heute 220 (Munich: Christian Kaiser, 1984).

5. A. Bürgsmüller and Rudolf Weth, *Die Barmer Theologische Erklärung* (Neukirchen: Neukirchener, 1982), 35. See here Jürgen Moltmann, ed., *Bekennende Kirche wagen: Barmen 1934–1984* (Munich: Christian Kaiser, 1984).

6. *Church Dogmatics* IV, 1–4, develops Christology in the framework of the doctrine of reconciliation.

7. English translation: 'Gospel and Law,' in *Community, State, and Church: Three Essays*, trans. A. M. Hall (New York: Doubleday, 1960), 71–100.

8. Translated into English as *Church and State* by G. Ronald Howe (London: SCM Press, 1939).

9. English translation: 'The Christian Community and the Civil Community', in *Against the Stream: Shorter Post-War Writings, 1946–52*, Ronald Gregor Smith, ed. (London: SCM Press, 1954), 13–50.

10. Karl Barth, *Church and State*, 29.

11. Ibid., 41.

12. Karl Barth, 'Die Kirche und die Kultur' in *Die Theologie und die Kirche*, Gesammelte Vorträge, vol. 2 (Munich: Kaiser, 1928), 364–91.

13. Karl Barth, 'The Christian Community and the Civil Community' (see n. 31 above), 38 (trans. altered).

14. Dietrich Bonhoeffer, *Ethics*, in Dietrich Bonhoeffer Works, Vol. 6, Clifford J. Green, ed. (Minneapolis: Fortress Press, 2004), 126–27; Arnold Albert van Ruler, *Droom en Gestalte: Een discussie over de theologische principes in het fragstuk van christendom en politiek* (Amsterdam: Uitgeversmaatschappij, 1947); van Ruler, *Gestaltwerdung Christi in der Welt: Über das Verhältnis von Kirche und Kultur* (Neukirchen: Kreis Moers, 1965); van Ruler, 'Das Leben und das Werk Calvins' in Jürgen Moltmann, ed., *Calvinstudien* 1959 (Neukirchen: Neukirchener, 1959), 84–94.

15. H. Richard Niebuhr, *The Kingdom of God in America* (New York: Willett Clark, 1937).

3. Separatist Eschatology

1. Guy Franklin Hershberger, ed., *Das Täufertum* (Stuttgart: Evangelisches, 1963); Hans-Jürgen Goertz, ed., *Die Mennoniten* (Stuttgart: Evangelisches, 1971); Jürgen Moltmann, *The Politics of Discipleship and Discipleship in Politics: Jürgen Moltmann Lectures in Dialogue with Mennonite Scholars*, ed. Willard Swartley (Eugene: Cascade, 2006).

2. Ernst Wolf, 'Schöpferische Nachfolge' in *Peregrinatio II: Studien zur reformatorischen Theologie* (Munich: Kaiser, 1963), 230–41. It was not until Dietrich Bonhoeffer that this subject was reintroduced into Protestant ethics.

3. Hans Denk, *Schriften II* (Gütersloh: Gütersloher, 1958), 45. Quoted in Goertz, *Die Mennoniten*, 41.

4. Heinold Fast, ed., *Der linke Flügel der Refomation: Glaubenszeugnisse der Täufer, Spiritualisten, Schwärmer und Antitrinitarier* (Bremen: Schünemann, 1962), 66–71.

5. Goertz, *Die Mennoniten*, 23ff., 32ff.

6. Ibid., 23.

7. John Howard Yoder, *The Politics of Jesus: Vicit Agnus Noster*, 2nd ed. (Grand Rapids: Eerdmans, 1994).

8. Fast, *Der linke Flügel*, 74–75.

9. Hans-Jürgen Goertz, ed., *Alles gehört allen: Das Experiment der Gütergemeinschaft vom 16. Jahrhundert bis heute*, (Munich: Beck, 1984). He rightly points to the link between the Anabaptists and the peasant revolts in the sixteenth century.

10. W. Klassen in Goertz, *Die Mennoniten*, 51.

11. Stanley Hauerwas, *The Peaceable Kingdom: A Primer in Christian Ethics* (Notre Dame: University of Notre Dame Press, 2002); Stanley Hauerwas and Samuel Wells, eds., *The Blackwell Companion to Christian Ethics*, 2nd ed. (Oxford: Wiley-Blackwell, 2011). See also Hauerwas's autobiography, *Hannah's Child: A Theologian's Memoir* (Grand Rapids: Eerdmans, 2010).

12. Stanley Hauerwas, *A Community of Character: Toward a Constructive Christian Social Ethic* (Notre Dame: University of Notre Dame Press, 1981), 74.

13. George A. Lindbeck, *The Nature of Doctrine, Religion, and Theology in a Postliberal Age* (Atlanta: Westminster John Knox, 1984; 25th Ann. Ed, 2009).

14. These points are put together by Jennifer M. McBride, *The Church for the World: A Theology of Public Witness*, diss. University of Virginia, 2008.

15. See G. Thomas's criticism 'Theologische Ethik im angelsächsischen Raum', *EvTh*. 68 (2008): 219–34.

16. Charles Marsh, *The Beloved Community: How Faith Shapes Social Justice, from the Civil Rights Movement to Today* (New York: Basic, 2004).

17. See Jennifer McBride, *The Church for the World*, with reference to Dietrich Bonhoeffer.

4. Transformative Eschatology

1. Text following *Martin Luther King Jr., 1929–1968: An Ebony Picture Biography* (Chicago: Johnson, 1968), 43–45. Comment in James H. Cone, *Martin and Malcolm and America: A Dream or a Nightmare?* (New York: Orbis, 1991).

2. The term 'anticipation' was introduced into the discussion well before Ernst Bloch's *Principle of Hope* of 1959. It already plays a leading role for the historical existence of human beings in Franz Rosenzweig's *Star of Redemption* (1921; 1930). Rosenzweig calls it 'the reversal of the objective relationship of time. For whereas the past presents what is already finished from its beginning to its end, and can thereby be told—and all "telling" begins from the beginning of the series—the future, as that which it is, namely future, can only be grasped by means of anticipation.... Here the last must in our thinking be the first' (170). 'Without this anticipation and the inner drive towards it, without "the will to bring the Messiah before his time" and the temptation " to take the kingdom of heaven by storm", the future is not a future but merely a past drawn out to unending length and projected forwards. For without such anticipation the moment is not eternal but a perpetual trudging on along the long road of time' (180f.).

3. *Uppsala Spricht: Die Sektionsberichte der Vierten Vollversammlung des Ökumenischen Rates der Kirchen in Uppsala 1968* (Geneva: World Council of Churches, 1968), 1–2. Quotation translated from the German text. See also Norman Goodall, ed., *Uppsala Speaks: Section Reports of the Fourth Assembly of the World Council of Churches, Uppsala 1968* (Geneva: World Council of Churches, 1968).

4. Philip Potter, ed., *Das Heil der Welt heute: Ende oder Beginn der Weltmission? Dokumente der Weltmissionskonfernz Bangkok 1973* (Stuttgart: Kreuz, 1973), 169–208.

5. In January 2005 the famous Pentecostal preacher Yonggi Cho acknowledged in his New Year's address to his Full Gospel Church in Korea that in his successful mission he had hitherto only had regard to the salvation of believers' souls, and he proclaimed the new year to be the 'year of social salvation'. 'I have concentrated only on the redemption of human beings and saw God's redeeming work too narrowly. Salvation is all-embracing. Up to now we were a Full Gospel congregation, but now we must

become a Full Gospel that embraces the world.' See the Family Newssheet of the Full Gospel congregation for March 2005. In the same issue I wrote for this a welcoming and endorsing commentary. This conversion of the best known Pentecostal preacher of the present time is remarkable and deserving of deep respect.

6. Jürgen Moltmann, *The Way of Jesus Christ: Christology in Messianic Dimensions*, trans. Margaret Kohl (London: SCM Press, 1990 and Minneapolis: Fortress Press, 1993). See also Bertold Klappert, *Worauf wir hoffen? Das Kommen Gottes und der Weg Jesu Christi—Mit einer Antwort von Jürgen Moltmann* (Gütersloh: Gütersloher, 1997).

7. For more detail, see Michael Welker, *God the Spirit*, trans. John F. Hoffmeyer (Minneapolis: Fortress Press, 1994).

8. Walter Rauschenbusch, *Christianity and the Social Crisis*, ed. R. D. Ross (New York: Harper & Row, 1964), 91.

9. These are the experiences of all resistance and liberation movements. See Jürgen Moltmann, *Experiences in Theology: Ways and Forms of Christian Theology*, trans. Margaret Kohl (Minneapolis: Fortress Press and London: SCM Press, 2000).

Part 2. An Ethics of Life

1. See John Paul II's encyclical *Evangelium vitae* of March 30, 1995; Gustavo Gutierrez, *The God of Life*, trans. Matthew J. O'Connell (Maryknoll: Orbis, 1991); Jürgen Moltmann, *The Spirit of Life*, trans. Margaret Kohl (Minneapolis: Fortress Press and London: SCM Press, 1992); Jürgen Moltmann, *The Source of Life: The Holy Spirit and the Theology of Life*, trans. Margaret Kohl (Minneapolis: Fortress Press and London: SCM Press, 1997); Geiko Müller-Fahrenholz, *Erwecke die Welt: Unser Glaube an Gottes Geist in dieser bedrohten Zeit* (Gütersloh: Gütersloher, 1993); and Konrad Raiser, *For a Culture of Life: Transforming Globalization and Violence* (Geneva: World Council of Churches, 2002).

5. A Culture of Life

1. Albert Camus, *The Rebel: An Essay on Man in Revolt* (New York: Knopf, 1961), 305.

2. 'Es zittern die morschen Knochen / der Welt vor dem großen Krieg.
Wir haben den Schrecken gebrochen, / für uns war's ein großer Sieg.
Wir werden weiter marschieren, / bis alles in Scherben zerfällt.

3. Günther Anders, *Endzeit und Zeitenwende: Gedanken über die atomare Situation* (Munich: Beck, 1972); G. Anders, *Die atomare Drohung: Radikale Überlegungen* (Munich: Beck, 1981).

4. Association for the Taxation of Financial Transactions and for Citizens' Action.

5. Donella H. Meadows, et al., *The Limits of Growth: A Report for the Club of Rome's Project on the Predicament of Mankind* (New York: Signet, 1972). Cf. Gregory Fuller's nihilistic book *Das Ende: Von der heiteren Hoffnungslosigkeit im Angesicht der ökologischen Katastrophe* (Zurich: Ammann, 1993).

6. Stuart Kauffman, *At Home in the Universe: The Search for the Laws of Self-Organization and Complexity* (New York: Oxford, 1995).

7. Paul C. W. Davies, *Cosmic Jackpot: Why Our Universe Is Just Right for Life* (New York: Houghton Mifflin, 2007).

8. Philip Clayton, *Die Frage nach der Freiheit: Biologie, Kultur und die Emergenz des Geistes in der Welt* (Göttingen: Vandenhoeck & Ruprecht, 2007).

9. Hans Jonas, *The Imperative of Responsibility: In Search of an Ethics for the Technological Age*, trans. Hans Jonas and David Herr (Chicago: University of Chicago Press, 1984).

10. Steven L. Weinberg, *The First Three Minutes: A Modern View of the Origin of the Universe* (New York: Basic, 1993).

Romano Guardini, *Freedom, Grace, and Destiny: Three Chapters in the Interpretation of Existence*, trans. J. Murray (London: Harvill, 1961). See also the comment by Klaus P. Fischer, *Schicksal in Theologie und Philosophie* (Darmstadt: Wissenschaftliche, 2008).

11. Robert Jay Lifton, *The Life of the Self: Toward a New Psychology* (New York: Touchstone, 1976). I owe the approach to these analyses to Geiko Müller-Fahrenholz, *Erwecke die Welt: Unser Glaube an Gottes Geist in dieser bedrohten Zeit* (Gütersloh: Gütersloher, 1993).

12. Tim LaHaye and Jerry B. Jenkins, *The Glorious Appearing: The End of Days* (Carol Stream: Tyndale, 2004), is the last volume in this latest pop-apocalyptic Left Behind series of Christian endtime stories, which created a stir in America but did not sell at all in Europe. See here Barbara R. Rossing, 'Prophecy, End-Times, and American Apocalypse: Reclaiming Hope for Our World', *Anglican Theological Review* 89, no. 4 (Fall 2007): 549–64. There is evidently a correspondence to Christian fundamentalist apocalyptic in the Islamic Hakkani movement and its spiritual mentor Ayatollah Mohammed Mesbah Jasdi in Ghom, Iran. These are 'Mahdists' who believe that the 'Twelfth Imam' 'disappeared' in the ninth century and will return at the end of the world, in order, after a catharsis of the world through a catastrophe, to carry off believers to paradise and unbelievers to damnation. Iran's president Ahmadinejad belongs to this movement (*Der Spiegel* 26 [2009]: 104–7).

13. Ernst Käsemann, *Perspectives on Paul*, trans. Margaret Kohl (London: SCM Press and Philadelphia: Fortress Press, 1971), 24–25.

14. Albert Schweitzer, *The Mysticism of Paul the Apostle*, trans. William Montgomery (original ed., 1931) (Baltimore: Johns Hopkins University Press, 1998) is still the only book on Paul's Christ-mysticism.

15. Eberhard Jüngel, 'Die Ewigkeit des ewigen Lebens,' in *Ganz werden: Theologische Erörterungen* (Tübingen: Mohr Siebeck, 2003), 345–54.

16. Boethius, *The Consolations of Philosophy*, Book V.1.

17. Søren Kierkegaard, *The Concept of Anxiety: A Simple Psychologically Orienting Deliberation on the Dogmatic Issue of Hereditary Sin*, Kierkegaard's Writings, vol. 8, ed. Reidar Thomto and Albert B. Anderson (Princeton: Princeton University Press, 1981).

18. Elisabeth Moltmann-Wendel, *Gib die Dinge der Jugend mit Grazie auf: Texte zur Lebenskunst* (Stuttgart: Radius, 2008) 51–60.

19. Martin Luther, 'hominem justificari fide' in Disputatio de homine, 1536, *WA* 39.1, 175ff. See also the comment by Ernst Wolf, *Peregrinatio II: Studien zur reformatorischen Theologie, zum Kirchenrecht und zur Sozialethik* (Munich: Kaiser, 1965), 135.

20. 'Die biologische Lebensbegriff' in the *Historisches Wörterbuch der Philosophie*, vol. V, Joachim Ritter, Karlfried Gründer, and Gottfried Gabriel, eds. (Basel and Stuttgart: Schwabe, 1980), 97. Alfred North Whitehead's definition 'Life is Robbery' (*Process and Reality: An Essay in Cosmology* [New York: Harper and Row, 1960], 160) is often cited, but it is related only to the nourishment of a 'living society'. His more comprehensive definition is: 'The primary meaning of life is the originating of conceptual novelty—novelty of appetition' (ibid., 156).

21. Max Scheler, *Die Stellung des Menschen im Kosmos* (Munich: Nymphenburger, 1947), 41: 'to become human is to be elevated to openness to the world by virtue of the spirit.'

22. Joachim Bauer, *Prinzip Menschlichkeit: Warum wir von Natur aus kooperieren* (Hamburg: Hoffmann and Campe, 2006).

23. Angela Adams and Willi P. Adams, *Amerikanische Revolution und Verfassung*, 1754–1791 (Munich: Dt. Taschenbuch, 1987).

24. G. W. F. Hegel, *Theologian of the Spirit*, trans. J. Michael Steward (Minneapolis: Fortress Press, 1997), 101.

6. Medical Ethics

1. Jürgen Moltmann, *Science and Wisdom*, trans. Margaret Kohl (Minneapolis: Fortress Press and London: SCM Press, 2003).

2. Helmuth Plessner, 'Conditio humana', *Opuscula* 14 (Pfullingen: Neske, 1964), 49–72.

3. For more detail on this point, see Jürgen Moltmann, *God in Creation: A New Theology of Creation and the Spirit of God*, trans. Margaret Kohl (London: SCM Press, 1993 and Minneapolis: Fortress Press, 1985), 215–43.

4. Dietrich Bonhoeffer, *Letters and Papers from Prison*, Dietrich Bonhoeffer Works, vol. 8, ed. John W. DeGruchy (Minneapolis: Fortress Press, 2009), 541.

5. Immanuel Kant, *Critique of Pure Reason*, Preface to the Second Edition, trans. Norman Kemp Smith, (London: MacMillan, 1929), 20.

6. See Søren Kiekergaard, Preface to *Sickness unto Death*, 1849.

7. Hannah Arendt, *The Human Condition*, 2nd ed. (Chicago: University of Chicago Press, 1998), 177. See also the comment in Eberhard Jüngel, *Anfänger: Herkunft und Zukunft christlicher Existenz* (Stuttgart: Radius, 2003).

8. On the following passage, see Konrad Hilpert and Dietmar Mieth, eds., *Kriterien biomedizinischen Ethik: Theologische Beiträge zum gesellschaftlichen Diskurs* (Freiburg: Herder, 2006). The contributions are for the most part written from a Catholic viewpoint.

9. G. E. W. Wolstenholme, ed., *Man and His Future* (London: Churchill, 1963); Robert Jungk, ed., *The Challenge of Life* (Basel: Birkhäuser, 1972). On problems of genetic regulation, see Amitai Etzioni, *Genetic Fix* (New York: Joanna Cotler, 1976); Volkmar Braun, Dietmar Mieth and Klaus Steigleder, eds., *Ethische und rechtliche Fragen der Gentechnologie und der Reproduktionsmedizin* (Munich: Campus, 1987).

10. Here I am following Eberhard Jüngel, Ernst Käsemann, J. Moltmann and D. Rössler, 'Thesen zur Diskussion über § 218 StGB: Annahme oder Abtreibung', in Jürgen Baumann, ed., *Das Abtreibungsverbot des § 218StGB: Eine Vorschrift die mehr schadet als nützt* (Darmstadt: Luchterhand, 1972), 135–48. I quote the texts I find important: 1. 'To the protection of human life [there belongs] not only protection against the annihilation of that life but also the protection of its human quality; the human quality is no less a constitutive element of human life than its vitality' (136). 2. 'Human life is only human life when and inasmuch as it is accepted life. Acceptance and recognition are as vital for a person's life, particularly a child's, as breathing, nourishment or the blood supply. Non-accepted life leads to illness, aggression and death. In the basic anthropological idea of acceptance the human quality of the developing life is communicated through the free decision of parents and society. The acceptance of parents and society belong constitutively to the engendering and bearing of the child. The liberty of the parents and the human dignity of the child are two sides of this acceptance' (140). For the interpretation and discussion of the Tübingen theses, see Christiane Kohler-Weiß, *Schutz der Menschwerdung: Schwangerschaft und Schwangerschaftskonflikt als Themen Evangelischer Ethik* (Gütersloh: Gütersloher, 2003), 133–74. In what follows I am taking the legal requirements from Jürgen Baumann's book on German criminal law reform of 1972.

11. 'Karl Barth, *Church Dogmatics* III/4, 417, 421.

12. Sung-Hee Lee-Linke, *Frauen gegen Konfuzius: Perspektiven einer asiatisch-feministischen Theologie* (Gütersloh: Gütersloher, 1995).

13. On the surmounting of the stigmatizing of disabled people and on the community of the disabled and the non-disabled, see Jürgen Moltmann, *Diakonie im Horizont des Reiches Gottes: Schritte zum Diakonentum aller Gläubigen* (Neukirchen: Neukirchener, 1984), 42–73, ed. and trans. Theodore Runyon as 'The Diaconal Church in the Context of the Kingdom of God' in *Hope for the Church: Moltmann in Dialogue with Practical Theology* (Nashville: Abingdon, 1979), 21–36.

14. Ludolf von Krehl, *Pathologische Physiologie* (Leipzig: Vogel, 1912).

15. Paul Lüth, *Kritische Medizin: Zur Theorie-Praxis-Problematik der Medizin und der Gesundheitssysteme* (Hamburg: Rowohlt, 1972).

16. Ibid.

17. Helmuth Plessner, *Lachen und Weinen: Eine Untersuchung nach den Grenzen menschlichen Verhaltens* (Bern: Francke, 1961); Plessner, *Die Stufen des Organischen und der Mensch* (Berlin: de Gruyter, 1928).

18. von Krehl, *Pathologische Physiologie.*

19. Viktor von Weizsäcker, *Der Gestaltkreis: Theorie der Einheit von Wahrnehmen und Bewegen* (Stuttgart: Thieme, 1950).

20. See Jürgen Moltmann, *God in Creation: A New Theology of Creation and the Spirit of God*, 270–75.

21. James McGilvray, *The Quest for Health and Wholeness* (Tübingen: German Inst., 1981).

22. Dietrich Rössler, *Der Arzt zwischen Technik und Humanität: Religiöse und ethische Aspekte der Krise im Gesundheitswesen* (Munich: Piper, 1977), 119; similarly Karl Barth, *Christian Dogmatics* III/4, 356ff.

23. For much in the following passage, I am indebted to Dietmar Mieth, *Grenzenlose Selbsbestimmung: Der Wille und die Würde Sterbender* (Düsseldorf: Patmos, 2008).

24. Jürgen Moltmann, *In the End—The Beginning: The Life of Hope*, trans. Margaret Kohl (Minneapolis: Fortress Press and London: SCM Press, 2004), 108ff.

25. Mieth, *Grenzenlose Selbsbestimmung*, 75.

26. Christine Swientek, *Letzter Ausweg Selbstmord: Was alte Menschen in den Tod treibt* (Freiburg: Herder, 2008).

27. Thus first Karl Binding and Alfred Hoche, *Die Freigabe der Vernichtung lebensunwerten Leben: Ihr Maß und ihre Form* (1920) (Berlin: Berliner Wissenschafts, 2006); for comment, see K. Dörner, *Andreas Frewer and Clemens Eickhoff, eds., 'Euthanasie' und die aktuelle Sterbehilfedebatte: Die historischen Hintergründe medizinischer Ethik* (Frankfurt: Campus, 2000).

28. Mieth, *Grenzenlose Selbsbestimmung*, 23.

29. Arnd T. May and Ralph Charbonnier, eds., *Patientenverfügungen: Unterschiedliche Regelungsmöglichkeiten zwischen Selbstbestimmung und Fürsorge* (Münster: Lit, 2005).

30. Rubem Alves, *Ich glaube an die Auferstehung des Leibes: Meditationen* (Düsseldorf: Patmos, 1983); Elisabeth Moltmann-Wendel and Jürgen Moltmann, *'Mit allen Sinnen glauben: Auferstehung des Fleisches' in Leidenschaft für Gott: Worauf es uns ankommt* (Freiburg: Herder, 2006), 22–43.

31. Jürgen Moltmann, *The Source of Life: The Holy Spirit and the Theology of Life*, trans. Margaret Kohl (Minneapolis: Fortress Press and London: SCM Press, 1997), esp. 70–88.

32. The theological concept of *Gestalt* can be found in Dietrich Bonhoeffer, *Ethics*, in Dietrich Bonhoeffer Works, vol. 6, ed. Clifford J. Green (Minneapolis: Fortress Press,

2004), 101f., and in Arnold Abert van Ruler, *Gestaltwerdung Christi in der Welt: Über das Verhältnis von Kirche und Kultur* (Neukirchen: Neukirchener, 1956).

33. Elisabeth Moltmann-Wendel, *Wenn Gott und Körper sich begegnen: Feministische Perspektiven zur Leiblichkeit* (Gütersloh: Gütersloher, 2000); Elisabeth Moltmann-Wendel, *Gib die Dinge der Jugend mit Grazie auf: Texte zur Lebenskunst* (Stuttgart: Radius, 2008).

34. Luthers Werke in Auswahl, ed. Erich Vogelsang, vol. 5, *Der junge Luther* (Berlin: de Gruyter, 1933), 392: Ideo enim peccatores sunt pulchri, quia diliguntur, non ideo diliguntur quia sunt pulchri.

35. Norman O. Brown, *Love's Body* (New York: Random, 1966), 206: 'Life is Phoenix-like, always born anew out of its own death. The true nature of life is resurrection.'

36. According to Luther *WA* 5, 128.

Part 3. Earth Ethics

1. *Gott und Gaja: Zur Theologie der Erde*, EvTh 53/5 (1993), with contributions by Leonardo Boff, Elisabeth Moltmann-Wendel, and Jürgen Moltmann; Rosemary Radford Ruether, *Gaia and God: An Ecofeminist Theology of Earth Healing* (San Francisco: HarperSanFrancisco, 1992); Leonardo Boff, *Von der Würde der Erde: Ökologie—Politik—Mystik* (Düsseldorf: Patmos, 1994). A pioneer work was Larry L. Rasmussen, *Earth Community: Earth Ethics* (Maryknoll: Orbis, 1997). A new ecumenical position is offered by Geiko Müller-Fahrenholz, ed., *Peace on Earth and Peace with the Earth: Serving the Goodness of God's Creation* (Geneva: WCC, 2008).

7. In the Space of the Earth, What Is the Earth?

1. James E. Lovelock, *Gaia—A New Look at Life on Earth* (Oxford, 1979); Lovelock, *The Ages of Gaia: A Biography of Our Living Earth* (New York: Norton, 1966, Revised Edition, 1995): See here Elisabet Sahtouris, *Gaia: Vergangenheit und Zukunft der Erde*, foreword by James Lovelock (Frankfurt: Insel, 1993).

2. *Christianity Today*, 11 January 1993: 'Saving Our World? How Christian Is the Green Agenda? Is the Earth Alive?'

3. Lovelock, *Ages of Gaia*.

4. Giovanni Pico della Mirandola, *Oration on the Dignity of Man* (1486).

5. See Lovelock, *Ages of Gaia*.

6. Ernst Ulrich von Weizsäcker, *Erdpolitik. Ökologische Realpolitik an der Schwelle zum Jahrhundert der Umwelt* (Darmstadt: Wissenschaftliche, 1991).

7. Jürgen Moltmann, *God in Creation: A New Theology of Creation and the Spirit of God*, trans. Margaret Kohl (Minneapolis: Fortress Press, 1993, and London: SCM Press, 1985), 158–84.

8. Bernd Janowski, *Die Welt als Schöpfung: Beiträge zur Theologie des Alten Testaments* 4 (Neukirchen: Neukirchener, 2008); Michael Welker, *Creation and Reality*, trans. J. F. Hoffmeyer (Minneapolis: Fortress Press, 1999).

9. That is why Sigmund Freud defined health as the capacity for work and for enjoyment.

10. Jürgen Moltmann, *God in Creation*, 276–96; Jürgen Moltmann, *God for a Secular Society: The Public Relevance of Theology*, trans. Margaret Kohl (Minneapolis: Fortress Press and London: SCM Press, 1999), 113–16.

11. Jürgen Moltmann, *Sun of Righteousnes, Arise! God's Future for Humanity and the Earth*, trans. Margaret Kohl (Minneapolis: Fortress Press and London: SCM Press, 2010), 67–74.

12. Ibid., 127–48. That is the Babylonian concept of the judging, rectifying and healing divine righteousness, which is taken up in the Old Testament and understood in a new way.

13. This is emphatically stressed by Hans-Joachim Kraus, *Systematische Theologie im Kontext biblischer Geschichte und Eschatologie* (Neukirchen: Neukirchener, 1983), 131–336. It is also emphasized in Celtic spirituality. See J. Philip Newell, 'God was celebrated as the life within all life. Creation was seen as the dwelling place of God', *The Book of Creation: An Introduction to Celtic Spirituality* (New York: Paulist, 1999), xxii.

14. John Calvin, *Institutio*, I, 5, 1. The reason for this, according to Calvin, lies in the creation in the Spirit of God. Spiritus Sanctus enim est, qui ubique diffusus omnia sustinet, vegetat et vivificat (*Institutio* I, 5, 14). If the whole creation is the work of the Spirit, then it is full of signs of the coming God and his glory.

15. Friedrich Nietzsche, *Also sprach Zarathustra* I.3, Kritische Studienausgabe, vol. 4 (Berlin: de Gruyter, 1993), 15. See also Jürgen Moltmann, 'Das Reich Gottes und die Treue zur Erde,' *Das Gespräch* 49 (Wuppertal: Jugenddienst, 1963).

16. Leonhard Ragaz, 'Der Kampf um das Reich Gottes' in *Blumhardt, Vater und Sohn– und weiter* (Zurich and Leipzig: Rotapfel, 1922), 60.

17. Johannes Harder, ed., *Christoph Blumhardt: Ansprachen, Predigten, Reden, Briefe 1865-1917*, III, (Neukirchen: Neukirchener, 1978), 295.

18. Dietrich Bonhoeffer, *'Dein Reich komme: Das Gebet der Gemeinde um Gottes Reich auf Erden'*, (Hamburg: Furche, 1957), 8–9.

19. Dietrich Bonhoeffer, *Letters and Papers from Prison*, Dietrich Bonhoeffer Works, vol. 8, ed. John W. DeGruchy (Minneapolis: Fortress Press, 2009), 372.

20. Dietrich Bonhoeffer, *Letters and Papers from Prison*, ed. Eberhard Bethge (London: SCM Press, 1971), 415 (trans. altered). See also Ruth-Alice von Bismarck and Ulrich Kabitz, eds, *Love Letters from Cell 92: The Correspondence between Dietrich Bonhoeffer and Maria von Wedemeyer, 1943–45*, trans. John Brownjohn (London: Harpercollins, 1994).

8. The Time of the Earth

1. See my outline 'Creation as an Open System,' in *The Future of Creation*, trans. Margaret Kohl (Philadelphia: Fortress Press and London: SCM Press, 1979), 115–30. Also R. Faber, 'Zeitumkehr: Versuch über einen eschatologischen Schöpfungsbegriff,' *ThPh* 75 (2000), 180–205.

2. John Polkinghorne, ed., *The Work of Love: Creation as Kenosis* (Grand Rapids: Eerdmans and Cambridge: SPCK, 2001).

3. Max Pohlenz, *Die Stoa: Geschichte einer geistigen Bewegung* (Göttingen: Vandenhoeck & Ruprecht, 1959), 64ff.

4. Jürgen Moltmann, 'Die Kategorie Novum in der christlichen Theologie,' in *Ernst Bloch zu ehren* (Frankfurt: Suhrkamp, 1965), 243–63; also in *Perspektiven der Theologie* (Munich: Kaiser, 1968); trans. M. Douglas Meeks as 'What Is "New" in Christianity: The Category Novum in Christian Theology,' in *Religion, Revolution, and the Future* (New York: Scribner's, 1969), 3–18.

5. Achim Stephan, *Emergenz: Von der Unvorhersagbarkeit zur Selbst-organisation* (Paderborn: Mentis, 2005).

6. Erich Jantsch, *Die Selbstrganistion des Universums: Vom Urknall zum menschlichen Geist* (Munich: Hanser, 1979, 1982).

7. Karl Marx, *Die Frühschriften*, ed. Siegfried Landshut (Stuttgart: Alfred Kröner, 1953), 330.

8. Jürgen Moltmann, *Sun of Righteousness, Arise! God's Future for Humanity and the Earth*, trans. Margaret Kohl (Minneapolis: Fortress Press and London: SCM Press, 2010), 189–208.

9. Reinhart Koselleck, *Vergangenen Zukunft: Zur Semantik geschichtlichen Zeiten* (Frankfurt: Suhrkamp, 1979).

10. "Mutual Aid in the Human and Animal World."

11. Joachim Bauer, *Warum ich fühle, was du fühlst: Intuitive Kommunikation und das Geheimnis der Spiegelneutrone* (Hamburg: Hoffmann and Campe, 2005); Bauer, *Prinzip Menschlichkeit: Warum wir von Natur aus kooperieren* (Hamburg: Hoffmann and Campe, 2006); Bauer, ed., *Das kooperative Gen: Abschied vom Darwinismus* (Hamburg: Hoffmann and Campe, 2008).

12. Carl Hinrichs, *Ranke und die Geschichtstheologie der Goethezeit* (Göttingen: Musterschmidt, 1954), 165.

13. Jürgen Moltmann, *The Coming of God: Christian Eschatology*, trans. Margaret Kohl (Minneapolis: Fortress Press and London: SCM Press, 1996).

9. Ecology

1. 'Ökologie' in *Historisches Wörterbuch der Philosophie*, ed. Joachim Ritter, vol. 6, 1146–49; 'Ökologie' in TRE, xxv (Berlin: Schwabe, 1995), 36–46.

2. Viktor von Weizsäcker, *Der Gestaltkreis: Theorie der Einheit von Wahr-nehmen und Bewegen* (Darmstadt: Wissenschaftliche, 1932).

3. Willy Hellpach, *Geopsyche: Die Menschenseele unterm Einfluss von Wetter, Klima, Boden und Landschaft* (Leipzig: Engelmann, 1939); Kurt Lewin, *Grundzüge der topologischen Psychologie* (Bern: Hans Huber, 1969).

4. Giovanni Pico della Mirandola, *On the Dignity of Man* (1486).

5. Johann Gottfried Herder, *Über den Ursprung der Sprache, 1770* (Berlin: Voss, 1959), 18.

6. Max Scheler, *Die Stellung des Menschen im Kosmos, 1927* (Munich: Nymphenburger, 1947); Arnold Gehlen, *Urmensch und Spätkultur* (Bonn: Athenäum, 1956).

7. Rosemary Radford Ruether, *New Woman, New Earth: Sexist Ideologies and Human Liberation* (New York: HarperSanFrancisco, 1975). On the previous history, see Carolyn Merchant, *The Death of Nature: Women, Ecology, and the Scientific Revolution* (San Francisco: HarperSanFrancisco, 1980).

8. Lester Russell Brown, ed., *State of the World: A Worldwatch Insitute Report on Progress toward a Sustainable Society.*

9. Bill McKibben, *The End of Nature* (New York: Random, 1989).

10. Leo Scheffczyk, *Der Mensch als Bild Gottes, Wege der Forschung 124* (Darmstadt: Wissenschaftliche, 1969).

11. Jürgen Moltmann, *God for a Secular Society: The Public Relevance of Theology*, trans. Margaret Kohl (Minneapolis: Fortress Press and London: SCM Press, 1999).

12. Gehlen, *Urmensch und Spätkultur*, 295.

13. This not-very-felicitous term goes back to the Hegelian Karl Christian Friedrich Krause (1781–1832).

14. Alfred North Whitehead, *Process and Reality: An Essay in Cosmology* (New York: Cambridge University Press, 1929).

15. Jürgen Moltmann, *The Trinity and the Kingdom*, trans. Margaret Kohl (London: SCM Press, 1981 and Minneapolis: Fortress Press, 1993); Moltmann, *God in Creation*, 94–98.

16. Hildegard von Bingen, *Lieder*, ed. Prudentiana Barth, Immaculata Ritscher, and J. Schmidt-Görg (Salzburg: Müller, 1969), 299:

> The Holy Spirit is life-giving life,
> Mover of the universe and the root of all created.
> He purifies the universe from all impurity,
> He cancels the guilt and anoints the wounds.
> Thus he is radiant life, worthy of praise,
> waking and reawakening the universe.

17. Thomas Aquinas, *STh* I q 8a 2 ad 3.

18. Jürgen Moltmann, *Sun of Righteousness, Arise!*, 189–208.

19. Thomas Aquinas, *STh* I q 8.

20. Christian Link, *Die Welt als Gleichnis: Studien zum Problem der natürlichen Theologie* (Munich: Kaiser, 1976).

21. Oswald Bayer, *Schöpfung als Anrede* (Tübingen: Mohr Siebeck, 1990).

22. H. Kessler, *Das Stöhnen der Natur: Plädoyer für eine Schöpfungsspiritualität und Schöpfungsethik* (Düsseldorf: Patmos, 1990).

23. Gernot Böhme, *Für eine Naturästhetik* (Frankfurt: Suhrkamp,1989).

24. Jürgen Moltmann, *The Way of Jesus Christ: Christology in Messianic Dimensions*, trans. Margaret Kohl (London: SCM Press, 1990 and Minneapolis: Fortress Press, 1995), 274–312.

25. *The Gospel of Thomas*, Logion 77.

26. G. van Leeuw, *Der Mensch und die Religion* (Basel: Falken, 1941). Similarly, K. Löwith, *Gesammelte Abhandlungen zur Kritik der geschichtlichen Existenz* (Stuttgart: Kohlhammer, 1960), 228–55.

27. Albert Schweitzer, *Die Lehre von der Ehrfurcht vor dem Leben: Grundtexte aus fünf Jahrzehnten* (Munich: Beck, 1966), 21.

28. Ibid., 32.

29. Ibid., 159.

30. Ibid., 36.

31. Alfons Auer, *Umweltethik: Ein theologischer Beitrag zur ökologischen Diskussion* (Düsseldorf: Patmos, 1984).

32. Ibid., 55.

33. Ibid., 56f.

34. Ibid., 289.

35. Klaus Michael Meyer-Abich, *Wege zum Frieden mit der Natur: Praktische Naturphilosophie für die Umweltpolitik* (Munich: Hanser, 1984).

36. Ibid. 99.

37. Christian Link, *Schöpfung: Schöpfungstheologie angesichts der Herausforderungen des 20. Jahrhunderts* (Gütersloh: Gütersloher, 1991); Celia E. Deane-Drummond, *Creation through Wisdom: Theology and the New Biology* (Edinburgh: T & T Clark, 2000); Medard Kehl, *Und Gott sah, dass es gut war: Eine Theologie der Schöpfung* (Freiburg: Herder, 2005).

38. I have discussed this a number of times. See *Creating a Just Future: The Politics of Peace and the Ethics of Creation in a Threatened World*, trans. John Bowden (Philadelphia: Fortress Press and London: SCM Press, 1989); *God for a Secular Society*, trans. Margaret Kohl (Minneapolis: Fortress Press and London: SCM Press, 1999), 117–34.

39. See L. Vischer, ed., *Rights of Future Generations—Rights of Nature, Studies from the World Alliance of Reformed Churches* 19 (Geneva: World Alliance of Reformed Churches, 1990), 62.

40. Albert Lorz, *Tierschützgesetz: Kommentar* (Munich: Beck, 1987); Gotthard M. Teutsch, *Mensch und Tier, Lexikon der Tierschützethik* (Göttingen: Vandenhoeck & Ruprecht, 1987).

41. 'Rechte künftiger Generationen und Rechte der Natur', *EvTh* 50, 1990, no. 5, with contributions by E. Giesser, P. Saladin, C. Zenger, J. Leimbacher, C. Link, L. Fischer, and Jürgen Moltmann; Vischer, *Rights of Future Generations*.

10. Earth Ethics

1. On the following section, see Heinrich Bedford-Strohm, 'Die Entdeckung der Ökologie in der ökumenischen Bewegung,' in Hans-Georg Link und Geiko Müller-Fahrenholz, eds, *Hoffnungswege: Wegweisende Impulse der Ökumenischen Rates der Kirchen aus sechs Jahrhunderten* (Frankfurt: Lembeck, 2008), 321–48.

2. *Der Spiegel* 31 (2009).

3. Jürgen Moltmann, *The Open Church: Invitation to a Messianic Lifestyle*, trans. M. Douglas Meeks (London: SCM Press, 1978), also under the title *The Passion for Life: A Messianic Lifestyle* (Philadelphia: Fortress, 1978).

4. Joachim Bauer, *Prinzip Menschlichketi: Warum wir von Natur aus kooperieren* (Hamburg: Hoffmann and Campe, 2006).

5. Uwe Jochum, *Kritik der Neuen Medien: Ein eschatologischer Essay* (Munich: Fink, 2003).

6. Dietmar Kamper and Christoph Wulf, *Die Wiederkehr des Körpers* (Frankfurt: Suhrkamp, 1982).

7. Jürgen Moltmann, *Spiritualità dei sensi vigili* (Modena: Fondazione Collegio San Carlo di Modena, 2006).

8. Stephen E. Toulmin and June Goodfield, *Die Entdeckung der Zeit* (Munich: Goldmann, 1970).

9. Jürgen Moltmann, *The Source of Life: The Holy Spirit and the Theology of Life*, trans. Margaret Kohl (Minneapolis: Fortress Press and London: SCM Press, 1997), 103–10; Rolf Heinrich, *Christliche Gemeinschaft leben* (Gütersloh: Gütersloher, 2001).

10. A wonderful example is the Open Door Community for the unemployed and homeless in Atlanta, Georgia. See Peter R. Gathje, *Sharing the Bread of Life: Hospitality and Resistance at the Open Door Community* (Atlanta: Open Door Community, 2006); Ed Loring, *I Hear Hope Banging at My Back Door* (Atlanta: Open Door Community, 2000), E. N. Loring, *The Festivals of Shelters: A Celebration of Love and Justice* (Atlanta: Open Door Community, 2008).

11. Jürgen Moltmann, 'Freedom in Community between Globalization and Individualism: Market Value and Human Dignity' in *God for a Secular Society: The Public Relevance of Theology*, trans. Margaret Kohl (Minneapolis: Fortress Press and London: SCM Press, 1999), 153–66

12. C. B. Macpherson, *The Political Theory of Possessive Individualism: Hobbes to Locke* (Oxford: Clarendon, 1962).

13. David Riesman, *The Lonely Crowd: Individualism Reconsidered* (New York: Anchor, 1953).

14. Martin Buber, *Dialogisches Leben: Gesammelte philosophische und pädagogische Schriften* (Zurich: Müller, 1947). The African concept of 'Ubuntu' goes beyond Buber: 'I am because we are' and 'we are because I am'. The I-We comes before the I-Thou.

15. Amitai Etzioni, *Die Entdeckung des Gemeinwesens: Ansprüche, Verantwortlichkeiten und das Programm des Kommunitarismus* (Stuttgart: Schäfer Poeschel, 1975). For the

basis in social philosophy, see Philip Selznick, *The Moral Commonwealth: Social Theory and the Promise of Community* (Berkeley: University of California Press, 1992).

16. For more detail, see Wolfgang Huber, *Folgen christlicher Freiheit: Ethik und Theorie der Kirche im Horizont der Barmer Theologischen Erklärung* (Neukirchen: Neukirchener, 1983).

17. Samuel P. Huntington, 'The Clash of Civilizations?', *Foreign Affairs* 72, no. 3 (Summer 1993): 22–49.

12. Divine and Human Righteousness and Justice

1. Jürgen Moltmann, 'Theologische Kritik der politischen Religion,' in Johann Baptist Metz, Jürgen Moltmann and Willi Oelmüller, *Kirche im Prozess der Aufklärung* (Munich: Kaiser, 1970), 11–52.

2. Arnold Anton Ehrhardt, *Politische Metaphysik von Solon bis Augustin*, Vol. 1: Die Gottestadt der Griechen und Römer (Tübingen: Mohr [Siebeck], 1959).

3. Ansgar Skriver, *Gotteslästerung?* (Hamburg: Rütten & Loening, 1962).

4. Adolf von Harnack, 'Der Vorwurf des Atheismus in den ersten drei Jahrhunderten', *Texte und Untersuchungen zur Geschichte der altchristlichen Literatur 28*, 4 (Heft, 1905), 10.

5. Hendrikus Berkhof, *Kirche und Kaiser: Eine Untersuchung der Entstehung der byzantinischen und der theokratischen Staatsauffassung im 4. Jahrhundert* (Zurich: Evangelischer, 1947).

6. Quoted in Skriver, *Gotteslästerung?*, 24.

7. Anselm von Feuerbach, 1832, quoted in Skriver, *Gotteslästerung?*, 27.

8. G. E. Lessing, *Education of the Human Race* (1780) § 88.

9. Reinhart Hummel, *Weltbilder des Reininkarnationsglauben und das Christentum* (Mainz: Matthias-Grünewald, 1988).

10. H. von Stietencron, quoted in Hummel, *Weltbilder des Reininkarnationsglauben*, 44.

11. Hummel, *Weltbilder des Reininkarnationsglauben*, 11.

12. Bernd Janowski, 'Die Tat kehrt zum Täter zurück. Offenen Fragen im Umkreis des "Tun-Ergehen-Zusammenhang"' in Bernd Janowski, *Die rettende Gerechtigkeit: Beiträge zur Theologie des Alten Testaments II* (Neukirchen: Neukirchener, 1999), 167–91.

13. K. Koch, 'Gibt es ein Vergeltungsdogma im Alten Testament?' *ZThK* (1955): 1–42.

14. K. Koch, 'Gibt es ein Vergeltungsdogma,' quoted in Janowski, *Die rettende Gerechtigkeit*, 170.

15. Janowski, *Die rettende Gerechtigkeit*, 190.

16. According to Koch, yhwh is thought of 'not as a Supreme Being who acts on human beings from outside' but as 'the morally determined ground of all reality and the positive power of the reality process ' (Janowski, *Die rettende Gerechtigkeit*, 172).

17. Jürgen Moltmann, *In the End–The Beginning: The Life of Hope*, trans. Margaret Kohl (Minneapolis: Fortress Press and London: SCM Press, 2004).

18. Ulpian, Fragment 10. See 'Gerechtigkeit' in *HistWdPh* III (Stuttgart, 1974), 329–38.

19. Hans H. Schmid, *Gerechtigkeit als Weltordnung: Hintergrund und Geschichte des alttestamentlichen Gerechtigkeitsbegriff* (Tübingen: Mohr, 1968).

20. This is rightly stressed by Bernd Janowski, with Jan Assmann, in Janowski, *Die rettende Gerechtigkeit*, 178.

21. See *Die Weisheit des Konfuzius: Aus dem chinesischen Urtext*, neu übertragen und eingeleitet von H.O. H. Stange (Frankfurt: Insel, 1994), 13, 52.

22. Heinrich Bedford-Strohm, *Vorrang für die Armen: Auf dem Weg zu einer theologischen Theorie der Gerechtigkeit* (Gütersloh: Gütersloher, 1993).

23. Hans Küng, *A Global Ethic for Global Politics and Economics*, trans. John Bowden (London: SCM Press, 1997 and New York: Oxford University Press, 1998).

24. Jürgen Moltmann, *Sun of Righteousness, Arise!*, 127–48.

25. A. Grund, 'Die Propheten als Künder des Gerichts,' in Ruth Heß and Martin Leiner, eds, *Alles in Allem: Eschatologische Anstöße* (Neukirchen: Neukirchener, 2006), 167–81.

26. Jürgen Moltmann, *Sun of Righteousness, Arise!*, 117–26.

27. Jürgen Moltmann, *History and the Triune God*, trans. John Bowden (London: SCM Press, 1991), 44–56; Moltmann, *In the End—The Beginning*, 53–78.

28. See Leonard Ragaz, *Die Gleichnisse Jesus: Seine soziale Botschaft* (1943) (Hamburg: Furche, 1971), on the self-righteousness of the good. On the following passage, see also Johann Baptist Metz, *Memoria Passionis: Ein provozierendes Gedächnis in pluralistischer Gesellschaft* (Freiburg: Herder, 2006).

29. John Paul II, encycical *Dominum et vivificantem* (May 18, 1986), 39: 'Out of the mouth of Jesus the Redeemer, in whose humanity the "suffering of God" was proved true, a word is to be heard in which the eternal love shows itself to be full of divine compassion: Misereor—I have compassion,'

30. Traditionally, there are three steps: confessio oris—contritio cordis—satisfactio operum—confession, contrition, satisfaction (or restitution). This last step is taken into account in § 64 of the German penal code in 'perpetrator-victim settlement: compensation for damage.'

31. See Martin Luther King Jr., *Letter from Birmingham City Jail* (1963), in *Strength to Love* (Philadelphia: Fortress Press, 1981), 138–46; *Stride toward Freedom* (New York: Ballantine, 1958), 135f.

32. Karl Barth, *Church and State*, trans. G. Ronald Howe (London: SCM Press, 1939); Barth, *Against the Stream*, trans G.T. Thomason and H. Knight, (London: SCM Press, 1954). More generally, see Wolfgang Huber, *Gerechtigkeit und Recht: Grundlinien christlicher Rechtsethik* (Gütersloh: Gütersloher, 1996).

33. Karl Marx, *Die Frühschriften*, ed. Siegfried Landshut (Stuttgart: Kröner, 1953), 216. Marx thought that this teaching is the ultimate criticism of religion, but it is in fact the prophetic hope leading to this demand.

34. Ernst Bloch, *Naturrecht und menschliche Würde* (Frankfurt: Suhrkamp, 1961), 14. John Rawls discusses more recent contractual theories in the concept of justice in *A Theory of Justice* (Cambridge: Belknap, 1971), 258ff.

35. For the thesis that righteousness means 'faithfulness to the community', see Gerhard von Rad, *Old Testament Theology*, trans. D. M. G. Stalker (Edinburgh: Oliver & Boyd, 1962).

36. G. Oestreich, 'Die Idee des religiösen Bundes und die Lehre vom Staatsvertrag' in *Zur Geschichte und Problematik der Demokratie* (Berlin: Duncker & Humblot, 1958), 11–32; Jürgen Moltmann, *God for a Secular Society: The Public Relevance of Theology*, trans. Margaret Kohl (Minneapolis: Fortress Press and London: SCM Press, 1999), 24–45, on Philipp Duplessis Mornay and Thomas Hobbes.

37. J. Wayne Baker, *Heinrich Bullinger and the Covenant: The Other Reformed Tradition* (Athens: Ohio University Press, 1980). On the further development of covenant politics, see Quentin Skinner, *The Foundations of Modern Political Thought, vol. 2: The Age of Reformation* (Cambridge: Cambridge University Press, 1978). On federal theology, see

Gottlob Schrenk, *Gottesreich und Bund im älteren Protestantismus vornehmlich bei Johannes Coccejus*, 1923 (Giessen: Brunnen, 1985).

13. Dragon Slaying and Peacemaking in Christianity

1. Heino Falcke, *Wo bleibt die Freiheit? Christsein in Zeiten der Wende* (Freiburg: Kreuz, 2009).

2. Hannah Arendt, *On Violence* (New York: Mariner, 1970).

3. Uwe Steffen, *Drachenkampf: Der Mythos vom Bösen* (Stuttgart: Kreuz, 1984).

4. Franz Georg Maier, ed., *Byzanz*, Fischer Weltgeschichte, vol. 13 (Frankfurt: Fischer, 1973), 21–4: Jörg Rieger, *Christ and Empire: From Paul to Postcolonial Times* (Minneapolis: Fortress Press, 2007).

5. This interpretation is wrong. According to Daniel 7 the despotic empires come from chaos, spread chaos, and sink into chaos, but the empire of the Son of man comes from heaven, is a humane empire, and remains. Anyone who adds the Christian empire on to the others, as the Quintomonarchians did, overlooks their qualitative difference, and with it the apocalyptic alternative. Thus also K. Koch, 'Spätisraelitisches Geschichtsdenken am Beispiel des Buches Danel', *HZ* 193, 1961, 7–32. Wolfhart Pannenberg followed him with his universal-history interpretation. See Wolfhart Pannenberg, ed., *Revelation as History*, trans. D. Granskou and E. Quinn (New York: Sheed & Ward, 1969).

6. Mariano Delgado, 'Die Metamorphosen des Messianismus in den iberischen Kulturen,' in *Zeitschrift für Missionswissenschaft*, vol. 34 (Münster: Aschendorff, 1994); Mariano Delgado and Klaus Koch, eds, *Europa: Tausendjähriges Reich und Neue Welt* (Stuttgart: Kohlhammer, 2003).

7. See Mary Kaldor, *Neue und alte Kriege: Organisierte Gewalt im Zeitalter der Globalisierung* (Frankfurt: Suhrkamp, 2000); Erhard Eppler, *Vom Gewaltmonopol zum Gewaltmarkt?* (Frankfurt: Suhrkamp, 2002).

8. Eppler, 120, on the commercialization of security.

9. Arthur Kaufmann, ed., *Widerstandsrecht* (Darmstadt: Wissenschaftliche, 1972; Jürgen Moltmann, *The Experiment Hope*, trans. M. Douglas Meeks (Philadelphia: Fortress Press, 1975), 131–46.

10. This is the formula of the constitutional lawyer R. Dreier in Peter Glotz, ed., *Ziviler Ungehorsam im Rechtsstaat* (Frankfurt: Suhrkamp, 1983), 60: 'Wer allein oder gemeinsam mit anderen, öffentlich, gewaltlos, und aus politisch-moralischen Gründen den Tatbestand von Verbotsnormen erfüllt, handelt grundrechtlich gerechtfertigt, wenn er dadurch gegen schwerwiegendes Unrecht protestiert und sein Protest verhältnismäßig ist.' See also W. Huber's important theological and ethical contribution, 'Die Grenzen des Staates und die Pflict zum Ungehorsam', *Ziviler Ungehorsam im Rechtsstaat*, 108–26. John Rawls has derived the following definition from the American civil rights movement: 'Civil disobedience is a public, nonviolent, conscientious yet political act contrary to law usually done with the aim of bringing about a change in the law or policies of the government,' *A Theory of Justice* (Cambridge: Belknap, 1971), 364.

11. Elisabeth Moltmann-Wendel, *The Women around Jesus: Reflections on Authentic Personhood*, trans. John Bowden (London: SCM Press and New York: Crossroad, 1982).

12. Jürgen Moltmann, *On Human Dignity: Political Theology and Ethics*, trans. M. Douglas Meeks (Philadelphia: Fortress Press, 1984, 2007).

13. H. Falcke, 'Theologie des Friedens in einen geteilten Welt,' in Jürgen Moltmann, ed., *Friedenstheologie–Befreiungstheologie: Analysen, Berichte, Meditationen* (Munich: Kaiser,

1988), 17–66. See also Donald W. Shriver, *An Ethic for Enemies: Forgiveness in Politics* (New York: Oxford University Press, 1995).

14. Shriver, *An Ethic for Enemies*.

15. The periodical issued for the fraternities (Brüderhöfe) is called Plough. Hospitality is the periodical published by the Open Door Community in Atlanta in solidarity with the homeless and those imprisoned on the deathrow. It is directed against the system of white male supremacy in the southern regions of the United States.

14. Control Is Good—Trust Is Better

1. Erhard Eppler, *Die tödliche Utopie der Sicherheit* (Hamburg: Bertelsmann, 1983).

2. Pä Ström, *Die Überwachungsmafia: Das gute Geschäft mit unseren Daten* (Munich: Carl Hanser, 2005).

3. Erik H. Erikson, *Identity and the Life Cycle*, 1959 (New York: Norton, 1980).

4. Reiner Strunk, *Vertrauen: Grundzüge einer Theologie des Gemeindeaufbaus* (Stuttgart: Quell, 1985).

5. Niklas Luhmann, *Trust and Power*, trans. H. Davis et al. (Chichester: Wiley, 1979), admittedly sees the matter quite differently. Cf. Onora O'Neill, *A Question of Trust* (Cambridge: Cambridge University Press, 2002).

6. See chapter 12 above.

7. The Basic Law of the Federal Republic of Germany, 1,2, states: 'The German people therefore acknowledge uninfringeable and inalienable human rights as the foundation for every human community, for peace, and for justice in the world.'

8. Martin Luther, *Large Catechism*, 1529. The First Commandment: 'You shall have no other gods.' The criterion of complete trust corresponds to the Sh'mah Israel: 'Your shall love the Lord your God with all your heart, and with all your soul, and with all your might' (Deut. 6.5). The counterproof can easily be provided: if I love earthly created things absolutely and totally, I am asking too much of them and am destroying their fragile beauty.

15. The Righteousness of God and Human and Civil Rights

1. J. Hersch, *Les Droits de l'Homme d'un point de vue philosophique* (Paris, 1968).

2. Wolfgang Heidelmeyer, *Die Menschenrechte: Erklärungen, Verfassungsartikel, Internationale Abkommen* (Paderborn: Schöningh, 1973); Eckehardt Lorenz, ed., '… *erkämpft das Menschenrecht.' Wie christlich sind die Menschenrechte?* (Berlin: Lutherisches, 1981).

3. Jan Milic Lochman and Jürgen Moltmann, *Gottes Recht und die Menschenrechte* (Neukirchen: Neukirchener, 1976).

4. Wolfgang Huber and Heinz E. Tödt, *Menschenrechte: Perspektiven einer menschlichen Welt* (Stuttgart: Kreuz, 1977).

5. Conference of European Churches, *Church and Society*, Brussels No. 6 (June 2009): Human Dignity vs. Christian Morality?

6. Claus Westermann, *Genesis 1–11*, trans. John J. Scullion (Minneapolis: Augsburg and London: SPCK, 1984).

7. Landrecht Buch 3, Article 42.

8. Martin Grabmann, *Die Grundgedanken des Heiligen Augustinus über Seele und Gott in ihrer Gegenwartsbedeutung* (Darmstadt: Wissenschaftliche, 1967).

9. Jürgen Moltmann, *Politische Theologie—Politische Ethik* (Munich: Kaiser, 1984), 170–72.

10. See chapter III.

11. See chapter III, 3, 4.

12. Dumitru Staniloae, *Orthodoxe Dogmatik*, vol. 1 (Gütersloh: Gütersloher, 1984), 293: In Western theology frequent attempts were made to divide the redemption of man from the redemption of nature. Eastern Christianity has never divided the two.... As we believe, every human person is in a certain way a hypostasis of the whole cosmic nature.... The whole of nature is designed for the glory of which human beings will partake in the kingdom of the consummation.'

13. L. Vischer, ed., *Rights of Future Generations—Rights of Nature*, Studies from the World Alliance of Reformed Churches 19 (Geneva: World Alliance of Reformed Churches, 1990).

14. Seyla Benhabib, 'Unterwegs zu eine kosmopolitischen Democratie?' *NZZ Outline*, June 13, 2009, 1–4.

15. Volker Rittberger, 'Weltregieren: Was kann es leisten? Was muss es leisten?,' in Hans Küng and Dieter Senghaas, eds., *Friedenspolitik: Ethische Grundlagen internationaler Beziehungen* (Zurich: Piper, 2003), 177–208. I am indebted to the Tübingen political scientist Volker Rittberger for access to the discussion described. See also Volker Rittberger, ed., *Wer regiert die Welt und mit welchem Recht?* (Baden-Baden: Nomos, 2009).

16. Josef Bohatec, *England und die Geschichte der Menschen- und Bürgerrechte*, ed. Otto Weber (Graz: Böhlau, 1956).

17. See the first section of this chapter, with the comment by All Kyrill, Patriarch of Moscow, *Freedom and Responsibility: A Search for Harmony* (London: Darton, Longman and Todd, 2011).

18. Staniloae, *Orthodox Dogmatik* I, 293.

Part 5. Joy in God: Aesthetic Counterpoints

1. When after the unrest of 1968 the necessary political and social-ethical emphasis of my political theology became too strong, I freed myself in 1971 from the total claim of the law in the little book *The Theology of Play*, trans. R. Ulrich (New York: Harper & Row, 1972; *Theology and Joy*, London: SCM Press, 1973) in order once again to give weight to the joy in aesthetics.

2. One of the spirituals begins, 'How can I sing the Lord's song in an alien land?' See James H. Cone, *The Spirituals and the Blues: An Interpretation* (New York: Seabury, 1972).

3. Jacqueline Aileen Bussie, *The Laughter of the Oppressed: Ethical and Theological Resistance in Wiesel, Morrison, and Endo* (New York: T&T Clark, 2007).

4. Friedrich Hölderlin, 'Hyperion'.

16. Sabbath—The Feast of Creation

1. I draw gratefully on Abraham Joshua Heschel, *The Sabbath: Its Meaning for Modern Man* (New York: Farrar, Straus and Giroux, 1951), and Franz Rosenzweig, *The Star of Redemption*, trans. William W. Hallo (New York: Holt, Rinehart, and Winston, 1971).

2. See Wolfgang Philipp, *Das Werden der Aufklärung in theologiegeschicht-licher Sicht* (Göttingen: Vandenhoeck & Ruprecht, 1957).

3. Martin Grabmann, *Die Grundgedanken des heiligen Augustinus über Seele und Gott* (Darmstadt: Wissenschaftlich, 1957). For the discussion about the restriction to the soul, see Jürgen Moltmann, *The Source of Life: The Holy Spirit and the Theology of Life*, trans. Margaret Kohl (Minneapolis: Fortress Press and London: SCM Press, 1997), 70–88.

4. Dietrich Ritschl, *Bildersprache und Argumente: Theologische Aufsätze* (Neukirchen: Neukirchener, 2008), 49–59.

5. A. Heschel, *The Sabbath*, 8.

6. Jürgen Moltmann, 'What Is Time? And How Do We Experience It?' in *dialogue* 39, no. 1 (2000): 27–35.

7. Today some people associate this way of looking at things with meditative contemplation, but as Plato said, it is the view which comes from astonishment. In pure theory we perceive in order to participate, not in order to dominate, exploit or utilize. We perceive things with our eyes, not with our grasping hand. We let things be what they are and do not claim them for ourselves.

8. Rosenzweig, *Star of Redemption*, part III, book 1.

9. For more detail, see Jürgen Moltmann, *God in Creation: The Gifford Lectures 1984–85*, trans. Margaret Kohl (San Francisco: Harper and London: SCM Press, 1985), 292–96.

10. Rosenzweig, *Star of Redemption*, 359.

17. The Jubilation of Christ's Resurrection

1. For more detail, see Jürgen Moltmann, *God in Creation* (London: SCM Press, 1985 and Minneapolis: Fortress, 1993), 292–96.

2. Franz Rosenzweig remarked on this connection. See Rosenzweig, *Star of Redemption*, 358–59.

3. A typical documentation of this is Benedict xvi's encyclical *Salvi Spes*, which is concerned with the soul and its future in eternal life. The proximity to gnostic redemption religion cannot be overlooked.

4. See Ernst Benz, Hans Thurn and Constantin Floros, *Das Buch der Heiligen Gesänge der Ostkirche* (Hamburg: Furche, 1962), 102, 103, 107, 114.

18. "And Peace in the Midst of Strife"

1. M. Grabmann, *Die Grundgedanken des heiligen Augustinus über Seele und Gott*, 11.

Index

259

brain function and death, 95
Buber, Martin, 160, 203
Buddhism, 53, 104
Byzantine rule and theology, 192

Calvin, John, 116
Calvinism, 7–8, 19–20, 24
Camus, Albert, 45
capitalism, 47–48, 178–79, 214
catastrophes
    causes of, 172
    ecological, 49–50, 133–34, 151–52,
        179, 221
    economic, 165, 221
    ethics and prevention of, 140–43, 166
    nuclear, 46–47
    solidarity and, 159
catechon, identity and function of, 13–15
Catholic doctrines, xiii–xiv, 72, 220
Catholic policies, 50, 85, 96, 195, 225–26
changing the world, guide for, 40–41
children, care and needs of, 76, 83–84, 86
children, obligations to have, 76
children, status of unborn, 79–81, 82
Cho, Yonggi, 246n5
Christianity
    acceptance by God, 127
    action and, 6
    ascetic, 103–4
    bodily behavior, 106
    imperialism and, 191–92
    liberal, 31
    roles of, 10–13, 19–21, 22, 55, 135, 193
    Roman empire and, 170, 192, 262n5
    Sabbath day in, 234, 235
    strategies for a just peace, 204–6
    "this-worldliness," 73
    universalism and, 192
Christocratic ethics, 21, 41
Christology, 19–24, 37–39, 69, 138–39
chronos, 58
church, the
    cosmic orientation of, 139
    future of, 21
    as model for the state, 22, 33
    peace churches, 204
    protection of, 171
    resurrection views of, 236–37
    roles of, 31–32, 225–28

separation from world of, 28–32
social services and justice, 184
state vs., 21–23
true church, the, 22–23
Church Dogmatics, 20
Ciba conference, 78–80
city farming, 157
city of God vs. city of the devil, 9–10,
    20–21
civil community vs. Christian community,
    21–22, 205
civil disobedience, 195–96, 262n10. See also
    resistance
climate catastrophe, 49–50, 179
clocks, 154–55
Club of Rome, xi, 49
cognition and recognition, 137–38, 151
coming of God, the Sabbath and, 234
common age of humanity, 64
communication, interpersonal, 127
communicative freedom, 161
Communist manifesto, 175
community
    civil, 184
    civil community vs. Christian, 21–22
    competition and sense of, 48
    freedom of humans and, 160–61
    mutual, importance of, 68, 158–59
    poverty and, 66
Confessing Church, the, 8, 20
confession of sins, public, 32
confidence, development of, 59, 62, 86
consciously lived life, 63
consequences and acts, link between,
    172–74
constant will, 175
Constantine I, Emperor of Rome, 235
Constantinian theology, 13, 30, 32, 191–92
constitutions, 186, 211–12
control and trust, 208, 213–15
Convention on the Rights of the Child of
    1989, 217–18
conversion to righteousness, 55
Corpus Christianum, 28
cosmocentrism, 136, 222
cosmos, humans as part of, 69
court systems, victims and perpetrators in,
    186–87
covenant of free and equal, 185